OVERVIEW

I will live in the Past, the Present, and the Future. The Spirits of all Three shall strive within me. I will not shut out the lessons that they teach.

CHARLES DICKENS

This is not a book on time management or personal productivity. No doubt we could all improve our effectiveness through better prioritisation and planning and the application of smarter systems to juggle the demands of our working day and life generally. But this is time management run by the clock and the calendar to squeeze more stuff into an already crowded schedule. We don't need another book announcing a new time management system; there are already more than 250 in publication. Indeed we think that time management may be part of the problem rather than the solution.

Now It's About Time is based on two fundamental insights:

- how we think about our **past, present and future** has a major impact on our life outcomes - our job satisfaction, career success and long-term life success
- the issue is less about the management of time and more about the **management of our minds** in how we think about yesterday, today and tomorrow

We believe that the feelings we have about our past, how we view the present, and anticipate our future are important indicators of our well being and key dynamics of our success in life. If time is a thread connecting what was, what is and what will be, "when the thread is stretched taut, there seems to be a flow of experience that reflects harmony among past, present and future." This is when we are at our best, when "the past, the present and the future are really one."

Alternatively our outlook on time is less a taut thread to connect the past to the future and more a tangled knot of three different strings.

We can allow our **past** to be a constraint, either to hold on to difficult and troublesome experiences that continue to dominate our life now, or look back wistfully to simpler and happier times. In the **present** we can find ourselves struggling to cope with competing demands, finding it difficult to stop and enjoy the moment. Alternatively we throw ourselves into today with reckless abandon with potential

risks for our long-term well being. Our **future** can provide energising purpose. Or we can contemplate the challenges that lie ahead with dread, frozen with fear as we anticipate life's hazards. For others, the future is a fantasy based on wishful thinking. Here our dreams of what "should be" avoid the tough challenges of engaging with the reality of "what is".

Now It's About Time asks three big questions:

- are we **connected to our past** seeing it as a source of valuable experience and learning; or resentful about its impact, or nostalgic for happier times?
- are we **operating in the current flow** optimising our enjoyment of the present; or avoiding pressing realities, or simply living for the moment?
- are we preparing to **build a better future**; or fearful of what lies ahead, or fantasising about unlikely possibilities?

How we respond to these questions have important implications for our current satisfaction and future success in life.

In beginning to answer these questions we will investigate the way our memory works and why it lets us down; the processes of attention, concentration and flow; why our imagination is a double-edged sword; the emotions of fear, confidence and courage; the inter-play of experience, learning and wisdom; and the dynamics of happiness, well being and success.

We also explore a range of themes, everything from absent mindedness, anger and anticipation, decision making, déjà vu and dreams, forgetfulness and Freud, planning, priorities and procrastination, regret, reminiscence and revenge, scrapbooks, sex and stress, to zen thinking.

Format

The structure of the book is based on the "conceptismo", the literary format popularised by Balthasar Gracian in "The Art of Worldly Wisdom". The shrewd 17th century Spanish priest provided 300 "bite sized chunks" of insight; simple, concise and direct observations and reflections to clarify the realities of human nature and social interaction and suggest the strategies and tactics for a wise life. For us this format seemed to work better when we started to post content on the www.now-itsabouttime.com site, than any attempt to provide a step by step "how to manual".

Some of the conceptismos are simply a quote or extended question, others highlight a research finding that illuminates a specific issue, or summarise the observations of an interesting thinker. We also draw on the biographies of fascinating individuals whose life experiences tell us something important about the nature of time.

Now it's about time

How the past, present and future shape our life success

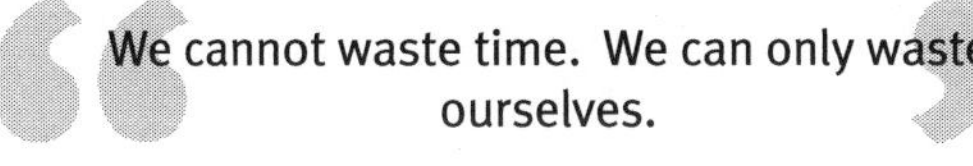

We cannot waste time. We can only waste ourselves.

GEORGE ADAMS

Munro, Andrew
Now It's About Time
www.now-itsabouttime.com

ISBN 978-1-4476-0776-2

Design
Eric Gaskell at EG Design
www.egdesign.co.uk

CONTENTS

We make no attempt at a structured learning sequence in linear A - Z fashion. It's a collection of 300 topics that ask important questions worth thinking about.

We do however provide over 500 reference points to articles and books, blogs and other on line resources for in-depth research and insight. Because of the fast changing nature of the Internet we've not embedded the links which are used on the website; Google the key words and you should find the reference. If you don't, the chances are you'll stumble on something even more interesting. Please do email us at admin@amazureconsulting.com with your finds and we'll update the site.

Above all, **Now It's About Time** is designed to help you think about time. If there is one thing we discovered in our explorations of the psychology of time it is that we rarely stop to think: what happened in our life, what is happening now and what might happen in future. Use the insights to prompt your reflections about your own life, discuss ideas with friends and colleagues, and explore the references and recommendations for more information and ideas, and practical guidance. We hope you enjoy dipping in and out of the book. In researching and writing it we've had a lot of fun and gained fresh insights. We hope you do.

As that wise sage Baltasar Gracian said: "All that really belongs to us is time; even they who have nothing else have that."

WHO

Andrew Munro is a Director of AM Azure Consulting, the talent management consultancy that often takes a contrarian view to how organisations design and implement processes for assessment, performance management, career development and succession planning. Author of "Practical Succession Management", Andrew has worked over the past 20 years with more than 300 firms to help identify and develop the leadership talent and character that builds great organisations.

He would like to thank the many people who, directly and indirectly, contributed to this book.

Progressive clients who asked questions and got him thinking more about the nature of leadership and why time might provide an important insight into the dynamics of success and failure, and happiness more generally in life. There are too many to list here, but special thanks to Neil Lewis at Working Transitions who prompted him to make it happen now, and Dr Tom Kennie at Ranmore Consulting whose wisdom is not always welcome, but is always valuable.

The research team at AM Azure (Tony Day, Michelle Jones, Angela Skears, Richard Munro) who kept hunting down fascinating articles and publications, and made life increasingly difficult for him as he attempted to finish this book. A special thanks to Fiona Jones who coordinated content management for the web site at www.now-itsabouttime.com.

The designers at PsyTech who coordinated the development of the web site and the on line TimeFrames assessment, in particular, Deryck Murphy, Alan Kitching and Lesley Morris who applied their typical creative brilliance and emotional composure in project management to accommodate last minute changes.

Eric Gaskell, the artist behind the graphical design; check out his work at the on line gallery at www.egdesign.co.uk.

His family - Susanna, Kit, Theo and Josceline - who often wondered why someone writing a book about time should have so little time for them. His only response is that one of the first writers about time and how we think about it - Benjamin Franklin - was also a hypocrite.

CONNECTED TO THE PAST

To be able to look back upon one's past life with satisfaction is to live twice.

MARCUS VALERIUS MARTIAL

We can look back negatively on our previous life, and in ruminating on the difficult and troublesome times, we find it hard to escape from this past. Alternatively nostalgia reinterprets our yesterday to create a wonderful place to which we want to return, and help us escape from the challenges of today and tomorrow.

When we connect to our past, we look objectively at previous events, able to take a better perspective on what happened and why it happened to see the broader forces at work in shaping who we now are and our expectations of the future. What we think we experienced at the time, we revisit now through the lens of greater life wisdom.

Mistakes and failings are not "too difficult" to think about, but are valuable experiences in which important lessons of life were learnt. And in connecting to our past we also reframe our achievements and successes to appreciate the influence of others. We also identify the impact of luck to maintain that life humility which avoids the hazards of the ego.

HOW CHARLES DICKENS' PAST PRODUCED A CHRISTMAS CLASSIC

I will live in the Past, the Present, and the Future. The Spirits of all Three shall strive within me. I will not shut out the lessons that they teach.

CHARLES DICKENS

We know the story of Charles Dickens' "A Christmas Carol". Written in Victorian England as it was discovering the nostalgia of forgotten Christmas traditions, Ebenezer Scrooge is a miserly businessman who has been warned by the ghost of his business partner, Jacob Morley, to change his ways.

On Christmas Eve Scrooge is visited by three more ghosts. The ghost of Christmas Past reminds Ebenezer of his boyhood and a time of youthful innocence. The ghost of Christmas Present transports Scrooge to different scenes including the dinner at his hard worked clerk Bob Cratchit's house. The third ghost, the ghost of Christmas Yet to come, foretells a harrowing future for Ebenezer: his neglected and untended grave is revealed.

Scrooge awakens on Christmas morning with joy in his soul. He has been transformed from a penny-pinching businessman into a compassionate individual, full of kindness and generosity.

In "A Christmas Carol" Charles Dickens drew on his own difficult past. After an idyllic few years of childhood, Dickens' life changed when his indebted father was sent to prison. Forced into lodgings, Charles found himself working ten hour days at a blacking factory, pasting labels on to shoe polish. Even when his father was released Charles had to continue his work at the factory.

Resentment about his situation would have been easy. But Dickens was also touched by the experiences of the poor he encountered. Escaping the blacking factory to become a legal clerk before moving into journalism, Dickens remembered his past to write remarkable novels of injustice and poverty.

WHAT WAS THE TIME OF NELSON MANDELA'S LIFE

The past, the present and the future are really one: they are today.

HARRIET BEECHER STOWE

Nelson Mandela knows the importance of time. Describing his time as a prisoner at Robins' Island, he said, "Every hour seemed like a year." And in the over-turn of apartheid to create a democratic society, he connected his personal past to the future of the South African nation.

Prison gave every reason for Mandela to reflect on previous injustices and remain stuck in that past. Instead his biographer writes; "He took the long view. He was thinking in terms not of days and weeks, but decades. He knew history was on his side."

This is life maturity, to see the past objectively for what it is, not to reinterpret it or pretend adversity never happened. Nor is it to allow the past to breed the kind of resentment that is destructive. It is the maturity that, as Nelson Mandela did, identifies better possibilities for the future.

"Ultimately, the key to understanding Mandela is those 27 years in prison. The man who walked onto Robben Island in 1964 was emotional, headstrong, easily stung. The man who emerged was balanced and disciplined. I often asked him how the man who emerged from prison differed from the wilful young man who had entered it. He hated this question. Finally, in exasperation one day, he said, 'I came out mature.' "

"Mandela: His 8 Lessons of Leadership"
Richard Stengel, 2008 Time

HOW TO BE STOICAL ABOUT TIME

One must always maintain one's connection to the past and yet ceaselessly pull away from it.

GASTON BACHELARD

Marcus Aurelius was the last of the five great emperors of Rome, ruling from 161 A.D. until his death in 180 A.D, a reign that was the "happiest and most prosperous". More than a proficient emperor, warrior or statesman, Marcus Aurelius was also a philosopher who in his quiet moments of leisure wrote his "Meditations", a personal document to himself to record and remind him of the wisdom of the stoics and to guide him in life. Marcus Aurelius was the first and maybe last philosopher-king.

Running through the Meditations are the themes of breaking free from the emotions that often imprison us, the cultivation of inner peace, the need to take personal responsibility, and above all, the way we think about time. "Time is a sort of river of passing events, and strong is its current; no sooner is a thing brought to sight than it is swept by and another takes its place, and this too will be swept away." For Marcus Aurelius we should think about:

- our past and why we need to detach ourselves from any feelings of resentment about what has happened or didn't happen
- our present and the importance of space and quiet to reflect and be mindful about the moment
- our future and why we shouldn't worry too much about the brevity of time. Death is something that will happen to everyone, and not to be feared

Some find the wisdom of Marcus Aurelius a bit too bracing. Others have suggested Meditations is the writing of a bad-tempered man in a state of existential despair.

Nonetheless, whatever we think of the stoic Marcus Aurelius, we need to work out our own life philosophy and how it shapes our attitudes to our past, present and future.

We all have a set of views about our past, present and future. The question is whether these attitudes are helping or hindering our progress in life.

"A Guide to the Good Life: the ancient art of stoic joy" William Irvine

"The Meditations" Marcus Aurelius

WHY LIFE MUST BE UNDERSTOOD BACKWARDS TO BE LIVED FORWARDS

Life can only be understood backwards; but it must be lived forwards.

SOREN KIERKEGAARD

Soren Kierkegaard, the Danish existentialist who emphasised the need for each individual to create meaning for their own lives (rather than accept any hand-me-down philosophical system) understood something fundamental about time and how we think about the course of our lives.

Our past is not our destiny. Our present and future is not determined by the dynamics of our upbringing, early relationships and life experiences. **But** the past does shape and influence our assumptions about the world, our beliefs about the nature of happiness and life success, and expectations of what can be achieved in life.

We don't have to "accept" our past, and its circumstances and constraints. But it's no bad idea to give our past the value it deserves.

And if we come to terms with our past, recognising the positives as well as acknowledging the negatives, we may recognise Kierkegaard's insight that "life is a mystery to be lived, not a problem to be solved."

"Time Travel 101: Techniques For Reliving The Past and Seeing The Future" Sid Savara

WHEN OUR HOUSE IS ON FIRE WHAT POSSESSION DO WE RESCUE

We don't just treasure our memories; we are our memories.

DANIEL GILBERT

Our house is ablaze. We have only a few seconds to rush back to recover one key possession. What do we choose?

For most people the answer is: "my photo album".

Why? Because we know that who we are now is a lot about who we were in the past. It's true that not every past is a happy past, and many people want to forget their past.

But we still know our past is important in our lives. We also know that memory plays tricks. When we look back in time we don't have access to a DVD box set of every day of our lives. Instead we have a set of "impressionist paintings rendered by an artist who takes considerable licence with his subject."

And because we know our memories are faulty, in the event of our house going on fire, we want something that reminds us of who we were, what we did and where we went.

IS IT DÉJÀ VU ALL OVER AGAIN

Of course, some people dismiss déjà vu as a lot of rubbish that never happens to them, but in the end everyone experiences it. Of course, some people dismiss déjà vu as a lot of rubbish that never happens to them, but in the end everyone experiences it.

GUY BROWNING

Neo: "A black cat went past us, and then I saw another that looked just like it."

Trinity: "A déjà vu is usually a glitch in the Matrix. It happens when they change something."

We encounter a new experience and it's so familiar we feel we're reliving a moment from our earlier life. This is déjà vu. It's the sudden feeling that we've had this experience, even though we know we haven't. And it's so familiar we know what's going to happen next. As one individual summarised: "The whole scene was so familiar I thought I knew what people were going to say before they said it. It was like I was in a movie I'd already seen."

For para-normalists, the déjà vu experience is evidence for reincarnation. "Déjà vu is the crack in time that suddenly grants us a glimpse of the eternal return of our own existence." In déjà vu our soul is experiencing something we actually experienced in a previous life. Other interpretations suggest that déjà vu is an experience meant to remind us of past mistakes or to predict good fortune.

What is more likely is that our mind is playing a trick on us. Our memory is a juggler. On the one hand it has to retain what we already know. Spotting what is familiar is quite a handy tactic to make life easier. It means when we walk into our office each morning we don't stand around wondering where things are. On the other hand, because our memory is limited, it is predisposed to remember what is new and different and activated by the unfamiliar.

Occasionally however the juggler of our memory finds it too difficult to sort out the familiar and unfamiliar. And when we perceive the unfamiliar as familiar we

experience déjà vu. Jamais vu is the opposite; we see a situation as if for the first time whilst knowing we have in fact been in the situation before.

Significantly the incidence of déjà vu seems highest in young adulthood and to fall off gradually through retirement age, arguably because we're shifting to a life routine of more familiarity.

So if we allow more novelty and freshness into our lives as we age, maybe we should expect to experience more déjà vu.

WHAT MOVIE ARE WE PLAYING

What types of movies are you projecting in your head? Are they inspiring adventures or depressing horror movies? Positive movies with good outcomes or negative movies with bad and sad endings? Movies that are mostly empowering or disempowering? And finally, and most importantly, do your internal movies support your success or sabotage it? Select your movies wisely!

DANIEL M. MURPHY

Our memories are not necessarily an accurate record of our past. Our brains don't hold a video of our past that is played back as the definitive story of our lives. Instead we recreate our past through the lens of our current feelings and expectations of the future.

We should check that we're not reinventing a past shaped by our current life circumstances.

If our movie of the past is one of either absolute delight or horror, either we've been very lucky or unlucky. Or we're projecting back from our present to redefine our past.

In any event it's worth asking if we need to play another movie reel that is providing a more uplifting life message.

IS IT ANOTHER GROUNDHOG DAY

What if there is no tomorrow? There wasn't one today.

PHIL CONNORS

Phil Connors, as played by actor Bill Murray in "Groundhog Day", is a self centred, defensive and grumpy weather forecaster, asked to head off to Punxsutawney, Pennsylvania to await the annual ritual of a groundhog emerging from its burrow. This signals whether or not the town will have an early end to the severe winter the town experiences.

Phil covers the story but a snowstorm traps him in the town for another night. Waking up in his guest room the following morning Connors is amazed to discover that it is the "morning of the day before all over again"; exactly the same radio announcement, conversations, meals, and reruns of the broadcast with the groundhog. And so it goes on, a time loop in which the day is replayed over and over again.

Initially depressed by his recurring life situation, Connors experiments with this new experience of time. Knowing that he has all the time in the world and knowing what will happen next in life, he takes piano lessons, learns the art of ice sculpture and becomes a Good Samaritan in the town.

Connors undergoes a transformation. "Trapped in a recurring day, a freezing day in Punxsutawney" in which nothing changes, only Phil can change. And he "undergoes a breakthrough to a more authentic self in which intimacy, creativity and compassion come naturally".

We don't live in a "groundhog day". We can't keep replaying the day until we get it right. But we can think about how the scripts of our past can keep us stuck in the same mind-set and habits that we experience as "rewind and replay". If we want today to be different we may need to go back to yesterday to work out what we want to change.

WHY BOB MARLEY WAS RIGHT ABOUT THE PAST

In this great future you can't forget your past. BOB MARLEY

We should look forward to the past.

The Western world spatialises time as a visual image in which the past is behind and the future is in front. We look forward to the future and we look back to the past.

The South American indigenous people, the Aymara people, living in the Andes highlands, hold a reverse concept of time. When asked about the past they point forward. The past summarises events they have experienced and known. The future is behind, because for the Aymara it isn't known and not worth speculation. Questions about what lies ahead are met with a shrug of the shoulders.

In a world keen to "move on" from the past to focus only on the future, the Aymara people may have identified an important truth. Our past is known but often we don't face it.

This isn't a life strategy of reminiscing with regret or finding comfort in nostalgia. Instead it's the reality that there are memories of our past that continue to be dynamics of our current happiness and future success.

"With the Future Behind Them" Rafael Núñeza & Eve Sweetser, 2006 Cognitive Science

WHO IS IN CONTROL

Who controls the past controls the future; who controls the present controls the past.

GEORGE ORWELL

In the nightmarish world of George Orwell's 1984, the totalitarian Ministry of Truth rewrites history. Because past events have no objective existence, surviving only as written records or human memories, the past can be whatever the records and memories agree upon.

In our minds, we operate our own Ministry of Truth through the experiences we repress, the memories we retain and exaggerate, and how we reinvent our past in light of current circumstances as well as our own future aspirations.

We can take control of our own present to ensure our past isn't becoming a tyrant that is running our lives.

WHAT WE CAN LEARN FROM HISTORY

Man is a history-making creature who can neither repeat his past nor leave it behind.

W.H. AUDEN

It helps us to see ourselves as part of our world's journey.

C WALSH

We can take the view that "history is a pack of lies about events that never happened told by people who weren't there".

Or, because we've bought into the hype about the speed and scale of change that is transforming our world, we can view past events as largely irrelevant to the challenges we now face. Because life is (and will continue to be) very different, there is not much to be learnt from old solutions to past problems; we need to find new solutions to a new set of problems.

Or we can see history as providing valuable insights to guide our thinking and decisions about the future. History can:

- **inspire us** to greater effort through the achievements of past pioneers and innovators. As Isaac Newton noted "If I have seen further it is by standing on the shoulders of giants." History reminds us of the giants
- **connect us to the spirit of human progress** to help understand the assumptions we hold about the way life has been, is and might be in future
- provide grounded examples of happiness and success and unhappiness and failure and **highlight the dynamics of how we might "live the good life"**
- **remind us of what we can change** quickly and what may take a bit longer given the realities of human nature and social interaction
- identify in a global world the **dynamics of cultural similarity and difference** and why and when we find it difficult to get along, and when countries and cultures have cooperated in harmony
- **shift our horizons** from the pressing day to day realities to see ourselves as part of a bigger life adventure and draw on past experiences to imagine new possibilities
- **learn humility.** If, as Edward Gibbon, suggested, "history is indeed little more than the register of the crimes, follies, and misfortunes of mankind" maybe we can avoid the hazards of stupidity and hubris

WHO DO WE THINK WE ARE

Committing yourself is a way of finding out who you are. A person finds their identity by identifying.

ROBERT TERWILLIGER

A tough question. Our identity - our sense of who we are - arises out of a complex dynamic of our life experience, career focus and status, our life style and hopes and aspirations.

Marshall Goldsmith suggests we think of our personal identity as the interplay of two dimensions:

- the first dimension spans our **past** to our **future**
- the second is the spectrum from the image **others** have of us to the image we have of **ourselves**

In simplistic terms we can adopt one of our four positions.

1. Self and Past: our remembered identity
This is our identity defined by us writing our autobiography. At best this is being connected to important family and cultural traditions and grounded in a solid sense of our life achievements. It may also be a personal identity caught up in difficulties from the past we haven't let go.

2. Others and Past: our reflected identity
This is our identity as defined by others' expectations of us based on our past. This is us being stereotyped by others' views of our past successes and failures. Here there is a risk that our identity becomes a kind of strait-jacket defined by others' perceptions of our previous achievements or disappointments, expectations that constrain our view of who we are and what is possible.

3. Others and Future: our programmed identity
This is us defined by others' expectations of what we can and will do in future. If this is an expectation from wise and supportive family members, friends and colleagues that we can achieve more in life, this identity may trigger greater effort. Alternatively, if our identity is a life script written by others and their views of what is possible, it may lack that authenticity that engages us fully in our future.

4. Self and Future: our created identity
This is the identity that we create for ourselves. This is the view of who we are that isn't controlled by our past or determined by others' view of what we can and can't do. This isn't personal identity as a Walter Mitty fantasy figure, out of touch with realities. It is an identity when we take charge of our personal destiny.

When we think about ourselves, it's worth checking what our identity is based on.

Is it one created for ourselves based on a positive view of our past, confidence about our current challenges and an optimistic outlook on the future and what is possible? Or one rooted in the past and others' out-dated views of our previous achievements?

"Are You Full of Mojo or Nojo?" Marshall Goldsmith 2009 Businessweek

WHY HAVE WE BEEN SUCCESSFUL

Those who have succeeded at anything and don't mention luck are kidding themselves.

LARRY KING

Success is entirely due to luck. Ask anyone who has failed.

OSCAR WILDE

In "Outliers", Malcolm Gladwell provides an alternative account of success. Instead of asking the usual questions:

- what are successful people like?
- what kind of personality do they have?
- how intelligent are they?
- what kind of life style do they have?
- what personal talents are they born with?

that might explain how successful individuals reach the top, Gladwell shifts the emphasis; "These kinds of personal explanations don't work."

"Successful people are invariably the beneficiaries of hidden advantages and extraordinary opportunities and cultural legacies that allow them to learn and work hard and make sense of the world. It is only by asking where they are from that we can unravel the logic behind who succeeds and who doesn't."

Although Gladwell's view may be disputed, his analysis is useful in reminding us that: success is an extraordinarily **complex** phenomenon. "Is it brains, education, personality, family relationships, skills, luck, etc?"

It's probably the interplay of all these factors (and it depends on how we define success in life), but luck makes a difference.

- **timing matters** in success. Success isn't about doing the right things, it's recognising the moments of greatest opportunity and moving at the right time to seize them
- **hard work is important** to success. This isn't the work of the unthinking slog; it is the hard work of continual and informed practice - the 10,000 hour rule - to keep improving to build mastery

- success is "dealing with things that go wrong, or better still, stopping things from going wrong." Failure often arises from the "cascading spiral of the trivial malfunctions"; success focuses on doing **lots of little things well**, and spotting when a little thing may be escalating into a bigger problem

Rather than framing our success as the deserved outcome of our innate brilliance, if we see success as a complex interplay of different factors, of which luck to have been born at a particular time and space is critical, then we might develop that humility that keeps us honest about our past and present.

WHY PROUST WAS RIGHT ABOUT THE POWER OF THE PAST

What we call our future is the shadow that our past projects in front of us.

MARCEL PROUST

From a well-to-do family, Proust was a critic, translator and socialite in Paris. After the deaths of his parents, Proust withdrew from a busy social life to his cork-lined room and worked the rest of his life on his semi-autobiographical novel Remembrance of Things Past.

The lengthy novel - around 3,200 pages - comprises memories from Proust's childhood, observations of aristocratic life-style, gossip and recollections of the closed world where he never quite found his place. In fact the description is "strikingly contemporary - networking, parties, infatuations, casual sex, capriciousness, impulse buying, celebrity worship."

And the book is a reflection of Proust's obsession with time. Where has it gone? Can it be restored?

Perhaps the most famous scene occurs as Proust dunks a Madeleine cake into a cup of tea, and his memory is triggered:

"No sooner had the warm liquid mixed with the crumbs touched my palate than a shudder ran through me and I stopped, intent upon the extraordinary thing that was happening to me. An exquisite pleasure had invaded my senses, something isolated, detached, with no suggestion of its origin. And at once the vicissitudes of life had become indifferent to me, its disasters innocuous, its brevity illusory..... I had ceased now to feel mediocre, contingent, mortal."

This is the stuff of memory, and we can revive our past by conjuring up memories. For Proust, the memories that counted the most were not the obvious experiences we easily recall. Instead it is the countless small incidents that we don't think meaningful at the time that turn out to be important. It is these involuntary memories - triggered by a smell, a taste, a burst of music - that have immense power to bring back our past.

At the end of his novel Proust observes: "a feeling of vertigo seized me as I looked down beneath me, yet within me, as though from a height of many leagues....at the long series of the years."

Our past is not passed. Our past is an ongoing source of our life meaning and purpose to give us power for the present and future.

SHOULD WE KEEP A SCRAPBOOK OF LIFE

And in the end, it's not the years in your life that count. It's the life in your years.

ABRAHAM LINCOLN

Making a scrapbook of our life story has become an increasingly popular activity, supported by dedicated websites and classes. Here the scrapbook is not simply an interesting collection of photographs and memorabilia but a reservoir of memories to connect our present to the past.

A study of reminiscence at Vanderbilt University showed that thinking about the past is one of the principal ways we continue to have a relationship with old parts of ourselves. Through reminiscing we maintain an "inventory" of the key images of ourselves from the past and weave "a thread of continuity among them." Reminiscing, the process of "life review," allows us to recall our accomplishments and come to terms with any past conflicts and disappointments.

Sharing the scrapbook of our life can also be an important element in our social lives. Time spent sharing life stories builds a greater understanding of others. The recall of enjoyable memories is pleasurable and even therapeutic.

Excessive reminiscence of course has its hazards; our personal and professional goals and relationships suffer when our focus is dominated by the past rather than the present and future. But if our life scrapbook is connecting us to our past - to put our past into perspective and to remind us of important memories - we should keep it up-to-date.

"Documenting your Memoirs with a Life Scrapbook"
Daniel Sklar

IS HOGMANAY WORTH CELEBRATING

> *Should auld acquaintance be forgot,*
> *And never brought to mind?*
> *Should auld acquaintance be forgot*
> *And auld lang syne!*

New Years Eve, and the stroke of midnight, and "Auld Lang Syne" - Old Long Ago - is sung. Robert Burns' first verse asks if our old acquaintances should be forgotten. As we face the end of one year and move into a new one, should we move on to forge new relationships and friendships?

Burns' response:

> *"For auld lang syne, my dear,*
> *For auld lang syne.*
> *We'll take a cup o' kindness yet*
> *For auld lang syne."*

We should "take a cup of kindness" to those who are part of our past. As Katherine Au points out "they deserve a toast, a mark of honour, of kindness in the present for what they mean to us."

This is life to be lived for the future in another year but with a recognition and appreciation of our past. Auld Lang Syne asks us to "be self conscious about the memories, the acquaintances and the influences from that past."

It's no accident that after the singing and dancing of New Year's Eve we then make resolutions at the start of another year in our lives. When we think about our future, our plans and hopes, and the changes we want to make, connecting to our past helps us understand who we are and what is important to us.

WHAT HOGMANAY SAYS ABOUT US

As the calendar changes, everyone experiences the anxiety of asking difficult questions: what have I done with my life? Why isn't my life happy? Where is my life going?"

HERBERT RAPPAPORT

New Year's Eve is a big deal. December 31st is more than just another date in the calendar. The passing of the old year and the arrival of the new one arouses a spectrum of emotions.

For some, it is the opportunity to **look back**, proud of the accomplishments of the last twelve months. Others review the year feeling sadness about disappointments and unfulfilled expectations, or mourning the loss of another year.

For other people, the chime of the bells is a vivid reminder that the "clock is ticking" and they feel anxious about the speed and turbulence of time. Some prefer to lose themselves in the festivities of the party, preferring to simply enjoy the **"here and now"** of the moment rather than think too much about the year that has gone or the challenges of the next one.

And there is another group that sees New Year's Eve as a time to take stock and **plan ahead** for the forthcoming year. The past is past, and the party will soon be over. Members of this group are mentally working through the resolutions they need to make to ensure a better future.

At the next Hogmanay celebration, it's worth checking if we are celebrating and what that celebration might say about us.

DOES PAST LIFE REGRESSION HELP US MAKE SENSE OF WHO WE ARE NOW

When you use past life regression it may be helpful for you to have an open mind.

ADMIN AT WWW.ALDOHAS.COM

If you open your mind too much, your brain may fall out.

FRANCIS WHEEN

If we're feeling dissatisfied with our current life it may be because we have become disconnected from the lives we have already lived. It may be difficult experiences we encountered as a child growing up. It may even be further back in time to discover the problems we faced as a slave in ancient Egypt or as a factory owner in Victorian Britain.

In past life regression, the negative feelings we have today - "our faulty thoughts" - are a "carry over" from the past. And the carry overs, the wrongs we have committed and the injustices we experienced, unless addressed, will block our future life development.

Past life regression (PLR), often involving hypnosis, takes us back on a journey to our previous lives, either experienced in our historical past or in a previous reincarnation. For PLR therapists the process is essential to healing.

At one level, the concept of past life regression has a certain intuitive appeal. Our past does shape who we are now. And our memories - positive and negative - do affect the way we now approach life. Of course, for example, it is important to let go and forgive.

What is less obvious, disturbing and potentially damaging is the way past life regression therapists:

- prompt the emergence of false memories
- treat every life problem as a voyage back to a troubled past
- exploit the anxious and vulnerable with a treatment process with no empirical foundation

If we want a better present and future there are better solutions than travelling back in our imagination to a world a past life regression therapist manufactures for us.

"Past life regression: a skeptic's guide" at Skeptic's Dictionary

"Self Conducted Past Life Regression" Ellen A. Mogensen at HealPastLives.com

"Review of "Crazy" Therapies" Bob Carroll 1997 in Science & Pseudoscience Review in Mental Health

WHY READING THE BUMPER BOOK OF WISDOM WON'T MAKE US WISE

If you were to read the bumper book of wisdom when you were very young, it wouldn't make any sense. You have to live through something to understand it properly.

GUY BROWNING

There are those who imagine that the unlucky accidents of life - life's "experiences" - are in some way useful to us. I wish I could find out how. I never know one of them to happen twice. They always change off and swap around and catch you on your inexperienced side.

MARK TWAIN

Reading the "Big Bumper Book of Wisdom" won't make us wise. Wisdom requires an engagement with the full flow of life experience. But wisdom gained only through experience can be slow, difficult and at times painful. It is true that human nature being what it is, some lessons we seem to learn only after we have failed the test.

But we can accelerate our progress by:

- applying **honesty about our failings and mistakes** to avoid repeating them. As Dale Turner notes: "Some of the best lessons we ever learn are learned from past mistakes. The error of the past is the wisdom and success of the future."
- reflecting on **what has worked well** and how to build on these achievements for the future. This isn't living based on repeating the same formula over and over again, but it is to recognise our fundamental talents and strengths and how to deploy them for future challenges
- **adopting the kind of humility** which is responsive to the insights of others from our past, looking to learn from individuals who have been on the path

"25 lessons I've learnt in 50 years" Barrie Davenport at www.marcandangel.com

WHY BURNING AFTER READING IS A MISTAKE

Report back to me when it makes sense. CIA SUPERIOR

Fired by the CIA, John Malkovich decides to write a memoir of his experiences. His whiskey-sodden ramblings find themselves on a disc in a bag left in a health club. Brad Pitt and Frances McDormand, the gym employees, assuming this is highly classified information, spot an opportunity to make money and resort to blackmail.

Malkovich refuses to play ball, and the gym employees go to the Russian embassy to sell the information. "Burn After Reading", a classic Coen brothers' film, is a screwball, dark and chaotic comedy, full of misunderstandings.

The film concludes at CIA HQ with the Director checking on the status of the various players in the episode (either dead or in hospital):

CIA Superior: What did we learn, Palmer?
CIA Officer: I don't know, sir.
CIA Superior: I don't ******* know either. I guess we learned not to do it again.
CIA Officer: Yes, sir.
CIA Superior: I'm ****** if I know what we did.
CIA Officer: Yes, sir, it's, uh, hard to say.

Chaos of course is confusing. But if we don't learn anything, we may find ourselves repeating the chaos.

HOW WE CAN MAKE THE EXPERIENCE OF LIFE A BIT LESS PAINFUL

There is only one thing more painful than learning from experience, and that is not learning from experience.

LAURENCE J. PETER

Experience is a brutal teacher, but you learn. My God, do you learn.

C.S. LEWIS

Experience is critical to our lives and progression. We might know the theory of "what should be done in principle", but until "we've been there, done it and got the T shirt"; there will always be a question mark about our capability and credibility.

But experience can be difficult. It's challenging and costly. Experience is about mistakes that can be embarrassing. Experience wastes time in futile endeavours we regret. And experience incorporates the risks of set backs and disappointments that might dent our confidence to tackle future challenges.

If we can't avoid the realities of life experiences, we can at least put in place processes that optimise our learning from experience.

The first is **reflective thinking to turn experience into insight**. If we don't understand what we did, why we did it and its impact, we may at worst, keep repeating costly mistakes or, at best, fail to leverage the knowledge from the experience.

The second is to **find a mentor** and establish the kind of relationship that is responsive to others' experience and life learning. We tend to over-estimate the uniqueness of our life situation, thinking that others' experiences and emotions are very different to our own. Often they're not. With humility we can discover from others' successes and failures, insights that may be painful and time consuming for us to learn first hand.

"44 Ways How to Find a Mentor" Mike Michalowicz

HOW GROOVES BECOME RUTS

If you look at every leading company that has ultimately lost, one of the things that will be consistent in all of them is that what was once a groove has become a rut, and ultimately becomes a cultural impediment for even thinking differently.

HARVEY GOLUB

When we're in the groove we're in the zone of excellence. Grooves provide consistency of purpose, focusing attention on what matters and avoiding distractions, and helping deploy our current strengths.

But grooves easily become ruts. Our success reinforces a way of doing things that we keep repeating. But the groove becomes a rut that constrains our thinking of new directions.

When our past is a groove that prompts excellence we continue to succeed. When the groove is in danger of becoming a rut we're in trouble.

WHY MISTAKES ARE GOOD

Mistakes are the portals of discovery.

JAMES JOYCE

Give me a fruitful error anytime, full of seeds, bursting with its own corrections.

VILFREDO PARETO

Ellen Langer asked Harvard students to give unprepared speeches to an audience. Students were assigned to one of three groups:

- mistakes are bad and shouldn't be made - the fear condition
- mistakes are OK and instructed to make a mistake - the forgiveness condition
- make mistakes and incorporate them into the speech itself - the openness to novelty condition

Speakers gave their talks knowing they would be judged on their performance. Those speakers in the openness to novelty group rated themselves as more comfortable and were evaluated as more effective by the audience.

If we cut ourselves some slack to accept our past mistakes in life, and accept we will make more mistakes in future, maybe we loosen up to operate with greater confidence and curiousity.

"Curiosity: the secret to your success", Rosie Ifould, Psychologies

WHY WE GET IT WRONG ABOUT OUR OWN AND OTHER' BEHAVIOUR

What this means is that we are not very good scientists, we tend to take things 'personally' - and it's normal! Our explanatory style is paranoid by default.

PAVEL SOMOV

We explain others' behaviour and actions as a reflection of their character. When others let us down, for example, our interpretation is they are inconsiderate and ill-mannered. But we tend to overlook the power of situations to shape behaviour (i.e. the person was extremely busy at the time and had a lot on).

However, with ourselves, we recognise the pressures of circumstances. When we make a mistake, we attribute it to the situation rather than arising from our personality (we're unlikely to explain our mistake by identifying our thoughtlessness).

If we remember this bias - "the fundamental attribution error"- in how we explain our and others' behaviour, we may find it easier to:

- maintain a sense of personal humility about our own successes and failures
- avoid the finger of blame in identifying who cocked up

WHY THE MANNERS OF MEMORY MATTER

There is no sound sweeter to most people than their own names.

When we meet someone for the first time we should make sure we get the name. One reason we don't remember names is that we didn't get it in the first place. Either we're preoccupied with what we're about to say or we get distracted by the general clamour of conversation.

If you don't hear the name, ask the person to repeat it. And after hearing it, repeat it back to confirm that you heard it correctly as well as to help you remember it. And try to use the name quickly in the conversation that follows. Don't be clumsy about it. Too much repetition and the person will get nervous! And when you get the opportunity, write down the name.

Make the name meaningful. Here memory association can be useful. Either create a visual image based on the name (e.g. Keith Sawyer becomes a sawmill with a large K sign at the front). Or associate the name with someone else you already know who has a similar name.

Focus on a distinctive feature of the person's appearance that will attract your attention the next time you meet the person. Studies show that studying the person's face and trying to make a personal judgment (such as honesty, kind, etc.) helps in remembering the person.

Review the association. The name and the face now need to be consolidated in your long-term memory. After your conversation, think about who you met - their name, face and the specifics of your conversation. Talk about this individual to others and describe them in detail. And it can be useful to make notes at this time to strengthen your memory as well as have a written record of the people you met which can be revisited before your next encounter.

"How to remember names and faces" at www.skillstoolbox.com

WHY IT'S GOOD TO BE GRATEFUL

Gratitude is not only the greatest of virtues, but the parent of all the others.

CICERO

Do we take ourselves and our past achievements and successes for granted? Are we taking others and the support they provide also for granted?

Gratitude is an antidote to the negative emotions we may feel about our situation. It is true there may be reasons to feel resentment and a sense of injustice. But gratitude - the appreciation of our life as it is today - helps translate the past into present.

"Count your blessings" may seem an old fashioned exhortation. But it works.

- start keeping a **diary to note five things** for which you are thankful. Do this once a week for ten weeks in a row and review your attitudes
- remember to **remember the good things** in life. Don't allow yourself to focus only on the mistakes and the problems
- make **gratitude part of your daily life**. Recognising others for what they have done for you, even the small acts of kindness, is necessary even when the person is family or a close friend
- **say "thank you"** for every act of kindness received. It's so simple to say and yet often unsaid
- take the time to **write a note** (handwritten is best) or send an email to express your appreciation, even if you already said thank you
- look for opportunities to **reciprocate favours** as soon as possible. Be observant to give spontaneous service instead of asking if help is needed
- provide ways to support others who are less fortunate. We never know when the tables might be turned one day

"The art of the thank you note" Trent Hamm at www.thesimpledollar.com

WHAT WAS MOREESE BICKHAM'S GLORIOUS EXPERIENCE

I don't have a moment of regret. It was a glorious experience.

MOREESE BICKHAM

So remarked Moreese Bickham upon being released from prison after serving thirty-seven years for defending himself against Ku Klux Klansmen who shot him.

On the evening of July 12, 1958, Moreese Bickham had an argument with two sheriff's deputies in a bar called "Buck's Place" in Mandeville, Louisiana. At approximately 11 pm the deputies drove Bickham's girlfriend home. The deputies wore street clothes, and many in the community believed the two deputies were associated with the Ku Klux Klan.

Later that night, the two officers arrived at Mr. Bickham's home. The deputies approached Mr. Bickham's front door, and fired at Mr. Bickham, striking him in the stomach. Mr. Bickham returned fire with a shotgun. Mr. Bickham was arrested several hours later at Baton Rouge Hospital. He was quickly convicted of two counts of first degree murder (premeditated homicide) and sentenced to death. For fourteen years, Mr. Bickham avoided execution, winning seven stays of execution. He lived on death row in the Angola State Penitentiary, in solitary confinement 23 hours per day. In 1972, after the U.S. Supreme Court determined that some death sentences were unconstitutional, the State of Louisiana converted Bickham's sentence to life without parole.

In 1994 corporate attorney Michael Alcamo accepted Bickham's case pro bono. On January 10, 1996, Alcamo escorted Bickham from the prison, as a free man, not subject to parole.

"It was a glorious experience."

Is this the delusion of someone who is rationalising a "wasted life"?

Like Pete Best, the original drummer of the Beatles who was dropped in favour of Ringo Starr, who said: "I'm happier than I would have been with The Beatles", it's easy for us to re-interpret our past and put a positive spin on previous events.

But the objective facts of our experience and the flow of life events are much less important to our happiness than **how we think** about this experience and these events. We think that failing an exam, losing our job, or the walk out of a partner, will have a devastating impact on our lives. And of course for some individuals these life disasters are damaging. But most of us seem to be remarkably resilient.

It's worth asking: is it a glorious experience?

"Why adversity is good for you" Melissa Karnaze at www.mindfulconstruct.com

"How not to be happy" Michele Connolly at www.happinessstrategies.com

HOW TO CREATE A PERSONAL TIMELINE

All that really belongs to us is time; even they who have nothing else have that.

BALTASAR GRACIAN

A timeline is a graphical representation of a period in time used to indicate change. Biographical and historical timelines also show context. A great research and study tool, timelines can also be used as a way of making sense of our own lives and the key episodes in the flow of our time. It helps us see key moments in our past life, highlighting our accomplishments (and darker moments of failure) and to establish a sense of continuity and purpose from our past to our present and future.

To create our personal timeline:

1. Start by making a few notes from your past. The day you were born is probably a good start. But some timelines go back a generation to begin with parents. Reflect on the key events in your life that in some way stand out as significant and important for you. Imagine you're writing your autobiography, which episodes would you write about?

2. Draw on a sheet of paper (landscape is best) a straight horizontal line near the bottom of the page with enough space to make notes below the line. This will be your timeline from your start point. Rather than end the horizontal point today leave enough space for your future. This is important. Now draw a vertical line on the left hand side from the start of your horizontal line to the top of the page. (Think back to the X-Y axes of school mathematics).

3. Write down the dates and a summary of the key events below the horizontal line. These are the facts of your time line. Don't worry if it gets messy. This is a working version which can be updated.

4. Once you've got a sense of the flow of events across the horizontal axis (e.g. early years, school, college, first job, and so on) it's time to label the vertical axis. It could be a happiness index (from low: unhappy to high: happy) but you may want to try something different (e.g. financial success, popularity). For each episode on the horizontal line plot its position on the vertical axis. Here you're indicating which events in the past have made you more or less happy (successful, popular etc).

5. Review your timeline to identify the pattern. No doubt there will be ups and downs and relative highs and lows as you move through the "time of your life". Is there any overall theme as you assess the trajectory of past to present?

6. Look again at the horizontal line. What about your future? Now is the time to map out your thoughts on future key episodes. This is the expression of your ideals and aspirations; a chart of your future life.

Now stand back. What is your timeline and the implications for your future? Looking to:

- build on the continuity of your past to stick with a winning formula?
- raise your game to improve upon your past?
- reinvent yourself to become a very different person?

CAN WE EVER START A NEW LIFE

Here lies Reginald Iolanthe Perrin. He didn't know the names of the trees and the flowers, but he knew the rhubarb crumble sales figures for Schleswig-Holstein.

REGINALD PERRIN

Well, I sort of staged a fake suicide and came back as my long lost friend.

REGINALD PERRIN

You can start over, but the biggest problem isn't the environment, but you.

KALEV OLIVE

John Darwin was seen paddling out to sea in his canoe on 21 March 2002, near Hartlepool on the North Sea. Later the same day, he was reported as "missing" after failing to report to work. Despite a large-scale sea search, there was no sign of Darwin, although a double-ended paddle was retrieved the following day. Later on 22 March 2002, the wreckage of John Darwin's canoe was found.

A death certificate was issued the following month, and his wife Anne made a claim on his life insurance, allowing a £130,000 mortgage to be paid.

On 1 December 2007, Darwin walked into a London police station, telling the police "I think I am a missing person" and claiming to have no memory of the past five years. His wife Anne - who had sold up her properties in England and moved to Panama three months before his re-appearance - expressed surprise and joy at the return of her missing husband.

When a member of the public typed the words "John", "Anne" and "Panama" into Google Images, a photograph revealed that the Darwins had been living in Panama. On 23 July 2008, John Darwin and Anne Darwin were both convicted of fraud, and sentenced to prison terms of over six years.

For some it's an appealing thought. Like Canoe Man, if we've made a mess of our life through financial troubles, work difficulties or marital problems, we can disappear to begin a new life. In another part of the world, with a different life style and new colleagues and friends, we can start all over again.

The key question however is the "who" that begins this new life. As Oliver Burkeman points out: "the concept of the fresh start suggests a very bizarre notion of the self...to try to escape entirely what makes you yourself is surely doomed by definition."

Of course we can and do change in life. Our past is not our destiny. But it's worth acknowledging that who we are now reflects the dynamics of our past, our genetic legacy, early upbringing, family dynamics, and so on in shaping our personality, motivations and aspirations.

We may find it difficult to start a completely new life if we're stuck with the person we were.

"How to Disappear Completely and Never Be Found" Doug Richmond

"Fresh Starts" Oliver Burkeman at www.guardian.co.uk

DOES OUR LIFE FLASH BEFORE OUR EYES

"About 13 years ago while flying from Quito, Ecuador to New York the plane I was in had an engine failure and we had to do an emergency landing in Bogotá, Colombia. It was insane at 30.000 feet, coming down really fast and everyone screaming and praying, the plane coming down sideways, shaking everywhere. When the plane is approaching the runway and ready to land and in those brief seconds all my life flashed before my eyes. Things from the time I was a newborn till then, things I done wrong, good moments, smiles, tears, ex-girlfriends, school time, parents, family, friends. It was an incredible experience. I do feel my entire life flashed before my eyes in a few seconds I saw everything like a fast forward yet strangely at the same time in slow motion as if time "stopped"."

NOSHA MCKENNA

The car in front of us suddenly brakes and, as we in turn stand on the brakes waiting for the impact, events seem to go into slow motion.

Survivors of near death experiences report a slowing down in time during moments of intense fear and often the experience in which their entire life is replayed in flash images.

David Eagleman, a neuroscientist at Baylor College of Medicine, Houston, was interested in exploring if our perception of time does slow down in the intensity of a frightening situation. In a dramatic experiment, volunteers jumped backwards 150 feet into a net without ropes or a harness. During the terrifying free fall - around 3 seconds - the volunteers looked at a screen on their forearm in which numbers whizzed faster than the normal mind could register. Eagleman argued that if time did slow down in a situation of intense fear, then the volunteers would be able to read the numbers. But they couldn't.

Although we record more memories when we experience extreme fear, time doesn't slow down. Instead the fear activates a key part of our memory. Either our brain goes into hyper-drive to scan its memory bank at phenomenal speed for a solution to a life threatening problem, or our brain is running an accelerated back up to consolidate the memories of a harrowing episode we want to avoid in future. In either case, our memory is creating the illusion of slow motion time.

Eagleman's findings are still a focus of academic dispute.

Perhaps the most practical conclusion was summarised by one flight crew member who had a near death experience.

> *My entire life flashed before me. My parents, grandparents, cousins, etc. were all as they were every time I had seen them. I remembered every last detail, colours, faces, everything from my entire life. This experience drastically altered my behaviour for the rest of my life.*

If our life is going to flash before our lives what images would we see?

"Does time really slow down during a frightening event" C Stetson et al, 2007 at PlosOne.org

"How can my life flash before my eyes" at www.wisegeek.com

Pummelvision lets you watch your life flash before your eyes Adam Dachis at LifeHacker.com

WAS IT A GOOD IDEA FOR BRIDGET JONES TO KEEP A DIARY

9st 4; alcohol units 4; cigarettes 12 (no longer priority); calories 3,752 (pre diet); self help books scheduled for dustbin 47

DIARY ENTRY, MONDAY 14 JULY, 1999 BRIDGET JONES

Whether we laugh or we cry, whether through sorry or joy, we can understand more about ourselves and each other, through keeping a journal or diary.

DOREENE CLEMENT

"Bridget Jones's Diary" is the book and film of a thirty-something, working in publishing, concerned about her weight, worried about her life, who decides on New Year's Eve "to turn it all around and start her diary. This is the record of her attempts to stop smoking, lose weight and catch Mr Right."

Is a diary an effective way, as Bridget Jones believed, to track life and kick-start change? Or is the record of our daily thoughts an exercise in introspection that does nothing other than encourage the replay and rumination of the difficult experiences of past life that can only make things worse?

The science seems to suggest that keeping a diary is a positive factor in life. Matthew Lieberman, using brain scan technology, investigated the "Bridget Jones effect". "Writing seems to help the brain regulate emotion. Whether it's writing things down in a diary, writing bad poetry, or making up song lyrics" it seems to build emotional maturity.

Expressive writing, according to psychologist James Pennebaker, helps us simplify and organise the fragmented memories of our lives. The process of "write it down" forms a coherent narrative to make sense of what we did and felt.

A diary, as the politicians and their associated spin doctors know, can be written to put a positive version on events, protect a reputation or simply be a way of cashing in on a past reputation. This is the Mae West theory of diary management: "if you keep a diary, one day it may keep you." Here diary entries are made with one eye on the past and the other eye looking to the future.

Alternatively, a diary written with authenticity is a way of slowing down time to keep track of events and make some kind of sense of our life experience. And in the future when we look back on our life we have an account of our past to trigger the memories of the wonderful episodes as well as the moments of difficulty and adversity.

For Bridget Jones, her diarising almost ended badly. Mark, one of her competing lovers, reads her diary and seemingly hurt about Bridget's entries about him, leaves. Bridget, distraught, rushes out in the snow to see Mark returning, holding a new diary.

"The new diary is a gift to give their relationship a fresh start. They kiss."

"Keeping a diary makes you happier" Ian Sample, 2009 Guardian

"A new reason for keeping a diary" Siri Carpenter, 2001, at apa.org

HOW TO LIVE TWICE

To be able to look back upon one's past life with satisfaction is to live twice.

MARCUS VALERIUS MARTIAL

> Blofeld: Allow me to introduce myself. I am Ernst Stavro Blofeld. They told me you were assassinated in Hong Kong.
> James Bond: Yes, this is my second life.
> Blofeld: You only live twice, Mr. Bond.

We can rush through life, caught up in the priorities and pressures of the moment, or charge on to prepare for future challenges. And in the process we forget the lives we have lived, and our experiences of our "seasons in the sun" as well as our periods of cold winter.

Sometimes it's good to stop and reflect on our two lives, the life we live and the life we can look back on, remembering who we were and what we achieved.

HELD BACK BY THE PAST

The stories that you tell about your past shape your future.

ERIC RANSDELL

When we look back on our past we do not sit as a movie goer passively watching the film of our previous lives. Our memories of who we were and what we did and felt are not a perfect record of past reality. When we look back to our past it's informative to check how our current mood and future expectations are now directing the movie we're watching.

When our reminiscences of the past are caught up in unfairness and injustice, regret and revenge are the responses that are triggered. Rumination over previous difficulties can either make us sulk about life's vagaries or trigger anger about those who offended or hurt us. In either case we are held back from living today to prepare for tomorrow.

This section examines how our memory plays tricks, the themes of negative emotions and why our previous relationships with others are often the reasons for our dissatisfaction, how past investments that didn't work are "sunk costs" and best forgotten, and when the "misery industry" of counsellors and therapists may do more harm than good.

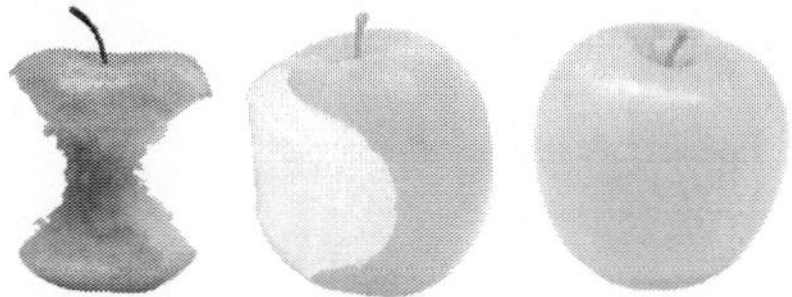

PAST

ARE WE SURVIVING OR THRIVING

In spite of all similarities, every living situation has, like a newborn child, a new face, that has never been before and will never come again. It demands of you a reaction that cannot be prepared beforehand. It demands nothing of what is past. It demands presence, responsibility; it demands you.

MARTIN BUBER

You can resent your bald spot or be glad you have a head.

PAUL PEARSALL

We have a repertoire of life responses to adversity and crisis.

Some reactions can make the crisis worse, some partly mitigate the effects, and others, strange though it may seem, provide a platform for greater life maturity. Paul Pearsall maps the spectrum of our responses including:

- **kindling** is when we add emotional fuel to the fire of the crisis. This is the reaction of anger and aggression, either to chastise ourselves for our own stupidity or to blame others and find fault. Venting might make us feel temporarily better, but expressing our anger causes the negative feelings to worsen and persist. In kindling, we flood our system with emotion and it becomes difficult to think clearly and make informed judgments

- in **suffering** we perceive ourselves to be the victim, feeling sorry for ourselves and our predicament, and withdraw into a state of self pity. This may be an inevitable part of the process in our reactions to trauma. When **** happens, it's not nice and it's easy to ask "why me?" Paul Pearsall points out that the "social sympathy and seductive calming effect of feeling victimised can feel soothingly good." But if we remain in the victim mode for too long, it damages our chances of thriving

- in **surviving**, we begin to enter the phase of "making it". Drawing on our courage and a sense that the "show must go on", we move to a point that helps us pick up the pieces and get on with things. But surviving seems to take a lot out of us; we tire easily and feel mentally drained

- **recovering** describes that response in which we bounce back to our pre-crisis state. We appear and feel none the worse for wear. Our energy levels return and we seem back to our formal selves again

- **thriving**. Here we thrive after the crisis. We not only bounce back, but we begin to flourish, operating at a higher level of mental and emotional functioning. And the remarkable thing is that we're flourishing, not in spite of the crisis, but because of it

It's important to ask: how are we doing emotionally?

- just about managing to stay in the game?
- or enjoying fulfilling our commitments and relishing the prospect of new challenges?

"The Beethoven Factor" Paul Pearsall

WHY DO WE FORGET HOW HAPPY WE ARE

I can guarantee you that while you look through so much ghostly contamination from your past; you will never know the beauty of living in the now.

SYDNEY BANKS

Sydney Banks asked by a friend, how he was feeling, mentioned he was a bit down. His friend said: "You're not really unhappy, Syd, you just think you are." A light bulb popped in Sydney's brain. He was in fact happy. He realised that a lot of the time we're unhappy because we choose to be unhappy.

Syd Banks recognised that we can spend time tracking back in time for explanations of our current life situation to explain why we don't feel as happy as we think we should be.

Banks' approach, refreshingly simple and direct, turns the philosophy of much mainstream therapy on its head. Instead of helping free people gradually from the early experiences that subconsciously influence their actions, Banks argues:

- the past is gone; today is the only day that exists
- previous experiences don't exist; our memories are only illusions
- take control of how you think to live in the now

Like the character Meursault in Albert Camus' novel "The Outsider" who, faced with death "suddenly" realises "I had been happy and I still was", if we let go of troubling memories from the past to focus on the "now", we might discover we're happier than we think.

"Health Realization" at Wikipedia
"The Enlightened Gardener" Sydney Banks

WHY A PICTURE IS WORTH A THOUSAND LIES

If memory is the diary we carry about, then it is likely to include truths, half truths, gaps and falsities.

K WADE & C LANEY

An interviewer shows us some personal photographs from our past. We are encouraged to recall the events depicted in each of the photos.

One of the photographs shows us as a child taking a hot air balloon ride. And the picture brings back a rush of memories as we relive the episode. "I was in year 6 at the local school. It would have been a Saturday. I'm pretty certain that Mum is down on the ground taking the photo."

The only problem is that the hot air balloon experience never happened. We are looking at a fake image which has been doctored.

Half of the participants in this research remembered something about the hot air balloon experience.

Our memories are of course inexact and unreliable. With a bit of digital trickery and interpersonal suggestion we can relive an event that never occurred. What is remarkable is that these false memories are held with as much detail, emotional power and conviction as our true memories.

This phenomenon suggests we develop a degree of healthy scepticism about what others say about their past and humility to accept that what we intensely remember may never have happened.

"Time to Rewrite Your Autobiography" Kimberley A Wade and Cara Laney, 2008 The Psychologist

PAST

WHY WE SHOULD MARVEL AT OUR MEMORY BUT RECOGNISE ITS FAILINGS

How do we cram the vast universe of our experience into the relatively small compartment between our ears.

DANIEL GILBERT

The difference between false memories and true ones is the same as for jewels: it is always the false ones that look the most real, the most brilliant.

SALVADOR DALI

Our memory is an amazing piece of mental tool-kit. Our memories can transport us back through the days, weeks, months and years of our lives to answer the question: remember when:

- we felt the anxiety of our first day of school
- the Christmas when snow began to fall on Christmas Eve and we hoped Father Christmas will remember to give us the Beano annual
- the shame of the first date that went embarrassingly wrong
- the elation and joy on passing our driving test
- the sun rose on Mount Batur

But because our brain capacity is limited, the marvel of our memory - given the amount of stuff it has to deal with - is that it works at all. It does work, and thanks to a sneaky evolutionary trick it works by cheating. We don't save every sensory association of every life moment. Instead our memory compresses the fullness of life experience into a few patterns.

And when we want to recreate a memory, the "tailor of our memory" doesn't rush out with the original suit. Instead it checks the pattern that is being triggered to then fabricate the experience. Our memory is good at this; it's quick and effortless. We feel we're wearing the original suit. But the memory tailor is assembling some kind of semblance of what we bought.

A brilliant solution by Mother Nature to the limitations of our brain capacity, the tactic of fabrication also has consequences. It means:

- **our current mood affects what we recall**. If the tailor is in a bad mood right now it affects the suits he produces. When he is negative he recalls the suits that didn't fit and made us feel awkward

- our **future expectations of life and its possibilities also distort our imagination.** When we're optimistic and full of hope about success, our memories construct examples of previous achievement, confirming our belief that we will succeed. And when we're pessimistic the tailor of memory fabricates episodes of past failure to remind us of our hopelessness

After millennia of evolutionary development, it's unlikely that we're going to rectify the limitations of our memories. But we can recognise how it constrains the way we think. It might help if we:

- check that our mood isn't distorting how we think about our past and future
- make use of a log or diary to record our experiences of events when they happen

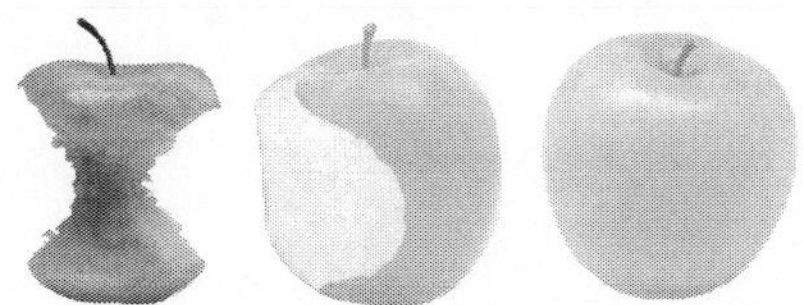

WHY WE SEEM PROGRAMMED TO RECALL THE MORE UNPLEASANT STUFF

Robert Plant may have been right: "good times, bad times, you know I've had my share." But it doesn't always feel like that. Van Halen asked: "where have all the good times gone?"

Why do we seem to remember the embarrassments, humiliations and unpleasantnesses of life in such vivid detail? Why are these episodes so easily played back from our memory?

This is the stuff of life that filters into our brains and keeps us awake at night. These are the memories of what we didn't do but should have, or what we did but shouldn't have. Rather than recall our accomplishments with pride, why are our memories more likely to revive the negatives?

In part it's driven by a smart evolutionary strategy that has served us well: the importance of fear in our survival. Mental software attuned to risk and threat is more likely to have kept us in the gene pool than an operating system that filtered out past hazards and left us only with memories of security and success. The problem is that this mental programming is better suited to the challenges we faced 10,000 years ago than the demands of life right now.

So why can't we simply forget the bad memories? One reason is that we revisit these episodes in an attempt to make sense of what happened. As Angela Londono-McConnell suggests "we're trying to answer the question why."

Sometimes it's good to know why we experienced set backs or did stupid stuff. Here we can review our past to gain important insights. Sometimes the reality is that there is no meaning.

Here we should just accept that replaying these moments from our past will only make us feel worse.

"Nature vs Nurture" Keith Hammonds, 2000 Fast Company

"Why memory lane is such a mortifying stroll" Diana Mapes, 2009 at msnbc.com

"Do-Over!" Jason Zasky at Failure Magazine

WHY AN ADVENTURE IS AN INCONVENIENCE RIGHTLY CONSIDERED

An adventure is only an inconvenience rightly considered. An inconvenience is an adventure wrongly considered.

G. K. CHESTERTON

Who remembers the conveniences of life? We don't seem to remember the times of peace, tranquillity and ease as well as the moments of awkwardness, awfulness and adversity. Whether it is the eccentric school teacher, the hurt of a break up, or the excruciating mistakes of a first job or the disaster of a camping holiday in Cornwall, it is the "inconveniencies" that stand out in our memories as somehow more vivid.

Embarrassing, dismal, or painful at the time, the inconveniencies of life seem to add a colour and texture to our lives that the happy times don't.

This isn't to agree with Joseph Heller, the writer of Catch 22.

Maybe a long life does have to be filled with many unpleasant conditions if it's to seem long. But in that event, who wants one.

But it is to suggest that G K Chesterton may be right when he suggests that we reframe life's inconveniences as part of the overall adventure.

PAST

HOW R D LAING'S PAST MADE THE FUTURE WORSE FOR OTHERS

From the moment of birth, when the stone-age baby confronts the twentieth century mother, the baby is subjected to these forces of violence, called love. These forces are mainly concerned with destroying most of its potentialities.

R D LAING

For a brief period in the early 1970s Ronald David Laing was the most famous psychiatrist in the world. His books, including the classic "The Divided Self", sold in millions. Laing attacked the psychiatric orthodoxy and its focus on genetics, biological treatment within grim and forbidding institutions in a bid to restore some kind of humanity to the therapeutic process. In a world in which "insulin induced comas, electric shocks, strait-jackets and padded cells" were the standard elements of "treatment", this was welcome.

The alternative view is that Laing was an unstable charlatan who "peddled anti-establishment opinions as a platform to advance his own career, and in the process, proposed views on schizophrenia that were dangerous nonsense", both for individuals and their families.

Laing's message however resonated with the radicalism of the 60's and the growing disillusionment with authority and the establishment. The idea that we can make sense of the baffling world of the schizophrenic, and that their incomprehensible behaviour and speech is rooted in disturbed family communication, took hold. In "The Divided Self", Laing argued that schizophrenia is the outcome when two identities come into conflict. If the identity defined for us by our families is very different to the authentic identity we experience for ourselves, the self is fractured. For Laing madness could be a voyage of self discovery, and when sufferers were freed of medical intervention and given enough support they could progress in their life journey of healing and growth.

Kingsley Hall, Laing's experiment of a new therapeutic community, attracted "visitors from all over the world as well as celebrities, poets, rock starts, misfits and former patients". Sean Connery, finding stardom difficult after appearing as James Bond in Goldfinger was encouraged by Laing to take LSD to help his anxiety. Predictably Kingsley Hall disintegrated into chaos and Laing headed off to Sri Lanka.

His later years were marked by dependence on alcohol and drugs, and he was forced to withdraw from the General Medical Council after accusations of drunkenness and assault.

In “The Wing of Madness”, Laing’s biographer traces his controversial ideas and erratic life style to a difficult childhood and adolescence. At the age of five, Laing’s mother told him that Santa Claus did not exist; an event that Laing later said triggered his first existential crisis. She also burned a little wooden horse to which Ronnie was becoming too attached. Later his mother began sticking pins into a “Ronald doll” with the aim of inducing a heart attack, although it’s worth noting, other family members did not support this claim. Undoubtedly, though, Laing grew up in an emotionally troubled world.

What perhaps is most striking about the life of Laing, given his conviction that mental illness arises out of family dynamics, is how extraordinarily badly he treated his own family. Abandoning his first five children and leaving them in penury, he “fathered five more children with three different women, had innumerable affairs and subjected them to violent drunken rages”. One son Adrian, writing his father’s biography, noted “it was ironic that my father became well known as a family psychiatrist, when in the meantime he had nothing to do with his own family.”

20 years after his death, R D Laing continues to stir controversy. A potential film, starring Robert Carlyle, is on hold whilst biographers battle over screen plays.

Disentangling the objective facts of Laing’s past and his reinventions from his present is impossible. What is clear is that Laing’s “past”, just like that of his own mother, who was “preparing herself emotionally and spiritually for the death of her father” at the time of Ronnie’s birth, cast a large cloud over his own life and that of his family.

“R D Laing revisited” Allan Beveridge, 1998 The Psychiatrist

“The Wing of Madness: Life and Work of R.D. Laing” Daniel Burston

“R. D. Laing: A Life” Adrian Laing

“The celebrity shrink who put the psychedelia into psychiatry” Jonathan Brown, 2008 The Independent

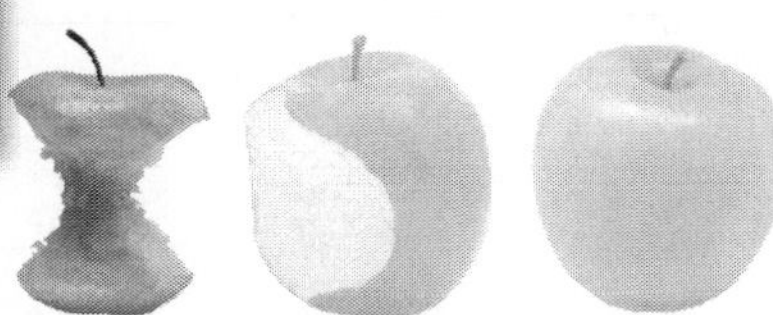

PAST

WILL IT EVER BE POSSIBLE TO GO BACK IN TIME

I'll be back.

ARNOLD SCHWARZENEGGER

Look back, live forward.

SUZANNE FINNAMORE

As physicists, our experiments deal with subatomic particles. How soon humans will be able to time travel depends largely on the success of these experiments, which will take the better part of a decade. And depending on breakthroughs, technology, and funding, I believe that human time travel could happen this century.

RONALD MALLETT, PROFESSOR AT THE UNIVERSITY OF CONNECTICUT, 2006

What a wonderful concept! Scientific theory turns into the reality of HG Well's Time Machine. We can go back to our past to relive our lives, replay the happy episodes of our life, undo our worst mistakes, and apologise to those we may have hurt.

No longer the stuff of scientific fiction which as Sean Redmond points out has always been about travel in time: "events either open in the altered past, the transformed present, or the possible future, transforming the reader to another age, place, dimension or world" - in time travel we can visit our past to conjure back again previous happiness and fix those times that set in train a process of unhappiness.

The physicists continue to debate the issues. In a bewildering world of theoretical possibilities it seems that travel into the future is more likely than into the past. After all, travelling back in time poses the infamous grandfather paradox. "If we can go back in time and kill our grandfather, who is the I that then goes back in time?"

Wormholes seem to be our best bet. By manipulating the black holes we sneak through the backdoor of the warp of space-time into an alternative universe. In this alternative universe(s), multiple selves become possible.

While the physicists conduct their experiments in space and time at the Large Hadron Collider and how to bend the laws of physics, it's worth asking if you could go back in time:

- would you really want to go back in time?
- to which period; why?
- how would you change the history of this moment?
- what would be the consequences?

Accepting that time travel to the past may not be possible in our generation, are we willing to let go of any difficulties to move on?

"Time Travel" at Wikipedia

HOW TO REGRET

My one regret in life is that I am not someone else.

WOODY ALLEN

People who say they regret nothing usually live to regret it.

GUY BROWNING

Regret for what almost happened can be the second most dangerous emotion after envy. And it's a safe rule that if you can't get your disappointments in perspective you will never last.

CLIVE JAMES

Envy is a destructive force. When others' successes, advantages or possessions make us discontented, envy is the dynamic at work, a dynamic with the potential to destroy us. But regret - that feeling of disappointment and loss about our past - isn't too far behind in the listing of damaging emotions. Regret keeps harking back to "what might have been...if only."

Like all emotions regret has a purpose: "it's supposed to be an indicator that something about our habits and behaviours must change." When we experience regret it's a sign that we need to shift our approach. The problem however with the feeling of regret is that rather than trigger action to move on to a better future, it often holds us back in the past. Allowed to dominate our thoughts, regret begins to imprison us.

Dave Navarro suggests we can turn regret into a positive dynamic when we:

- **listen to our regrets as the voice of an inner friend** rather than as a nagging adversary. Treat regret as a message of "tough love" to avoid future mistakes
- **confront our regrets head on**. Rather than allowing our regrets to catch us unawares and take us down a counter-productive spiral of thoughts, take the initiative to ask: what do I regret about my choices and behaviour in life? This helps put us back in the driving seat
- **attend to the message**. "What is this regret telling you about how you are living your life?" If the regret is a rumination about the past that is irrelevant to our current situation and future plans, let it go. If it's a signal that something needs to change, pinpoint the change that will make a difference

- **do something with the message**. We can either dwell over the message, reliving the memories of what might have been, or we can take action to avoid future mistakes

Regrets are "missed opportunities". When we see them as learning lessons to prepare us for future opportunities, we advance in life. If we remain caught up in regrets, ruminating over past losses, we are held back. When we acknowledge and come to terms with our regrets we move to a better past and future.

"How to Regret" Guy Browning, 2003 The Guardian
"How to Stop Regretting the Past and Start Building Your Future" Dave Navarro, 2008 at www.rockyour-day.com

HOW TO ACCEPT THE ODDS OF BAD LUCK

Nothing is a waste of time if you use the experience wisely. RODIN

If you are going to fail, you might as well fail at a difficult task.

AVINASH DIXIT

Because all decisions involve risk, we will sometimes be faced with the negative consequences of a decision that didn't work out. Here we can only accept the odds and deal with the bad decision outcomes.

- accept the situation
- tell others (e.g. our partner, boss, customers)
- analyse the reasons
- if we did the right thing, be prepared to take another risk

We shouldn't over-react to negative outcomes if we've worked through a robust decision making process.

Accept the odds, manage the consequences and be prepared to make another decision. And if our decision making process was flawed, we should track back to identify what went wrong.

"Past experience is invaluable for complex decision making" Dr Zoe Kourtzi, 2009, at www.sciencedaily.com

WHY WE SHOULD ADMIT MISTAKES AND NOT MAKE THEM WORSE

There are no failures - just experiences and our reactions to them.

TOM KRAUSE

Nowadays most people die of a sort of creeping common sense, and discover when it is too late that the only things one never regrets are one's mistakes.

OSCAR WILDE

It's not a good tactic to defend the indefensible. If we've made a mistake, we should say so and say it quickly.

But we don't have to elaborate on what we did or why we did it. It's better to focus on what we need to do in future.

Invariably it is our response to mistakes rather than the mistake itself that creates the bigger problem. None of us are perfect. So we shouldn't beat ourselves up if and when we do get it wrong. But we should find ways to put things right.

"The 6 critical mistakes done after a mistake was done" at www.lessoninlife.com

WHY SOME MISTAKES MATTER MORE THAN OTHERS

Mistakes are a part of being human. Appreciate your mistakes for what they are: precious life lessons that can only be learned the hard way. Unless it's a fatal mistake, which, at least, others can learn from.

AL FRANKEN

Mistakes are inevitable and an integral part of our development. But some mistakes will destroy our credibility overnight.

Mistakes made in the attempt to push ahead into new areas and part of the process of learning are understandable. And mistakes arising out of excessive commitment are usually forgiven.

But mistakes of judgement, particularly in the area of personal ethics and morality will permanently damage our credibility. And by jeopardising our reputation, they won't be forgotten.

"Worst leadership mistakes" at www.leadership-trainingtutorials.com

HOW TO MASTER THE ART OF THE APOLOGY

An apology isn't an apology unless you experience a change in heart.

There is an art to apologising. It isn't:

- the **excuse**: "I'm sorry...but...it happened but it wasn't really my fault; something else happened."
- the **denial of intent**: "I'm sorry...I wanted to...my intentions were good but I'm really a victim of events."
- **blame**: "I'm sorry...someone else let me down...I did my best but others didn't."

Politicians have mastered the art of the apology that isn't an apology. And in the process they damage their credibility. An effective apology incorporates:

- **recognition**: this is the apology that acknowledges something has gone wrong and identifies the severity of the problem. This is the apology that empathises with others to see the issue through their eyes and doesn't dismiss it as "one of those things"
- **responsibility**: a meaningful apology accepts personal responsibility. Rather than look around to point the finger of blame, an apology says, "I screwed up". We might not have personally got things wrong, but accountability may require us to accept responsibility
- **remorse**: this is the apology as empathy with others, seeing the consequences that have resulted from the problem. This is the apology as the genuine and heart felt expression of emotion
- **restitution**: "I'm sorry" is easy. More difficult but genuine is: "what do I need to do to put things right?" This is the apology as the swift response to do whatever needs to be done to restore credibility and reassure others that we are genuine in our commitment

We apologise with grace when we accept responsibility and express our commitment to put things right.

"Why can't more people just say sorry?" Matthew Parris, 2008, The Times

"The do's and don'ts of apologising" Shari Brewer at suite101.com

"How to apologise" at www.wikihow.com

PAST

WHAT WILLEM VAN DEN HULL SHOULD HAVE PUT BEHIND HIM

I felt the urge to set a few things straight. WILLEM VAN DEN HULL

Willem van den Hull was born in 1778 in Holland. A postman's son, with financial backing from some wealthy citizens, he trained as a school master, eventually becoming the owner of an independent boarding school. So far so good. Willem's school was the place where the children of aristocratic Amsterdam were educated.

We know a lot about Willem because he wrote an immense autobiography; 320,000 words in total. In it Willem records the detail of his life, the prizes he won as a child, the time he spent double-entry book keeping, and his progression in the teaching profession. Willem recounts his social advancement, the clothes and conventions that reflected his growing social status.

Why so much detail for what is largely an unremarkable life? Of course Willem did well in life, but there is little evidence of philosophical inquiry, scientific innovation or creative contribution to suggest so much biographical output. Why should this school master devote a large part of his later years to the writing of his life story?

Because Willem experienced humiliation and disgrace. Unable to pay a four cent fare on a tow barge trip, his reputation suffered as word got around of the embarrassing episode. When the maid of the minister of one church refused to allow him entry into the house - "how indelibly the impertinent face of that maid is etched in my soul" - Willem grew bitter about his standing within the Amsterdam elite.

Willem just couldn't let it go. And because he couldn't let it go, he devoted his life to an exercise in self justification: the writing of his story.

Sometimes we just need to let it go. However badly we might feel we've been treated in life, resentment that endures can only be damaging to our long-term well being.

"Why Life Speeds Up As You Get Older: How Memory Shapes our Past" Douwe Draaisma

"Forget the past: Let It Go to Fly Higher" Jeff Nickles at mysuperchargedlife.com

HOW TO AVOID THE RISKS OF RUMINATION

Never let yesterday use up today.

RICHARD H. NELSON

Rumination is the process whereby cows vomit up digested matter and digest it again, several times over.

Rumination is when we think about the meaning, origins and consequences of our negative feelings. It starts when something bad happens. We then think about how bad that thing is. Our minds then move to other bad things that have happened. From there, we're now thinking about how unfair life is.

The next thing we know a huge slice of time has gone by and our mood is sour.

Rumination has an initial appeal. We feel as if we're working toward a solution to our problem. In fact we're in danger of passive thinking that allows negative thoughts to escalate, reinforcing our initial negative feelings. As we keep "chewing the cud", rather than find a practical solution, we've probably exaggerated and distorted the problem. And we feel even less happy.

Worse still, the tendency to ruminate is an indicator of vulnerability to adversity, including episodes of depression.

To manage the habit of rumination:

- **catch yourself**. When you're about to chew the cud, admit and say out loud: "I'm beginning to ruminate"
- **remind yourself that you want a practical solution** to a specific problem, not to rehearse the range of possible causes to the problem
- **distract yourself**. Do something else. Jog, listen to music, take the dog for a walk, read a book; anything that will make you feel better than another round of rumination

- **schedule in an allocated time** - if you must - for rumination. This is a slot in your diary to think about what's worrying or upsetting you. Once the time is up, stop

- remind yourself of the positives in life. **"Count your blessings"** might seem old fashioned and patronising advice. But it works

"Probing the depression-rumination cycle" Bridget Murray Law, 2005 at www.apa.org

"How to stop ruminating" at www.ehow.com

Rumination: How just thinking about the problem can make the problem worse" Michael Anestis, 2009 at www.psychotherapybrownbag.com

"Smile and count your blessings – it'll make you happier" Karen McVeigh, 2009, The Guardian

WHY DID BUZZ ALDRIN SULK ON THE MOON

As the air clears it's absolutely vital not to say, "That was a big sulk, wasn't it?" This is the quickest possible way of launching the world's largest, longest and deepest sulk.

GUY BROWNING

600 million TV viewers watched the first moon landing, hearing the classic line "one step for man, one giant step for mankind". But the audience had to wait a while. Neil Armstrong, a meticulous man, was tidying up and doing the dishes. And then wait a while longer for his fellow astronaut, Buzz Aldrin, to emerge.

Originally scheduled to be the first to exit the landing module, Buzz was unhappy to discover he had been demoted, and Armstrong was now to be the first man on the moon. The TV viewers had to wait until he finished his sulk. And when asked to photograph Armstrong, Aldrin refused, claiming to be "too busy". Armstrong had to take his own picture.

As one fellow astronaut commented "Buzz resented not being first more than he appreciated being second."

Buzz's mood worsened on return to earth. As a consequence of the three day NASA debriefing, he and Neil missed the media storm, which he recognised would be the "real event".

The man who fell to earth rejoined the US air force - he had been a fighter pilot - but his role as commander of a test pilot school didn't work out. He quit the armed services at 42, had an affair, suffered depression, his marriage broke up, he went through another brief marriage, and eventually found himself selling Cadillacs in Beverly Hills and becoming dependent on drink.

We begin to sulk when we dwell on perceived injustices or past grievances. Apart from the downside of short-term ill humour, sulking may also have adverse long-term consequences on our well being and happiness.

"The Man Who Fell to Earth" Stephen Moss, 2009, The Guardian

"How to... sulk" Guy Browning, 2002, The Guardian

"Moondust: In Search of the Men Who Fell to Earth" Andrew Smith

IS REVENGE A DISH BEST SERVED COLD

Revenge may be a dish best served cold but it will probably leave you with a nasty aftertaste.

VAUGHAN BELL

We've experienced a wrong and an injustice. Someone has offended us, betrayed us or hurt us. So our minds turn to retribution. The guilty person should be punished. Only until there is the closure of seeing justice done can we move on with our lives. This is revenge as "catharsis".

The problem is that revenge may make life even worse for us. Or as Albert Schweitzer dramatically put it: "revenge is like a rolling stone, which, when a person has forced up a hill, will return upon them with a greater violence, and break those bones whose sinews gave it motion."

Part of the problem is rumination. If we forget the issue we begin to trivialise the episode that ignited our need for vengeance. It wasn't that big a deal, and we move on. But if we keep looking for ways to exact revenge our thoughts begin to exaggerate the significance of the incident. And even if our attempts at revenge are successful our minds can't forget it.

The sense of fairness and need for justice are of course powerful motivations. But the desire for personal revenge can be damaging.

It's useful to check what incident has triggered our emotions. If we're stirred by the injustice experienced by specific individuals and groups in society, we can channel our anger productively. But if it's about us - our status, feelings of personal offence or loss of face - maybe we should just let it go.

"Revenge is sweet but corrosive" at Mindhacks.com

"100 ways to get revenge" at 100waystogetrevenge.wordpress.com

"Why revenge feels sweet" Gina Simmons, 2010 at www.manageangerdaily.com

"How a broken guitar became a smash hit" Chris Ayres, 2009, The Times

"Revenge: the psychology of retribution" John Grohol at psychcentral.com

WHY SUNK COSTS SHOULD BE SUNK

Sunk cost: a cost which has been irreversibly incurred or committed prior to a decision point, and which cannot therefore be considered relevant to subsequent decisions.

You pre-order a non-refundable ticket to a sporting event. However, on the night you don't feel like going anymore: you're tired, it's raining, and there is a rail strike. And you can watch the event live on TV. You regret the fact that you bought the ticket because, you would prefer to stay at home, get comfortable on the sofa and watch it on TV. But you did buy the ticket. It was expensive and hard to get.

What do we do? If we go to the event, even though we would rather stay at home, we've been caught up in the thinking trap of "sunk cost".

Sunk costs are costs that are irrecoverable. You've spent the money and you won't get it back, regardless of future outcomes. The money is gone, so now you are better off doing what pleases you best. So, unless you can sell the ticket, just forget about what you paid for it. Spend the evening doing what you want to do - watching the game on TV.

The sunk cost factor is played out when we persist in an unfulfilling job or career (but I've worked so hard to get to this point), sticking with a bad relationship (but we grew up together), persevering with a business that will never be successful (but I invested so much in it; I can't walk away now). And the sunk cost factor explains **why we stick with an activity because we made an initial investment, even though that investment isn't going to produce a positive return.**

To avoid the sunk cost bias

- check that you're not sticking with a project only because of the investment you made in the first place. If it's a bad decision or project (and you can't make it better), get out of it, whatever your initial investment in time, effort and cost. Cut your losses and move on

- allow yourself to make mistakes. Quickly admitting your mistakes is much more productive than persevering with a losing position. Don't worry about "saving face"; worry about the costs of persisting with an unsatisfactory project
- ask: would you still do it? Apply the same rigour in examining current activity as you would in planning future commitments. Be prepared to abandon those activities that don't meet the test: "would I do it now?"
- don't confuse your long-term goals with the specific means you've chosen to achieve the goals. Don't stick with a project that isn't helping progress your goals, however emotionally and financially committed you feel about the plan

"Sunk cost bias - how it hinders your life and 4 ways to overcome it" at litemind.com

WHAT TO DO WHEN WE EXPERIENCE INERTIA

It's easy to carry the past as a burden instead of a school. It's easy to let it overwhelm you instead of educate you.
JIM ROHN

Inertia sounds like the name of a newly privatised energy company. If it was, you wouldn't want to get your energy from them. In real life, inertia is what stops things happening.
GUY BROWNING

As Marshall Goldsmith points out: the most reliable predictor of what we'll do is what we're doing now. Our default response in life is to experience inertia.

This is the life of habit. And while good habits have the potential to maintain our focus and discipline, bad habits hold us back from taking on new challenges, challenges that will broaden our repertoire of skills.

Try an experiment as you go through your day. Rate each activity on a 1 - 10 scale (1= low and 10 = high) to ask:

- how much long-term benefit did I experience from this activity?
- how much short-term satisfaction did I experience in this activity?

Record your activities for at least one day, preferably a week, and review the results. This is your chart of your experience of happiness and meaning. But it is more than a chart.

Knowing we will evaluate every activity against these two simple questions makes us more alert and mindful to what is providing short-term satisfaction or long-term meaning. It helps us stop doing stuff that isn't enjoyable and fulfilling.

And for the stuff we can't stop, it may help us approach the activity in a more positive spirit, determined to gain some personal benefit.

"Mojo: How to Get It, How to Keep It, How to Get It Back When You Lose It" Marshall Goldsmith, 2010

WHAT ARE THE REALITIES OF HUMAN NATURE

Science changes but human nature does not. SHERWIN NULAND

The master key to human nature is vanity. C G L DU CANN

Our attitudes about the past are often caught up in our thoughts and feelings of those we grew up with, played with, went to school, and worked with. Mixed in with the nostalgia of positive relationships we still value, there is also a potential for resentment towards those we now see as having held us back in life.

We come in different shapes and sizes, with distinctive talents and strengths, weaknesses, foibles and idiosyncrasies, shaped by our varying cultural histories, family backgrounds, life experiences, values and personalities. However we can make some generalisations about others:

- **most people don't care all that much about you**. "Never blame malice for what can easily be explained by conceit". It's not because most people are mean; it's because they are mostly focused on themselves. You only matter when it matters to others. It's not all about you - don't take it personally

- **most intentions are unknown**. We see the behaviour and how it impacts on us, but often we misread the underlying motivation. Don't over-interpret others' behaviours; there may be 101 reasons for their actions. Listen and get to know others before you jump to conclusions

- **selfish altruism explains a lot**. This isn't to say that everyone is selfish, only interested in their own interests. But it is to suggest that you will understand and interact more effectively with others if you recognise the principle of win-win, and how your actions help others, and others' actions assume help from you in future. If you're expecting others to help you simply because of generosity of spirit, you may be disappointed

- **bad memories**. Others have a lot of stuff to remember. If they forget you and your priorities, it isn't about you. But do make it easy for others to remember you and your priorities. You are competing with lots of other airtime in peoples' lives

- **emotions call the shots**. You might conclude a conversation, assuming a rational discussion. But most people have stronger feelings about the issues than is evident from the conversation. Because strong emotions aren't usually expressed (anger at the one end of the spectrum to sadness at the other), you won't know how others feel about you and your proposals. Don't assume all is well if you haven't recognised the emotional agenda

- **people need reassurance**. This is a mix of confusion about the complexity of life, the need for attention and social approval, and the fear of isolation and loneliness. Others want to feel a sense of belonging and social validation. If we're not making others feel welcome, safe and secure, we won't connect to them

Of course there are the exploitative rivals, neurotic fiends and horrible bullies who we've encountered in our past. There are also, for the most part, people like us.

"Teach Yourself to Live" C G L Du Cann

"The critical 7 rules to understand people" Scott Young at www.scotthyoung.com

"How to understand people better" at www.relationshipmatters.com

WHO WE SHOULD TRUST AND AVOID

If they tell it to you, they'll tell it about you.

The breach of trust shakes the foundations, not only of our friendships, but of our past and present.

Some people will break confidences and share information we regard as private.

Don't allow your motivation to build close relationships and share intimacies backfire on you. If your "friends" are willing to pass on information about other friends, the chances are they're also going to pass on information about you.

Some people can't be trusted. These are the:

- **loose cannons**, individuals with no concept of discretion, who will pass on confidential information to others
- **schemers** who exploit your willingness to share openly your concerns and worries
- **foolish**, with no insight into good manners and business etiquette
- **resentful**, those individuals envious of your success and who want to damage you

Spot these individuals and know how to manage your relationships with them but keep a distance.

Suspicion of others - their motives and intentions - is bad for the soul. But if we assume that everyone operates within our best interests at heart we may become disappointed and disillusioned.

HOW TO IDENTIFY LIFE'S MANIPULATORS

There are two types of people. Those who come into a room and say, "Well, here I am!" and those who come in and say, "Ah, there you are."

FREDERICK COLLINS

It's difficult to free ourselves of any past resentments if the "neurotic fiends" hold sway in our lives.

Awkward people and neurotic fiends come in many shapes and sizes, but perhaps most destructive to our current happiness are the manipulators. These are the individuals quick to take advantage of a trusting nature. The Machiavellian operator can be difficult to spot. Be alert to the indicators.

Manipulators:

- open up and talk freely of their own plans, ideas and feelings. In fact they don't. Their apparent self disclosure is calculated to encourage you to reciprocate and provide information to be used to your disadvantage
- begin the conversation with lots of "yes" questions to encourage your responsiveness before shifting to the killer question where they anticipate resistance
- use expressions such as "don't you think..., don't you feel...would you agree that...?" to push you into what they want
- have little hesitation in asking you personal questions at an early stage in your relationship
- ask your views about others and are keen to exchange gossip
- utilise flattery to make you feel good about yourself before making some demand on you
- want to force you into making quick decisions about something that is important to them

"Ten Types of Difficult People" J.D.Meier at sourcesofinsight.com

"Eight ways to spot emotional manipulation" Fiona McColl at www.cassiopaea.com

"Manipulation @ Work - how do you get what you want?" Jamie Showkeir and Maren Showkeir, 2008 at www.careerknowhow.com

HOW TO END RELATIONSHIPS

Stand with anybody that stands right, stand with them while they are right and part with them when they go wrong. ABRAHAM LINCOLN

Loyalty is an admirable virtue but misplaced, it can be hazardous. Loyalty to our "friends" can hold us back from advancing our plans.

It is difficult to break well-established relationships but we should recognise when our aims and our interests are diverging from those of our colleagues and friends.

Rather than be dragged down through a misguided loyalty to those previous friends and colleagues whose values we now question, we should be willing to end those relationships that are becoming counter-productive with the risk of undermining our personal credibility.

"How to decide when to end a long-term relationship" Steve Pavlina, 2005 at www.stevepavlina.com

WHAT DID BILL CLINTON ASK NELSON MANDELA

Forgiveness does not change the past, but it does enlarge the future.

PAUL BOESE

Bill Clinton once asked Nelson Mandela how he was able to forgive his jailors.

Mandela responded: "When I walked out of the gate I knew that if I continued to hate these people I was still in prison."

At his inaugural acceptance speech, he shook the hands of the four prison guards who had kept him captive for years as he went on stage. A key moment in helping South Africa address its past and move towards a better future.

Forgive. There is no shortage of "reasons" for resentment and bitterness. We all have experienced hurt and encountered injustice. But these emotions have great potential for self destruction. **Forgiveness is good and resentment is bad for the soul**. Forgiveness, as well as helping us manage the inevitable ups and downs of relationships, improves our own personal well being.

We become our own worst enemy when we hold on to past grievances. This kind of anger will hurt us more than our perceived adversary.

"Create a culture of forgiveness in the workplace"
Alexander Kjerulf, 2007 at positivesharing.com

PAST

HOW TO KEEP THE CHATTERING MONKEY QUIET

A man is going to borrow a lawn mower from his next-door neighbour. On the way there he imagines his neighbour saying "why don't you buy one of your own?" to which he replies:

Because I can't afford it.
Then why not get one on hire purchase?
I don't like being in debt.
Yet you're willing to come and borrow mine

*At this point he meets his neighbour in the front garden and shouts: Keep your ****** lawn mower!*

COLIN WILSON "ACCESS TO INNER WORLDS"

Buddhism compares the untrained mind to a chattering monkey that jumps from one branch to another. The monkey is constantly on the move. The 'Chattering Monkey' sits on our shoulder and chatters non-stop in our ear. This is the conversation we have in our head, lying in bed at night, in the shower, on the bus, everywhere.

The chattering monkey takes a slightly negative remark and engages our minds in a long discussion with amazing exaggeration. The chattering monkey will always convince us of the absolute worst possible outcome to the slightest problem. The chattering monkey also likes to go back into our history and search out similar events and add them to the argument. The monkey also looks into the future, identifying each and every hazard, exaggerating them into the worst possible scenario.

The chattering monkey makes for a stressful life. Take the initiative with the monkey. Don't let it set the agenda and take control of your inner conversation. Usually, the monkey needs to be told to go away. But sometimes we need to manage the conversation, applying clear headed logic to address the monkey's arguments.

"The chattering monkey" at www.reinventingmyself.com

"Are your thoughts helpful?" Stephen Mills, 2009 at www.ratracetrap.com

HOW TO PUT THE BRAKES ON A BLAME CYCLE

Our task is not to fix the blame for the past, but to fix the course for the future.

JOHN FITZGERALD KENNEDY

Put the brakes on a blame cycle before it escalates.

Sometimes it is easier to look for the guilty party (and psychologically satisfying in bolstering our self esteem) rather than find a practical solution to the problem. But blame takes conflict into destructive thought processes that become increasingly less relevant to our future plans.

When things are getting out of hand and we want or need to maintain a constructive dialogue the only responses are:

- I've made a mistake/offended you; **I apologise**
- We seem to have got into a misunderstanding; **can we start again**
- I want to understand your position. **I'm listening**
- **I want to work with you** to put things right and find a solution

"How to take responsibility and stop blaming others (even if others are to blame)" at www.sixwise.com

WHY WE SHOULD GET OFF THE COUCH

In “Sleeper” Woody Allen’s character has been cryogenically frozen for 200 years. When he’s woken, he says:

> *Two hundred years! I missed all those therapy sessions. I would have been cured by now.*

The expression “it’s good to talk” is firmly established in our culture. This is the appeal to work through the issues, explore our thoughts and feelings about past events, particularly if they have been unpleasant or traumatic. Talking it through makes sense of past events, and gives us new insights to move on and progress in life. Talking is now a standard practice in much counselling and psychotherapeutic practice, owing much to the original insights of Sigmund Freud and psychoanalysis.

In the world of psychoanalysis, our past is often a barrier to a happy and productive life. Difficult memories and thoughts are suppressed which unless revealed will continue to block our mental energies. Psychoanalysis has no shortage of terms for the ways in which this past is played out: fixation, repetition compulsion, regression. In summary, the excessive emotional pressures of our past deploy different tactics to block our present and future.

On the couch, the psychoanalyst will help us uncover these difficult thoughts and memories. We, as the patient, say whatever comes into our head and our analyst will explore these dreams, fantasies and remembrances and help make sense of our interpretations of the world. And eventually we will achieve that level of insight into our past that helps us move on for the future.

Or, as Sándor Ferenczi, one of the more astute founders of the psychoanalytical movement noted “while the patient lies there in misery, we sit comfortably in our armchair quietly smoking a cigar.”

No one doubts that an attentive, sympathetic and intelligent friend or advisor is an important asset to put life into perspective and help us gain new insights into our problems. And few dispute the benefits of evidence based psychotherapy that focuses on solutions to current problems.

What is problematic is the continuation of the psychoanalytical myth that until our past is uncovered and revealed we can't make real progress in maturing in life. For the died-in-the-wool psychoanalyst, most psychotherapy is the simple treatment of symptoms but doesn't address the fundamental causes, specifically from our early years and the dynamics of our family relationships.

In fact there is good reason to believe that the rehearsal of our past rather than opening up new insights to live fuller lives simply makes us feel worse. One reason perhaps why psychoanalysis's therapeutic track record as a treatment at best is dismal, and at worst damaging.

As Virginia Ironside, after thirty years in analysis, argues: "When therapy is offered for such commonplace, if horrible, life experiences as divorce and redundancy, it can actually makes things worse. Therapy makes these events seem extraordinary rather than just the everyday miseries that we all have to endure. Therapy encourages people to look at the bad and miserable things in their lives, to focus on their misfortunes, which usually makes people feel worse and ends up inflaming their anger."

Sigmund Freud suggests that "hysterics suffer mainly from reminiscences." Karl Kraus remarks that, in reminiscing on these reminiscences, "psychoanalysis is the disease whose cure it purports to be."

If we're stuck on the couch of "psychological archaeology" to uncover our past, it may be time for us to find more constructive solutions to life's difficulties.

"Psychoanalysis" at Wikipedia

"Madness on the Couch: Blaming the Victim in the Heyday of Psychoanalysis" Edward Dolnick

"Desperation nation - Britain in therapy" Brendan O'Neill, 2003 at news.bbc.co.uk

"6 ways to open up and talk in therapy" John M Grohol at psychcentral.com

WHY LOOKING BACK IN ANGER MAY MAKE US ANGRIER

They spend their time mostly looking forward to the past.

JIMMY PORTER

Anybody can become angry - that is easy, but to be angry with the right person and to the right degree and at the right time and for the right purpose, and in the right way - that is not within everybody's power and is not easy.

ARISTOTLE

When it first appeared on the London stage in 1956, John Osborne's "Look Back in Anger" revolutionised British theatre. For the first time, a harsh, brutal realism was evident in which characters felt and spoke like "real" people.

The story is a love triangle involving an intelligent but disaffected working class young man (Jimmy Porter), his upper-middle-class, emotionless wife (Alison), and her snobbish best friend (Helena Charles). Jimmy can be seen both as a noble rebel against an awful society that is bearing down on him, as well as cruel and misguided. His sarcastic and sometimes merciless taunts are directed at the two women and the class from which they emerged.

Jimmy Porter functions in a world of anger. His anger is directed at those he loves because they refuse to have strong feelings, at a society that did not fulfil promises of opportunity, and at those who arrogantly take up their places in the social and power structure and disregard others.

Many of the critics were offended by Jimmy Porter, but not on account of his anger; a working-class hero is expected to be angry. What annoyed them was something quite different: his self-confidence. "Oh heavens, how I long for just a little ordinary enthusiasm. Just enthusiasm that's all. I want to hear a warm, thrilling voice cry out Hallelujah. Hallelujah, I'm alive!"

If we look back to our past with anger, we should ensure this anger is being directed positively to our future.

"15 simple ways to overcome anger" at thinksimple-now.com

"Catharsis" David McRaney, 2010 at youarenotsos-mart.com

WHY STUBBORNNESS MAKES US FEEL GOOD BUT DOES US LITTLE GOOD

Stubbornness does have its helpful features. You always know what you are going to be thinking tomorrow.

GLEN BEAMAN

Stubbornness has its benefits. It provides consistency of purpose. What we once believed we still believe, whatever the evidence might say to suggest we shift our opinions. And psychologically it isn't too demanding. If we're right, then we can maintain our current life strategy in the knowledge that we will of course succeed.

Stubbornness also comes with a price. Stubbornness is the habit that:

- assumes we are always right and others are wrong, and blocks thinking that is different to our current beliefs
- shuts down debate about new possibilities because it challenges our preferred solutions
- persists in a misguided course of action because the admission of any mistakes would be personally threatening

We can maintain our current fixed position that we were right (and have been right all along).

Or we can accept that either we may have got things wrong from time to time, and that the future may be very different and require a new way of looking at the world.

"How to be open minded" Tammyrose at www.ehow.com

"Dealing with stubborn people and how to persuade them" Paul Hancox at ezinearticles.com

WHY HONESTY ABOUT OUR EMOTIONS MATTERS

By their nature, emotions are consuming.

HARRY MILLS

Our emotions can take over easily. One minute we're feeling cool and composed. The next minute - on hearing some bad news - we become a raving and ranting monster, or withdraw and detach ourselves from events.

Self awareness isn't the introspective preoccupation with ourselves. Self awareness is that capacity to recognise how our emotions shape events, to stand back from ourselves and observe the nature and intensity of the emotion we're experiencing. It helps if we pay attention to:

- our **physical reactions**, our speech patterns, body posture and specific signs (e.g. crossed arms, clenched fists)
- our **thoughts and beliefs**. This is recognising the "chattering monkey" who sits on our shoulder providing a non-stop narrative, telling us the stories that interpret events and shape our feelings
- our **triggers**. Self awareness is reinforced when we identify the situations, people, places and issues that get us feeling something we wouldn't otherwise have felt. Check the patterns of your triggers to work out what initiates positive and negative emotions
- our **motives**. We all have our standards of conduct, expectations of how we should behave in different situations. And when we find ourselves failing to meet these standards, it can provide an important insight into our emotional responses

Recognising the impact of our emotions on our behaviour is the first step. More importantly the next step is to understand and identify these specific emotions. Key prompts such as:

- what am I feeling now?
- what are my senses telling me?
- what judgements am I making; are they accurate?
- what might this emotion be trying to tell me that is useful?
- how might this emotion be deceiving me into interpreting events in a particular way?

help in making our emotions work for us rather than against us.

HOW BAD IS EMBARRASSMENT

When you're 18, you worry about what everybody is thinking of you; when you're 40, you don't give a damn what anybody thinks of you; when you're 60, you realise nobody's been thinking about you at all.

THE 18/40/60 RULE

We're rarely in the spotlight. In one research piece, students were asked to put on T-shirts, before being introduced to a group. The downside: emblazoned on the T-shirts was a large photograph of Barry Manilow. The students joined, then left the group after a few minutes. They were asked to estimate the percentage of the group who had noticed the T-shirt. 50% was the response. The group the students had briefly met were also asked if they noticed the appearance of the Barry Manilow T-shirt. Only 20% had.

We think we're in the spotlight when we're not. And we over-estimate the impact of embarrassing moments. The "spotlight effect" explains why people think their shortcomings and failings are far more noticeable than they actually are. Most of the time, most people don't notice. They're caught up in their own "spotlight". So don't over-react if you commit a gaffe. Others will probably not have noticed, but they will note your over response to your mistake when you draw attention to it. Don't make a minor mistake become a major embarrassing episode - for you and others.

Get past the point of embarrassment. The fear of embarrassment, that sense of social shame when we blunder, commit some gaffe or create awkwardness, is a major barrier to progress. Don't let it hold you back. If you are easily embarrassed then say so in managing any differences and disagreements. "I don't know why I am embarrassed in saying this. But I am. But it is important to me to say it so you understand my views..." Don't allow others to exploit your embarrassment. Acknowledge it and use it to your advantage.

Don't be embarrassed. Don't allow any sense of social awkwardness stop you from doing what you want to do. And if you do get embarrassed, so what? It is a small price to pay if it helps you achieve your goals.

"Overcoming the fear of embarrassment" Bruno Baceli at ezinearticles.com

HOW OLD DOGS DO LEARN NEW TRICKS

Whoever said: 'you can't teach an old dog new tricks' obviously never met a hungry dog.

When we find ourselves saying:

- "I am who I am."
- "I can't learn that."
- "That's not for me."

we're in danger of closing down opportunities to grow and develop in life.

We can define ourselves by our past experience and current skill-set, or we can be willing to keep discovering new facets of our personality and character, and find ways of opening up new options in life.

Research on mental functioning in old age provides lessons for all of us. Contrary to the prevailing assumption of decay, the aged brain shows a remarkable and enduring capacity to absorb new data, make new connections and acquire new skills. The MacArthur research identified the three factors that predict strong mental functioning in old age:

1. regular physical activity
2. a strong social support system
3. the belief in one's ability to handle what life has to offer

So, to help us keep learning new tricks it might be worth finding smart, up-beat jogging companions who we like and will maintain our curiousity about life and its possibilities.

"Successful aging: optimising life in the second half" Sol Stern and Richard O'Boyle at www.ec-online.net

WHAT IS THE ETERNAL SUNSHINE OF THE SPOTLESS MIND

How happy is the blameless vestal's lot
The world forgetting, by the world forgot
Eternal sunshine of the spotless mind
Each pray'r accepted, and each wish resign'd.

ALEXANDER POPE

Please let me keep this memory, just this one.

JOEL

We want to forget a painful event in our lives, a difficult relationship, a terrible job, a disastrous business venture or a minor embarrassment that still brings us out in a cold sweat. With the power of medical science, it must be possible to erase the memories to give us "spotless minds".

Two people, Joel and Clementine, meet on a train out of New York. Despite their very different personalities they are inexplicably drawn to each other. In fact Joel and Clementine are former lovers who broke up after two years together.

In the "Eternal Sunshine of the Spotless Mind", Clementine, after a nasty spat with Joel, had hired the mysterious bio-engineering firm Lacuna Inc, to erase all her memories of the relationship. Joel, on hearing the news, decides to undergo the same process, but as it's happening as he sleeps, he "remembers" he doesn't want to lose his memories.

The plot gets a bit more complicated as Lacuna employees begin to join the story of Joel and Clementine as they start their new relationship. Discovering the files which Lacuna has been keeping, the new couple accept the fact of their previous relationship, despite the absence of memories, and decide to build a new life together.

Rated the third best film of the decade, "Eternal Sunshine of the Spotless Mind" raises some important questions:

- does familiarity breed contempt?
- how much do we lose in the living?

- what do we forget and remember in life?
- can we break out of established habits and routines in our relationships?
- is it possible to start all over again?

As one reviewer suggests the film "is a parable on the futility of trying to escape the past".

Perhaps the key issue of the film is the inter-linkage of "experience, memory, pain and wisdom". Can we develop wisdom without the memories of the life experiences that are difficult?

WHY THERE ARE NO RULES WHEN WE HAVE TO GRIEVE

"Learning to deal with grief is learning to live again."

Grief comes in all sorts of shapes and sizes. The notion that we all have to work through the phases of the grief cycle - from denial, anger, bargaining, depression and acceptance - is largely discredited. Indeed, counselling provided to navigate us through these stages may do more harm than good.

All we can do in the words of the leading grief researcher, George Bonanno, is "cope ugly" in our own different ways.

Some of us will need quiet reflection, others the distractions of busyness. Some individuals will still feel acute pain many years after the loss, and others will "recover" after three months. Encouragingly, most of us are remarkably resilient in the event of the loss of a loved one. But a number of us - 10-15% - will experience profound and lasting suffering, a suffering that becomes debilitating.

In grieving there are no rules. Indeed there are many myths. And we shouldn't allow what has been described as the "grief police" tell us what and when we should feel.

But if we sense that we can't cope, that our grief is becoming distressing we should seek out proper and attentive professional support.

"Grief and loss" at www.caregiver.org

"Five fallacies of grief: debunking psychological stages" Michael Shermer, 2008, Scientific American

"An Interview with George Bonanno on Bereavement" David Van Nuys, 2010 at www.mentalhelp.net

"How to grieve: 5 myths that hurt" Paula Spencer at www.caring.com

"Words to comfort someone grieving" at www.healthy-holistic-living.com

NOSTALGIC FOR HAPPIER TIMES

The world is full of people whose notion of a satisfactory future is, in fact, a return to the idealised past.

ROBERTSON DAVIES

If our past life was a series of wonderful experiences, we should appreciate that fact. The problems start when we reinvent our past as a way of avoiding today's pressures and tomorrow's challenges. Because our memory is fallible it's tempting to recall only the positive moments and forget the times of embarrassment, difficulty and awfulness.

Our memory directs the movie of our past life to transform previous events into a cheerful romantic comedy or action-packed adventure in which we lived in the best of all possible worlds.

When nostalgia creates an ideal world we begin to rely on what we know, what is certain and comfortable and we start to fall back on familiar habits and routines. Nostalgia, enjoyable as a short excursion in time, incorporates longer-term risks in the journey of life. When our life is a series of comparisons between "what is" to an idealised "what was", it may limit our curiousity to keep exploring and our commitment to progress.

WHY LIBRARIANS AREN'T RICH

If past history was all there was to the game, the richest people would be librarians.

WARREN BUFFETT

Warren Buffett, the second richest individual in the world, and certainly, the shrewdest investor of all time, knows the importance of time. His investment strategy is about backing the long-term.

If you don't feel comfortable owning something for 10 years, then don't own it for 10 minutes. Only buy something that you'd be perfectly happy to hold if the market shut down for 10 years.

But Buffett also knows the hazards of forecasting the future. Buffett keeps within his circle of competence, only investing in businesses he understands.

Buffett also knows the peril of looking back to assume that past performance will predict future investment returns.

In the business world, the rear view mirror is always clearer than the windshield.

We should value our past but not assume it will provide the formula for future success.

"Help me find my "circle of competence!" Susan M Hayes and Ardle Joseph Culleton at ezinearticles.com

IS NOSTALGIA WHAT IT USED TO BE

Nostalgia is wishful thinking in reverse. It's a mental makeover that makes everything in the past seem better.
GUY BROWNING

I prefer the mystic clouds of nostalgia to the real thing, to be honest.
ROBERT WYATT

Those who know their past are tempted to repeat it but on the winning side.
DILLON WARDIAN

Most people have discussed with friends the comics and confectionary of childhood, the music of their school years, the TV programmes of their teens or early family holidays. Somehow life seemed happier then.

Once diagnosed as an illness among Swiss mercenaries who were fighting away from home, nostalgia is defined as the yearning for the past. Usually through rose-tinted glasses, nostalgia has a utopian element due to the power of our imagination to invent a better place and time. Our mind takes us back to a time and place when life was less complex, uncertain or challenging to a happier life episode of simplicity, certainty and ease.

Research from the University of Southampton found nostalgic memories to be potent mood boosters. It was found that people who write about good memories are more cheerful compared to people who write about everyday events, report higher self-esteem and feel more positively about their personal relationships.

Clay Routledge says that "nostalgia is a way for us to tap into the past experiences that we have that are meaningful, to remind us that our lives are worthwhile, that we are people of value, that we have good relationships, that we are happy and that life has some sense of purpose or meaning."

Nostalgia does however have a flip side. We can easily get lost in our past world and begin to feel all the good times are over. Here we feel that life was better, more fun and happier than now and we begin to experience regret.

But if we use nostalgia as a reminder of what has led us to where we are today and that there will be more good times in future, then why not.

"How to ... be nostalgic" Guy Browning, 2007, The Guardian

"What is nostalgia good for?" 2010 at news.bbc.co.uk

"Naturally nostalgic people have high self-esteem and are less prone to depression" Marina Krakovsky, 2006 at psychologytoday.com

"Neuroscience and Nostalgia" at VeryEvolved.com

HOW TO AIRBRUSH OUR LIVES

I can't tell you how many covers of magazines I've been in when my eyes were blue. I don't have blue eyes. I have green eyes.

KATE HUDSON

No one wants to look back over a difficult past to ruminate over difficult times or rehearse unpleasant experience. It's tempting therefore to use Photoshop psychology to airbrush our past. It's easily done, through any permutation of the following tactics:

- we conduct a **physical de-clutter** to remove those items (e.g. diaries, photographs, music) that may trigger any awkward and unpleasant experiences. Here we remove from our current physical environment (office and home) any reminders of difficulties from our previous lives
- our memories **sharpen and level** the facts of our lives. We level - hammer down the uncomfortable facts - to downplay the detail of events that were troublesome. In levelling some items and incidents are cropped out to accentuate the positives. Sharpening allows us to highlight and exaggerate specific events to point up some favourable aspects of the experience. Exposure is adjusted and red eye is fixed to translate past events into a wonderful previous life
- we **abandon those friends and colleagues** who have criticised us in some way or another (even though we suspect their feedback was well intentioned and probably accurate) to maintain a familiar and comfortable network which loves to reminisce about the happy times
- we believe all **the positive comments** from our old school friends and ex-colleagues on Facebook, LinkedIn and other social networking sites (although deep down we recognise it's part of a game of social reciprocity)

Well implemented, this psychological airbrushing creates a perfect past in which we never made any mistakes or experienced any failure (or only if they helped us on a journey to be the wonderful person we now are). In these airbrushed photographs of our past we were successful and always destined to succeed.

We should look back on our past with fondness. But if we're reinterpreting our past to create an identity that didn't in fact exist there may be potential hazards. We run the risk of maintaining an unrealistic persona of our current effectiveness and impact that becomes too demanding. Alternatively, in looking to relive a wonderful past, we create for ourselves a set of future goals that can only disappoint.

"Toward a psychology of memory accuracy" A Koriat et al, 2000, Annual Review of Psychology

"The art of airbrushing" Margarita Tartakovsky at psychcentral.com

WHY ARE EVENTS IN OUR ADOLESCENCE AND EARLY ADULTHOOD SO MEMORABLE

We do not remember days; we remember moments.

CESARE PAVESE

Hearing one word does it for me and the nostalgia all comes flooding back. The word? Bagpuss.

DAVE WICKS

When we flip back through the pages of the book of our life, some pages seem to have more writing on them than others. It is the events of our teens and early twenties that stand out as more memorable and important. Experts call this the "reminiscence bump": we recall a disproportionate number of life episodes between the ages of 10 and 30.

Why? For the full-on Darwinist the answer is easy. As we move towards the peak of our reproductive potential, our cognitive functions, including our memory, need to be at their most acute if we are to secure the "best mate" for our genetic legacy. We are hard-wired to optimise our memory at our most fertile. A possible explanation, but like many other evolutionary "just so" stories, probably not.

What are the main theories?
After the relative stability of our childhood, **things begin to change rapidly.** And faced with the novelty of adolescence our memories have to work harder to encode the stream of new experiences. There is a lot going on in our lives; the many firsts of attending a football match, the kiss at the disco, passing our driving test, the test of our courage to fight the school bully. These "first" memories, firmly consolidated, therefore become more vivid.

It is in adolescence that, typically, our **identities are formed**. As we progress through our teens into early adulthood we begin to discover who we are and who we want to be. During this phase we begin the narrative of our life. And of course beginnings are memorable.

Because our **cognitive processes slow down** as we age, we become progressively worse at encoding new information. So we remember those life events when our

memory was at peak performance. Over time, as we age, life's episodes don't get the same brain power and the experiences aren't consolidated in our memory banks.

The decline of memory theory seems to offer the best explanation. Our adolescence and early adulthood are more vivid only because our later life experiences aren't encoded as powerfully.

Part of the appeal of nostalgia are the vivid memories from our teens and adulthood. It is why our favourite books, music and films typically are associated with this period.

Either we can conclude that few things in future can ever be as good again. Here there is a danger we become part of the "rerun generation", revisiting the past to fix on the happy associations from our youth to avoid the challenges of the present and future. Or we can find ways to move from reruns to look-forwards.

"Things learned in early adulthood are remembered best" 1998, D Rubin at PubMed.gov

"We remember more from our teens and early twenties than we do from any other time of life" 2007, S Janssen, European Journal of Cognitive Psychology

"Re-run generation of 28-40s more concerned with nostalgia than planning for the future", 2010 at www.prlog.org

IN HINDSIGHT WAS EVERYTHING WONDERFUL

Well, as we all know by now, hindsight is twenty-twenty, but it is possible to turn your hindsight into foresight. ELLEN MOORE

Hindsight is a double-edged sword. Too much of it and the past seems inevitable. With too little hindsight, a panoramic perspective is impossible. LANCE KURKE

The hindsight bias: "the tendency to overestimate our own ability to have predicted or foreseen an event after learning about the outcome." With hindsight we knew it all along. We predicted with certainty that property prices would fall, our friend's marriage was going to be a disaster, and that the stock market was heading for a crash. The snag is: we didn't say so at the time before the event happened.

With the benefit of hindsight and our knowledge of what in fact did happen we reconstruct our past to make it consistent with what we now know in the present.

If things don't quite work out for us we look back to say "I was always going to be a failure." And if life goes well for us, we always knew we "were destined for great things."

The reality is of course we couldn't predict with certainty how events would unfold. But hindsight gives us a sense of reassurance that we did in fact know what would happen.

The problem with the hindsight bias is that it reduces our capacity to learn from experience. Because we now know what was inevitable, we rarely stop to reflect on events, why they turned out the way we did, or ask what we could have done differently or better.

Combine the hindsight bias with the appeal of nostalgia, and in the present we look back on a past in which we lived in the best of all possible worlds. It may have been "a wonderful life", or it may be that we are rationalising our previous life to avoid thinking about the challenges we now face.

PAST

WHAT IS IT ABOUT MUSIC THAT TAKES US BACK IN TIME

The times you lived through, the people you shared those times with - nothing brings it all to life like an old mix tape. It does a better job of storing up memories than actual brain tissue can do. Every mix tape tells a story. Put them together, and they can add up to the story of a life.

ROB SHEFFIELD

Music moves us for a number of reasons. It isn't simply as evolutionary thinker Steven Pinker states: "auditory cheesecake."

Philip Ball in "The Music Instinct" points out that music is more than a series of sounds in our ears. Music has immense power to comfort us when we are feeling low and to energise us to face the challenges of the future. It also connects us directly to the times and experiences of our past lives. When we hear the opening chords of (name that specific tune) we are transported back in time. And we are reminded of important events in our lives.

With the popularity of YouTube, the choice of music download sites, and the proliferation of TV channels based on "reeling in the years", it's easy to revel in the music of our past. It takes us back to a time when life was simpler, easier and happier.

Music has the capacity to remind us of who we once were, what we loved and lost, what we once hoped and dreamt of, and trigger the authentic emotions of regret.

But if we're trapped in a world of the music of our past, replaying the songs of our previous life, maybe we should change the channel to sometimes play different music to connect to a changing world.

"The Music Instinct" Philip Ball

HOW DO WE STOP THE MYSTERIOUS ACCELERATION

The older an hour glass the more quickly it runs. In hour glasses the grains of sand increasingly rub one another smooth until finally they flow almost without friction from one bulb into the other, polishing the neck wider all the time.

DOUWE DRAAISMA

Uninterrupted uniformity can shrink large spaces of time. When one day is like every other, then all days are like one, and perfect homogeneity would make the longest life seem very short.

THOMAS MANN, "THE MAGIC MOUNTAIN"

If you want to lengthen the perspective of time, then fill it, if you have the chance with a thousand new things.

JEAN-MARIE GUYAH

Why does life speed up as we get older? Why does a year in our fifties seem to last but a fraction of the year we experienced as a fifteen year old? And is there anything we can do about it?

The theories (galactic cycles aside):

- **as we age our memories interprets experience differently**. In our youth each day is a new experience filled with different events and unknown possibilities. But as the years pass, this freshness of experience moves to an automatic routine in which "weeks resemble one another, months resemble one another, and the monotony of life drags on." Because our estimates of time are in large part shaped by perceived differences (after all time has no meaning if nothing changes), the reducing number of life changes as we age creates the sense of speeding time
- **our memories are sharper when we were younger**. We're discovering more, learning more and our memories are bulging with life experience. Because our memories are busier consolidating lots of new stuff it feels like a great deal of time has passed. As we age and have fewer new and different encounters, our brain isn't having to do as much work and time seems to be pick up the pace

- **as a child much of our life is spent on anticipation**, looking forward to key events such as our next birthday, Christmas or the prospect of a summer holiday. Waiting of course helps slow time down. As adults we're less in the mode of anticipation and more in the mood of crisis management to deal with stuff as it happens. Our sense of urgency to manage our schedule and get things done quickly speeds up our experience of time
- we look at **our lives as a fraction of the potential life span**. A year in the life of a 10 year old is a tenth of their life time. That same year for a 50 year old is a fiftieth of their life time. Because that feels a shorter period, we experience the acceleration of time as the fractions of life shorten

Each theory has its pros and cons, all debated vigorously on the internet. But what does seem true is that we can slow down the passing of the years as we age if we keep our minds active, are mindful of each and every experience, keep engaged in new and different life events, and look forward with purpose to the next adventure.

"Why Life Speeds Up as You Get Older" Douwe Draaisma

"The seventh day of the Galactic cycle starts today", 2010 at Projectavalon.com

"How to make time slow down" 2008, Brian Hines at hinessight.blogs.com

WHY WE REMEMBER 31ST AUGUST 1997

Flashbulb memory: a vividly detailed memory of the circumstances under which one first learned of a surprising, consequential, emotionally involving event.

R BROWN & J KULIK

Time it was, and what a time it was. It was a time of innocence, a time of confidences; long ago, it must be, I have a photograph. Preserve your memories; they're all that's left you.

PAUL SIMON

Asked to recall a day at random in the last ten years the chances are we would struggle to recall what happened. But some dates trigger powerful and vivid detail.

Not only do we remember Princess Diana's tragic death, we remember where we were when we heard the news, what we were doing, who else was with us and our own responses and others' reactions.

Shocking news seems to create flashbulb memories.

It's partly the surprise and emotional distinctiveness of the event. It's also the fact that these are life events we've shared with others, either directly at the time or in discussion later. The process of recall and repetition ensures the memory is stored and can be recovered easily.

If we want to establish a photograph album of memories we can recall later in life, it will help if we live a life that incorporates novelty and variety, emotional lows and highs, and is shared with others.

"Flashbulb memory" at Wikipedia

PAST

WHAT THE PEARL OF LOVE REMINDS US OF

We were making the future, he said, and hardly any of us troubled to think what future we were making. And here it is!

H G WELLS

A young prince in northern India met and fell in love with "a young maiden of indescribable beauty and delightfulness" and made her his queen. "Love was theirs, full of joys and sweetness", but only for a year. Because of a venomous sting, the queen died.

The prince spent two days and nights in mourning as his servants worried. He emerged and ordered the servants to place his wife's body in a coffin of silver and lead. The coffin was placed within a second made of precious, scented woods wrought in gold. The second coffin was laid in an alabaster sarcophagus inlaid with precious stones. The Prince then announced that he planned to construct a vast monument to commemorate his beloved: the monument to be called the Pearl of Love.

Years followed as the Prince constructed the monument. He built a vast pavilion surrounded by a dome, pinnacles and copulas. He placed the sarcophagus in the center of the pavilion and reviewed his work. But he was not pleased.

More years follow as the Prince learnt more construction techniques. Entire structures were torn down and removed. Alterations were made, then reversed in favor of original designs. The sight of the Pearl awed visitors from around the world. The Prince would often "stand there and look at the vista, deeply moved and yet not fully satisfied." He decided that the sarcophagus would be better accentuated if he had the pavilion removed.

More time passed before the Prince decided that the Pearl was nearly complete. He took a small retinue to survey the final alterations and discovered that only one thing marred the Pearl's perfection. Only one thing had remained unchanged since construction began.

Long the Prince mused. At last he spoke. And pointing to his wife's sarcophagus he commanded: "Take that thing away."

Sometimes we forget our original purpose.

"The Pearl of Love" H G Wells, at Gutenberg.net.au

WHY REMEMBERING EVERYTHING DOESN'T MAKE US HAPPY

The advantage of a bad memory is that one enjoys several times the same good things for the first time.

FRIEDRICH NIETZSCHE

A person should keep their little brain attic stocked with all the furniture that they are likely to use, and the rest they can put away in the lumber-room of his library, where they can get it if they want it.

SHERLOCK HOLMES

Blessed are the forgetful, for they get the better even of their blunders.

MARY IN "ETERNAL SUNSHINE OF THE SPOTLESS MIND"

"Gazing on a blackboard of elaborate and meaningless equations, he would recall exactly the full detail - minutes, months and years later without any difficulty." The Russian journalist Shereshevsky possessed an exceptional intellectual gift: he could remember everything: words, numbers, figures and letters.

But these exceptional talents in memory were accompanied by a major drawback in life; his pathological memory interfered with his ability to hold a regular job, enjoy literature, or even to think in the abstract without being distracted by the sensory associations of his phenomenal memory. When an ice cream seller asked Shereshevsky what he wanted, his memory "saw" a stream of coal and black cinders pouring from her mouth. Unsurprisingly he lost his desire for the ice cream.

After a degree of fame as a mnemomist, dissatisfied with his performing life, Shereshevsky left the stage to work as a taxi driver.

Frederich Nietzsche may have been right: "The ability to forget is a key sign of health."

Jill Price, the woman who remembered everything said: "My memory is too strong. It's like a running movie that never stops. Most have called it a gift. But I call it a burden. I run my entire life through my head every day and it drives me crazy!"

No one wants to live a life in which our past is erased, but it is to accept the evolutionary wisdom that allows our memories to:

- filter the trivia that otherwise might linger and constrain our current cognitive capacity. (It is no coincidence that those individuals higher on neuroticism have a higher recall of the detail of negative past events)
- repress the traumatic and unpleasant experiences of life

"The woman who can remember everything", 2008, The Telegraph

"How memory works and why we forget certain things and not others" at Factoidz.com

"Why do we dream?" 2009 at Psychologytoday.com

WHY MARSHALL GOLDSMITH GOT IT RIGHT

The illiterate of the 21st century will not be those who cannot read and write, but those who cannot learn, unlearn, and relearn.

ALVIN TOFFLER

I behave this way, I am successful, therefore I am successful because I behave this way. That's the success delusion. They're where they are because they do many things right, and in spite of screwing things up. And what I try to do is help people sort out "because of" and "in spite of."

MARSHALL GOLDSMITH

The drivers of our past success will not guarantee our future success. "More of the same" will not be enough to succeed through the next phase of our development. Success may require us to abandon previous expertise and operating styles, not just acquire new skills.

Review your outlook to identify the shift in priorities and where you may need to stop doing old things before you begin to do new things.

"The Success Delusion" Marshall Goldsmith, 2007 at Marshallgoldsmithlibrary.com

PAST

WHY THE FUNDAMENTAL LAW IS FUNDAMENTAL FOR A GOOD REASON

If you always do what you've always done, you'll always get what you've always got.

SUSAN JEFFERS

Continuing to do what we've previously done is comfortable and easy. And for the most part, predictable.

But if we want something different and better, we may need to rethink our game plan and tactics. This requires high levels of personal honesty to review our past successes and failures, and exceptional courage to take risks in embarking on new activities.

Nostalgia has its appeal but if it's a dynamic that keeps returning to "how things used to be better", it may be holding us back from the kind of personal change that faces up to new and different challenges.

"Ideas for nostalgia" at Laterlife.com
"10 essential tips to change your life" Gail Sheehy at Lifeoptimizer.org

WHY MODEST SUCCESSES MAY BE HAZARDOUS

Success is not built on success. It's built on failure. It's built on frustration. Sometimes its built on catastrophe. SUMNER REDSTONE

Difficult though it may be, we should monitor our failures. Failures may be reminders of past mistakes, humiliations and embarrassments.

Modest successes provide the promise of a bright future and encourage greater investment. Modest successes can also lull us into a false sense of security about what will work and endure for the long-term.

Sometimes it is failure that drives genuine innovation. Spectacular failure suggests that someone has pushed into new areas, and we might learn something important for long-term success.

PAST

HOW THE POWER OF SAVOUR EXTENDS OUR EXPERIENCE OF THE GOOD TIMES

The happier the time, the more quickly it passes.

PLINY THE YOUNGER

Time has many paradoxes and ironies, not least that the best moments of our lives may be the briefest. Just when we are enjoying life it seems to rush past so quickly we feel we barely experienced it. And why do those periods of unpleasantness never seem to end?

It isn't surprising that nostalgia has so much appeal. Our memories allow us to enjoy experiences that we didn't appreciate fully at the time.

It helps if we develop the power of "savour" to "generate, intensify and prolong our enjoyment" of life. This is noticing and appreciating the positive aspects of life, and the mindfulness to attend to the experience of pleasure.

And we can savour across different time frames, anticipating future pleasures, experiencing present pleasures, and reminiscing about past pleasures. Each type of savouring is associated with self confidence and emotional maturity. Significantly, in several studies it is those most adept at reminiscing about their past, looking back on happy times and "rekindling joy from happy memories" who were found to be best able to deal with stress in life.

To savour:

- **share positive feelings**. According to Fred Bryant, the expert in the science of savouring: "Sharing is the strongest predictor of the level of enjoyment someone feels. People who do share their feelings with friends have higher levels of overall happiness than people who do not share their feelings."
- **take a mental photograph**; notice and highlight those things which are positive
- **congratulate yourself**; pat yourself on the back for the good things that have occurred

- **sharpen your sensory perceptions**; block distractions and concentrate on what you're savouring
- **say it out loud**; if something positive happens, express your feelings outwardly
- **be mindful**. For example, immerse yourself in the situation
- **count your blessings** and practice gratitude; this is a way to remember what's good in life
- **stop any negative thoughts** that spoil the moment you're enjoying right now; avoid the "shoulds" and "what ifs"

"How to cheer up savouring memories" 2008, Jerry Lopper at Suite101.com

"The art of savouring" Fred B Bryant at Naturalsolutionsmag.com

"Savoring: in praise of slow" Bridget Grenville Cleave at Personalgrowthinformation.com

WHAT WE LEARN FROM THE HAPPY ENDING OF A COLONOSCOPY PROCEDURE

> *We judge our past experiences almost entirely on how they were at their peak (pleasant or unpleasant) and how they ended. Virtually all other information appears to be discarded, including net pleasantness or unpleasantness and how long the experience lasted.*
>
> DANIEL KAHNEMAN

Colonoscopy is a painful medical procedure. Researchers keen to examine patients' attitudes to pain (hopefully to find ways to minimise it) tested a number of patients. Half of the group had the colonoscopy procedure extended by leaving the colonoscope in place 30 seconds after the examination was completed. The extra 30 seconds was mildly uncomfortable (and clearly less preferable to having the instrument removed immediately).

However this group reported a more positive (less negative) experience of the entire process. And patients in the extended examination were more likely to comply with calls for follow up colonoscopies than patients in the standard examination.

How we review our past - what we liked and disliked, enjoyed or hated - shapes our future. We want to do more of what was pleasurable and avoid those experiences that were unpleasant. It's useful then to know how our minds interpret the past.

What we don't do is evaluate the detail of each life episode to sum up the entire experience objectively. Asked "how was the party?" or "did you enjoy the conference?" our mind deploys short cuts to make sense of the experience. And among the idiosyncrasies of our memory is our "obsession with final scenes".

The "peak end rule" suggests that when we think about our past experiences our feelings can be predicted by a simple average of two moments: the most intense moment of the experience - the peak - and the feeling we experience at the end. The entire duration of the full experience is less important than our most intensely experienced feeling and the one that concludes the experience.

We expect the "peak" of our experiences to matter. What is remarkable is the power of the "end" to influence our memories of how happy or unhappy an experience was.

To build greater happiness, and have more positive memories to draw on for those times of nostalgia, it helps then if, for example, we:

- organise our working day to conclude with a good experience, an accomplishment we can take satisfaction from
- leave enough time in our conversations and meetings to emphasise the positives
- plan our holidays to end, not start, with the most pleasurable experiences

"Extracting meaning from past experiences"
Barbara L Fredrickson, 2000 at Unc.edu

WHEN IT'S BEST TO KNOW NOTHING

As for me, all I know is that I know nothing.

SOCRATES

Socrates was surprised to discover that the Delphic oracle had pronounced him the wisest person in the world. Bemused, Socrates determined to find a person who was wiser than he. After much discussion with other philosophers, politicians, craftsmen and poets, Socrates realised the oracle was correct. Although others possessed much certainty, it was a certainty that seemed to amount to little on questioning.

Socrates understood that the fact he knew nothing - and was open to new knowledge - did mean he was wise.

Our personal identity is often bound up in our past achievements, know-how and expertise. Others - our family, friends and colleagues - come to us for our views and opinions. And it becomes tempting to assume that we know it all; or if we don't, to imply that we do.

It may be a better strategy to enter conversations and discussions and participate in meetings with an attitude of "know nothing".

This isn't the calculated impression management of feigned ignorance to flush out any ideas that might oppose our own. Instead it is a mindset that asks rather than answers, listens rather than talks, checks understanding rather than assumes a common understanding, and is prepared to rethink rather than defend existing beliefs.

And when we know nothing, we may discover something new, fresh and original.

WHY WHAT WE KNOW CAN GIVE US TROUBLE

It isn't what we don't know that gives us trouble, it's what we know that ain't so.

WILL ROGERS

Nostalgia keeps us attached to a world we know.

And this familiarity makes us confident about ourselves and our life situation. But maybe we're holding on to knowledge, expertise and skills that aren't relevant to our future. This is us clinging on to a world that is changing and may be disappearing.

It helps if we rethink our existing expertise and skill to check how much is based on a familiar past and how much is relevant to a different future. We can't know it all. But we can keep interested and curious. So we should keep alert to what is changing and different.

The novel and the unexpected make us curious. What happened? Why? How did that work? But sometimes the best insights emerge from that curiosity which explores and rethinks what we thought we already knew.

Adding to our knowledge base and building greater expertise is important. But it also helps if we are willing to revisit our current assumptions to look at our existing knowledge from a different perspective to challenge our existing beliefs.

PAST

HOW GOOD IS GOOD

So give me a turbulent world as opposed to a quiet world and I'll take the turbulent one.

ANDY GROVE, FORMER CEO INTEL

We are at risk of lapsing into complacency when we rely on past successes? Or thinking that "good is good enough."

As Jim Collins points out "good is the enemy of great" and the dynamic that explains why previously successful organisations experienced decline and failure.

If we're thinking that was as good it gets, we shouldn't be surprised when our prediction turns out to be correct.

"Good is the enemy of great" Pat Morgan at Ezinearticles.com

WHEN WE SHOULD LET THE PLUG OUT

At some point everything gets a little stale and you have to step away from it.

LES CLAYPOOL

It is easy to let our thinking become stale.

Bombarded by the information overload of a relentless media generating a stream of the "new and next big thing", it is tempting to fall back on what is familiar and comfortable. And because the "new and next big thing" is often a repackaging of the obviously sensible or over-hyped nonsense, we can rationalise away new ideas.

We reinforce our existing views and beliefs by limiting our information intake to familiar sources. It helps if we:

- talk to others, particularly those involved in interesting projects
- are selective in listening to radio and TV programmes
- read decent newspapers and books with a very different perspective to our current opinions

Sometimes we need to pull out the plug to let the old water out and turn on the tap of fresh thinking.

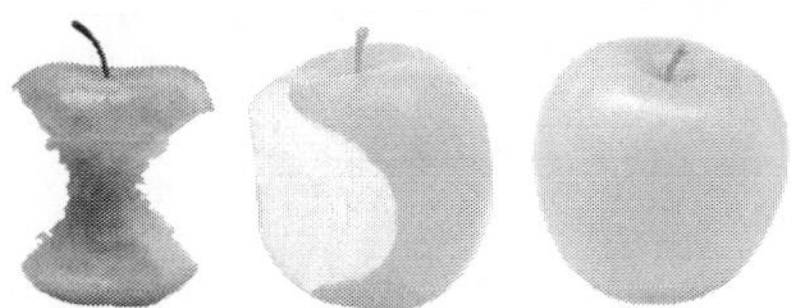

WHAT IS THE PERFECT DAY

The world is full of people whose notion of a satisfactory future is, in fact, a return to the idealised past.

ROBERTSON DAVIES

Who is "you"?

Is "you" a preservation of the past and an identity based on the familiar and comfortable? Or is the future "you" a different individual, willing to develop new skills and reinvent yourself for a different future.

Conduct the **"perfect day"** exercise to help you identify the key themes of your future life. What would your perfect day look like? In this exercise you are given the "blank sheet of life" to describe:

- where would you be (you can be anywhere in the world)?
- who would you be with (you can be with whoever would make your perfect day)?
- what would you be doing (there are no constraints)?
- what kind of person would you be (again, no constraints)?

This is not your good day. This is your version of the most perfect day you could ever imagine. Put in as much detail as possible. Be specific with the specifics. And it's **your** perfect day, not the day you think you should describe to others. You're not writing for an essay examination; don't worry about your vocabulary or grammar. But do put in enough creative effort to make your day "come alive".

Put your page to one side for a while. Then come back to it after a few hours.

- what key themes strike you?
- which life goals seem most significant?
- which don't feature at all?
- how does your "perfect day" now feel? Is it still perfect or is something missing?
- how similar and different is your perfect day to your current life situation?

ARE WE HAVING FUN YET

I don't want to get to the end of my life and find that I lived just the length of it. I want to have lived the width of it as well.

DIANE ACKERMAN

Given the rate of economic and social progress over the last few decades, and the increase in leisure time, are we now spending our time in more enjoyable ways in comparison to previous generations? Using an imaginative time sampling methodology economist Alan Kruegel and Nobel laureate Daniel Kahneman asked if we're spending more time on those activities associated with life satisfaction and meaning.

The answer unfortunately is no.

There might have been a decrease in time devoted to the mundane chores of life, but on net, we're not spending more time on the activities that make us feel more positive.

In the pie chart of life time, 20% of time is spent in unsatisfying activities (commuting, waiting); 31% on working; and 14% on the mundane. Another 22% is spent on the "mental valium" of TV and other passive activities. 12% of time is spent on activities such as walking and reading that we find enjoyable, and only 17% on the highly enjoyable and rewarding stuff (e.g. music, parties, sex, being in nature, spiritual practice).

We should rethink our approach to time management to ensure we build the kind of life style and working schedule that factors in more enjoyment, fun and meaning. Without this dimension in our lives, we may lose something of the quality that keeps us curious and confident about life's possibilities.

"Are we having more fun yet?" Alan Krueger at Brookings.edu

"6 tips for better time management" John Casey at Webmd.com

PAST

WHEN WE SHOULD RETHINK OUR LIFE ROUTINES AND HABITS

Habit converts luxurious enjoyments into dull and daily necessities.

ALDOUS HUXLEY

Don't look back on happiness, or dream of it in the future. You are only sure of today; do not let yourself be cheated out of it.

HENRY WARD BEECHER

We become accustomed to a certain way of operating, typically brought forward from our past. And this familiar routine defines our possibilities of happiness and success.

But habits can become a hindrance to new approaches, holding us back from shifting to more effective working styles.

It's easy to keep repeating what worked: meeting familiar friends, returning to the same holiday destination, and so on.

Do something different and see what happens. Vary your plans and schedule to build greater novelty and freshness into life.

"8 ways to get yourself out of a rut" Ellen Glasgow at Shiftyourmind.com

"7 life changing ideas" at Thechangeblog.com

WHAT DID LESTER BURNHAM LEARN

In less than a year I'll be dead...in a way I'm dead already.

LESTER BURNHAM

"American Beauty" is the film of Lester Burnham's mid life crisis and a tale of the pursuit of success, and how skewed notions of happiness can lead to unhappiness and a lack of life meaning.

Awakening from the "sleepy malaise that has come to define his life" in the emptiness of suburbia, Lester begins a new life. He looks at himself and wonders how he got there and what he needs to do to get back to the person he once was, someone who once loved life.

Quitting his job as a magazine writer he applies for a part time position at a fast food restaurant; "I'm looking for the least amount of responsibility." In his new life, he smokes pot, lusts after his daughter's girl friend, buys a sports car and starts getting into shape "to look good naked". Lester becomes friends with his new neighbour's son with a set of consequences that culminate in Lester being shot by the boy's father.

Lester can be viewed as a hero who attempted to break free from his current situation. Here, American Beauty is a tragic tale of redemption lost. But it's difficult to know what Lester was escaping from and to, apart from greater self indulgence that could only worsen his problems.

As the film closes, Lester's voice is calm and peaceful, as he expresses "nothing but gratitude for every moment of my stupid little life." Looking back he realises what was important and sees the beauty of his entire life.

Lester's tragedy was a nostalgia to look back on a self that had gone and couldn't be relived.

PAST

WHY EXTENDING OUR NETWORK EXTENDS OUR LIFE OPTIONS

Never answer the question 'What do you do?' with a job title and a company, but rather something interesting that guarantees the answer, "How do you do that?"

PATRICIA FRIPP

Review your professional and social circle. Are you spending time with like-minded people sharing similar views and opinions to reinforce your current beliefs and opinions?

Make it a priority to meet new people from different walks of life with fresh ideas to challenge and stimulate your thinking. You may disagree with their views but it will open up your horizons.

Tactics to build and cultivate your support network:

- make a list of those whom you would currently regard as part of your network and those who could potentially be added to it
- be proactive. Don't wait for someone else to make the first move. If you meet someone you think could be a good friend, invite him or her for coffee
- stay in touch. Answering phone calls, returning e-mails and reciprocating invitations quickly lets people know you care
- be open to new people you meet. Don't always fall back on those you already know. Welcome new faces; they may be potential friends for your support network
- be a good listener. Don't centre discussions around your issues. Interact by listening carefully to what others say, showing a genuine interest in their views
- show appreciation to those who consistently support you. Be grateful and display your gratitude openly
- don't overdo it. In your zeal to extend your social network, be careful not to overwhelm friends and family with phone calls and e-mails. Save those high-demand times for when you really need them

"Social support: tap this tool to combat stress" at Mayoclinic.com

"Safe social networking" Chris Denholm at Thesite.org

"Managing your support networks" at Mindtools.com

"12 great tips to improve your business networking skills" Ian Cowley at Cowleyon.com

HOW TO BEGIN A HAPPINESS PROJECT

One of the best ways to make yourself happy is to make other people happy. One of the best ways to make other people happy is to be happy yourself.

GRETCHEN RUBIN

Gretchen Rubin wasn't depressed or having a midlife crisis. She wasn't even unhappy, but she felt dissatisfied, and that something was missing in her life.

Remembering the words of the writer Colette, "What a wonderful life I've had! I only wish I'd realised it sooner", she began a happiness project: a programme of learning and activity to optimise her happiness and flourish more in life.

Her experiences and conclusions include:

- go to bed earlier. Know how to sleep and get up early
- exercise better. Find a programme that works for you, but take a minimum of 20 minutes a day three days a week
- tackle the clutter of life to get organised. Take on a nagging task you've been putting off
- act more energetic. "Fake it till you feel it" sounds false, but adding more zip and zest raises our energy levels
- don't expect praise or appreciation; do what needs to be done without looking for recognition
- fight right; manage any conflicts with wisdom.
- enjoy the fun of failure; to have more success, be more accepting of failure
- ask for help; there is a lot of people with similar interests and aspirations to our own. Find them and connect to them
- work smart; develop a working schedule and routine that increases your efficiency
- enjoy now; be happy in the journey rather than postpone happiness until the arrival. "The fun part doesn't come later, now is the fun part."
- make time for friends. Cultivate and nourish friendships. Remember birthdays and other significant times in others' lives. Be generous of your time and resources.
- pursue a passion. Make time for something that interests and inspires you and treat it as a key life priority
- laugh out loud. Not only is laughter physiologically good for us, it is an important element of social bonding

Reviewing her year's experiment in living, Rubin concludes with her **"splendid truths"**:

- happiness is often boosted most by eliminating the bad stuff, the patterns and behaviours that make us unhappy
- feeling and doing what is right is key
- happiness flourishes in an atmosphere of growth and when we're making progress towards new challenges
- to make ourselves happy is to make others happy, and the best way to make others happy is to act happy
- stay in the moment, appreciating life's events as they unfold rather than anticipate and rush ahead. "The days are long but the years are short."
- happiness is "hard work". A shift in life style to build in greater levels of happiness requires discipline and sustained follow through

We're all different. What works for one person in optimising happiness won't necessarily work for everyone. Begin your own happiness project to go from hankering back to better times to optimise your present and future.

First identify what matters to you, engages and inspires you and brings satisfaction and joy.

Second, make specific resolutions to commit to the practical actions that will boost your happiness. Third, review your progress to track what is and isn't working. Fourth, update and keep to your resolutions.

"Happiness Project Toolbox" Gretchen Rubin at Thehappinesstoolbox.com

WHY IT'S USUALLY A BAD IDEA TO READ AN AUTOBIOGRAPHY

It is said that Zaphod Beeblebrox's birth was marked by earthquakes, tidal waves, tornadoes, firestorms, the explosion of three neighbouring stars, and, shortly afterwards, by the issuing of over six and three quarter million writs for damages from all of the major landowners in his Galactic sector. However, the only person by whom this is said is Beeblebrox himself, and there are several possible theories to explain this.

THE HITCHHIKER'S GUIDE TO THE GALAXY

I am being frank about myself in this book. I tell of my first mistake on page 850.

HENRY KISSINGER

I don't think anyone should write their autobiography until after they're dead.

SAMUEL GOLDWYN

Autobiography is probably the most respectable form of lying.

HUMPHREY CARPENTER

The bookshelves groan with the weight of the autobiography genre. Politicians justify their policy decisions and record in office. Footballers want to build their brand to become celebrities. The disgraced look for redemption and forgiveness from the public. And the has-beens search for a new appeal and audience.

We've become so familiar with the format that we've forgotten the sheer arrogance of the individuals who think their life story should be told and read. Apart from the tedium of reading through details, significant to the writer but no one else, perhaps the main problem is the self serving bias that spins a story to put the individual in a positive light.

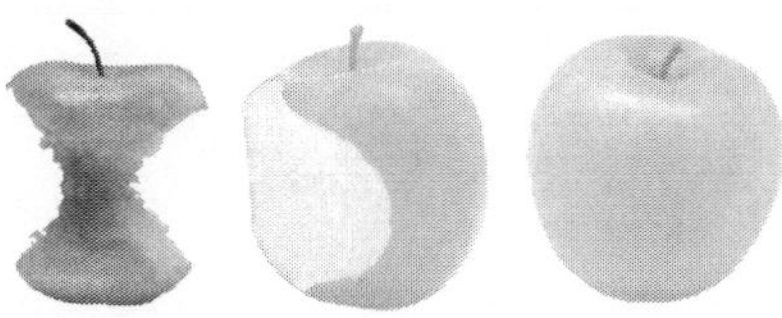

Even when failings and follies are recounted, it is always part of the learning on a journey to greater wisdom and success. With few exceptions most biographies are an exercise in self deception and impression management.

Typically, the autobiography is a rewriting of the past to make us feel better about the present in the hope that we will be remembered in future.

"You Cannot Live As I Have Lived And Not End Up Like This" Terence Blacker

"Autobiography" at Wikipedia

"Condemned by their words: the 10 worst autobiographies" 2006, The Independent

"Top ten biographies and autobiographies" at Thebookbag.co.uk

BUT WHY WE SHOULD WRITE OWN AUTOBIOGRAPHY

When you put down the good things you ought to have done, and leave out the bad ones you did do - well, that's memoirs.

WILL ROGERS

Autobiographies can be an exercise in self-justification. Or they can be a powerful way to review and reflect on the lives we've lived, living and want to live in future. It might not hit the bestseller charts, but our autobiography can be a useful device to stop and think and note down:

- how we would describe ourselves from different perspectives; how do others view us
- how we resemble and differ from our parents/family
- the dynamics of our family
- our sexual history
- school and work
- friendships, loves and social life
- how we have handled life's challenges
- crises, regrets and peak experiences
- the future changes we would like to make in life
- how significant others viewed and view our future
- our realistic expectations; what is most likely to happen next in our life

This doesn't have to be an exercise in literary perfection. It's probably better if it isn't. Instead it is our way of combining emotional honesty about our past, detachment from the pressures of the present and life curiousity about our future.

"How to write an autobiography" at Ehow.com
"Listmania; autobiographies" at Amazon.co.uk

OPERATING IN THE CURRENT FLOW

Whether it's the best of times or the worst of times, it's the only time we've got.

ART BUCHWALD

When we operate in the current flow we are engaged fully in the challenges of the present. Our minds aren't flickering back to what we forgot to do yesterday or running ahead to worry about tomorrow's challenges. This is the mature attitude that recognises that we can only act now.

This section suggests that while elements of time management can be helpful to optimise our efforts productively, the biggest gain is achieved not through a better personal organiser or project planner, but when we rethink our attitudes to time and manage our psychological energies.

Our work productivity and enjoyment of life is enhanced when we shift mental gear. Instead of the stop and start of brake and acceleration, we develop the art of attention, concentration and mindfulness to select the gear that is right for today.

PRESENT

WHY NOW DOES MAKE US HAPPIER, AND SEX HELPS

Happiness is found by living in the now, particularly if the now involves having sex.

GUARDIAN

It's official.

A Harvard University research team collected information on the daily activities, thoughts and feelings of over 2,000 people to find out how often they were focused on what they were doing and what made them most happy.

They found that people were happiest when having sex, exercising or in conversation, and least happy when working, resting or using a home computer. And although people's minds were wandering nearly half of the time, this consistently made them less happy.

The team concluded that reminiscing, thinking ahead or daydreaming tends to make people more miserable, even when they are thinking about something pleasant.

Even the most engaging tasks failed to hold people's full attention. Volunteers admitted to thinking about something else at least 30% of the time while performing these tasks, except when they were having sex, when people typically had their mind on the job around 90% of the time.

Research coordinator, Matthew Killingsworth observed: "Sex is one of the few broad categories of activity that requires and perhaps benefits from our full attention." No mention however of Ms Killingsworth's opinion.

Our minds have an extraordinary ability to wander. At best this is the power to free ourselves from the present to look back and reflect on the past and learn from it, and to anticipate and plan for the future. But "a wandering mind doesn't seem to be a happy mind."

Living in the moment really does make people happier.

IAN SAMPLE, 2010 GUARDIAN

WHY WE SHOULDN'T SAVE SEX FOR OLD AGE

I asked him what he wanted to do for his career, and he replied that he wanted to go into a particular field, but thought he should work for McKinsey for a few years first to add to his resume. To me that's like saving sex for your old age. It makes no sense. WARREN BUFFETT

Sacrifices now to build a better future are of course part of our progress in life. Rather than slump in front of the TV, we know it will be better for the long-term if we complete the tax form, read an article of professional interest, or clear out the garage.

But there are other "sacrifices" we make that are less about building for a successful future and more about living a life now that doesn't feel real or authentic. And in the process of living a life that doesn't connect to our deep-seated motivations and passions, it has the potential to undermine our long-term purpose.

Warren Buffet the "sage of Omaha" knows a thing or two about time. His entire investment strategy is based on the long-term, but he knows that some short-term sacrifices compromise us in our progress in life.

Do what you love and work for whom you admire the most, and you've given yourself the best chance in life you can.

WARREN BUFFETT

WHAT WAS EINSTEIN'S INSIGHT ABOUT THE IRONY OF TIME

When you sit with a nice girl for two hours it seems like two minutes. When you sit on an oven for two minutes, it seems like two hours.

ALBERT EINSTEIN

Einstein knew something about the mathematics of the relativity of time. He also understood the psychology of time.

While we sit in the doctor's reception area, the clock ticks and we are aware of each moment. At a lively dinner party with entertaining company we glance at a clock and are amazed it's two in the morning.

We know that time speeds up when:

- our minds are preoccupied with activity and we become immersed in a task
- we forget to attend to what's happening and don't register the signals of passing time
- we're relaxed and not fretting and worrying

Time slows down when:

- we do nothing but simply listen to the tick of the clock
- we wait for something unpleasant to happen and experience fear
- the unexpected happens and we need to process new information

This is the irony of time. As Stefan Klein points out: "the most beautiful hours of our lives appear to be briefest, yet the same period of time in an unpleasant situation never seems to end."

If we want to live a long life (extend our experience of subjective time) we should organise our lives to spend a lot of time in the reception area of a mad and unpredictable dentist with an obsession with clocks.

If we want to have a pleasant and fulfilled life we might have to accept the rapid passage of time. But at least we'll have lots of positive memories.

WHAT JAMES JOYCE KNEW ABOUT THE IMMEDIACY OF THE MOMENT

I am tomorrow, or some future day, what I establish today. I am today what I established yesterday or some previous day.

JAMES JOYCE

James Joyce's Ulysses tells the story of Leopold Bloom in the course of one day in Dublin in the early part of the twentieth century. Not much happens in the novel, at least not in the way we expect of the driving plot narratives of modern thrillers. Instead it is about three characters and their "stream of consciousness" as they interact.

With its abandonment of literary forms, Ulysses baffled many people (and still does). Others saw it as an imaginative experiment in the attempt to describe what our "participation in life is like, or rather what it seems to moment from moment to live."

As Michael Foley summarises: Joyce's aim was to "transform every reader's insignificant days into adventures as strange, rich, heroic and mythical as those in Homer - to turn every day into an Odyssey."

In a world of abstractions, where the management information of spreadsheets, the business jargon of meetings, or the consultancy-speak of process maps, is less about illuminating reality and more about obscuring direct experience. Ulysses and its "slurping of food and the smell of sweat" is a vivid reminder of the need to connect to day to day realities and the immediacy of experience in life's great adventure.

"Fighting the Bull" Brian Fugere

PRESENT

ARE WE BUSY DOING GREAT WORK

No one has yet said to me: "I've got too much Great Work. I'm overloaded with meaningful, engaging work that really makes a difference.

MICHAEL BUNGAY STANIER

We're all busy. The issue is what we are busy doing:

- **bad work**: those activities that take up time, consume emotional energy and make little impact
- **good work**: tasks we enjoy and work productively at to make progress
- **great work**: activities that are both meaningful and challenging. These are the tasks that make a difference to us and have a positive impact on others, leaving us energised and enthusiastic

It's useful to check where we're spending the balance of our time. If we're preoccupied with the "stuff of bad work" we're coping and not enjoying the process.

To create a sense of urgency about our time and how we're spending it, complete the death clock test. Statistically, it checks how long we have left to live. However scientific (or not), the display of the number of seconds before D day focuses minds on how we might need to shift our tactics to reduce bad work and increase great work.

Michael Bungay Stanier provides some suggestions to change the balance:

- think projects rather than job descriptions. Our job description is a guide to more good work; projects give the opportunity for great work
- schedule our days to achieve one "high impact" action that we will complete
- say yes - slowly. We shouldn't confuse the manners of life with the acceptance of others' problems. But rather than saying no, use questions before saying yes to clarify the personal commitment
- organise the working environment. Great work requires a different operating style. Find a time and space that helps you think creatively
- adequate is OK. Don't strive for excellence in everything you do. The strategy of perfection is a strategy that keeps us stuck on enhancing good work rather than increasing time for great work
- don't worry about making everyone happy. If everyone is happy, the chances are that we're not. Caught up in bad work we're not focusing on the few people that matter

- clear meetings out from the diary. Prioritise the ones that genuinely matter and make a difference and stop attending those that don't

You've got to find what you love. Your work is going to fill a large part of your life, and the only way to be truly satisfied is to do what you believe is great work.

STEVE JOBS

"It's your final countdown" at FindYourFate.com
"Stop the busywork: seven ways you can do more great work" Michael Bungay Steiner, 2010 at ChangeThis.com

WHAT ARE THE WARNING SIGNS OF WORK-AHOLISM

One of the symptoms of an approaching nervous breakdown is the belief that one's work is terribly important. BERTRAND RUSSELL

Workaholism is viewed as the "respectable addiction" and indeed is a highly valued quality in many organisations. It can be, however, as dangerous as many other addictions. In Japan, it's known as "karoshi" - death by overwork - and is estimated to cause 1,000 deaths per year.

There is a world of difference between hard work and workaholism. Hard work underpins any level of exceptional performance and outstanding achievement. Workaholism is that obsession that loses a sense of perspective about what matters in life, and becomes caught up in a vicious cycle of declining productivity.

It is true that much creative achievement has arisen out of a relentless passion. It is also true that many workaholics have looked back on their careers wondering why they didn't get to know their children, find the time to pursue their love of water colour painting, or just enjoy the smell of the roses.

The warning signs of workaholism:

- **strained relationships** as the workaholic loses focus on the important relationships in life
- **health problems**, and headaches, sleep disorders, gastric problems and the constant fatigue of a hectic schedule
- **the office intrudes on home life**. Paperwork takes over the dining room and conversations are dominated by "another tough day"
- **an unwillingness or incapacity to switch off**. Emails are to be checked and the phone is always on. On-call surgeons have an excuse. Most of us don't need to be available 24/7

Alcoholics have a twelve step programme. To avoid or start recovery from workaholism:

- **accept there may be a problem** that is affecting your mental and physical well being

- **plan your time**. Start by scheduling the right priorities. Make time for your important relationships. Relationship experts advise that a minimum of 20 minutes each day of quality time is needed to maintain a healthy relationship. But also plan longer breaks to get away from it all and really switch off
- **look after your health**. Keep fit and healthy. Check your vital signs (heart rate, blood pressure, weight, blood sugar, etc.) to see if you have room for improvement. Get plenty of sleep and watch your intake of alcohol, cigarettes etc.
- **delegate**. Allow other people to help you as often as possible. Workaholics often are perfectionists who want to maintain control and reluctant to allow others to assist
- **separate work and home**. Make a conscious effort to switch off from work. Don't take work home. Plan other activities that interest you and schedule in the downtime of relaxation

What work I have done I have done because it has been play. If it had been work I shouldn't have done it.

MARK TWAIN

"How to stop being a workaholic" Leo Babauta at ZenHabits.net

"Reclaim your life: twelve steps to stop being a workaholic" Deborah S. Hildebrand at OfficeArrow.com

PRESENT

ARE WE BURNING OUT

The No. 1 cause of burnout is doing the same thing over and over again and not seeing results. You need to do something different, whether it's increase your weights or do a different exercise.

STEVE KACZMARSKI

Life is too short, whatever the short-term financial gain, to persevere in an activity that is creating persistent stress. It will impact negatively on our long-term life outcomes.

Assess the "burn-out" element of your role. Does it:

- involve working for an exploitative organisation which "hires and fires" at will?
- pull you in different directions with conflicting goals, with no feedback on how you are performing?
- require you to "fake it" i.e. express emotions that aren't the authentic you?
- demand that your entire life revolves around its priorities but doesn't seem a meaningful or worthwhile activity in its own right?
- tire you out to the point that when you get home, all you want to do is switch off, watch a couple of hours of TV and go to bed?

If the answer is "yes", we should review our career options, and begin searching for another job.

"Out of juice? recharge" Todd Balf 1998 at FastCompany.com

IS BALANCE BULLSHIT

Balance is bullshit.

KEITH FERRAZZI

Life is about balance and compromise. No one can ever "have it all.

DALE WINSTON

The work life balance is a much admired goal. It highlights a life style in which work tasks are planned and scheduled effortlessly, and we work steadily and productively to meet our commitments, every now and again glancing at our social calendar, to remind ourselves of a rich array of forthcoming leisure and cultural activities.

This is the life of "Goldilocks", not too much, not too little, not too fast or too slow.

But it's probably a world that exists for only the most wealthy, who surrounded by an entourage of assistants and flunkies, glide effortlessly from the film set to the TV studio, and then out to supper at Claridges.

For the most part, for most of us, life is a series of "ups and downs" of different demands, and of the panics and emergencies of a child with a pencil in one nostril, a friend calling late at night upset by a messy divorce, and our company announcing a head count reduction.

We shouldn't expect each day, week and month to follow a regular and stable pattern. Imbalance is the name of the game. After all, our "hunter-gatherer" ancestors had to manage the "alternating periods of stress and ease". After the busyness of planting, there was downtime to allow the plants to grow, followed by the rush to bring in the harvest and rest throughout winter.

But if we feel our lives are running out of control, we rarely see our partner and children, don't find the time for physical exercise, want to slump on the sofa in the evening because we're too tired to contemplate anything other than TV, then we need to find greater balance.

And it starts by admitting we can't "have it all."

"You can't have it all" at LeadingToday.org

WHAT ARE THE 7 QUESTIONS WE SHOULD ASK EVERY WEEK

The only questions that really matter are the ones you ask yourself.

URSULA K. LE GUIN

- did I make a difference?
- did I laugh?
- did I attempt something new and different?
- did I have one scary moment?
- did I gain a new insight to make me wiser?
- what do I need to forget and put behind me?
- what do I want to achieve now?

When we're caught up in the rush of day to day events, it's good to find a slot of time each week for a moment of self reflection to take stock of our past, present and future.

"25 beautifully illustrated thought-provoking questions" Marc, 2010 at Marcandangel.com

WHY WE HAVE MORE TIME THAN WE THINK

Don't say you don't have enough time. You have exactly the same number of hours per day that were given to Helen Keller, Pasteur, Michelangelo, Mother Teresa, Leonardo da Vinci, Thomas Jefferson, and Albert Einstein.

H. JACKSON BROWN

If we have 168 hours in a week, why do we feel so starved for time?

LAURA VANDERKAM

There are 168 hours in a week. Even if we are in a demanding job, working 50 plus hours a week, and sleep 8 hours a night, that leaves over 60 hours for other activity in life. So why do we constantly feel we don't enough time?

The key reason is that we don't think strategically enough about time. And because we don't take the initiative to think and plan our time proactively, we get caught up in the busyness of unproductive distractions.

A strategic approach to time works out how best to optimise a key resource, the 168 hours we all have, starting by:

- logging how we currently spend our time. The results will surprise you. We work less than we think. And we don't direct our time to the things we say are important (e.g. our families)
- asking ourselves what we would like to be doing during the 168 hours of next week, and the week after. This is the tough question that asks us: what activities will have most impact on our career, financial and life success? What activities will "create happy memories for you and your children?"
- getting ruthless about eliminating anything that doesn't add value. Like a business consultant who analyses a firm's practices to focus efforts, this is time management as a discipline to overhaul the fundamentals of our current goals and activity

"If you find yourself saying I don't have time to do X, try changing your language. Instead say, I don't do X because it's not a priority."

"168 hours: the blank slate of time" Laura Vanderkam, 2010 at ChangeThis.com

PRESENT

CAN WE BEAT THE CLOCK

Until we can manage time, we can manage nothing else.

PETER F. DRUCKER

Until you value yourself, you will not value your time. Until you value your time, you will not do anything with it.

M. SCOTT PECK

Keep a log of how you allocate your time. Review this log at the end of each week to identify the productive and unproductive use of your time. Give time the respect it deserves. Once you've spent it, you can't get it back again. What is your efficiency ratio: time achieving meaningful outcomes vs. time spent on activity?

See the big picture. Don't strive to achieve your immediate objectives, concentrating your efforts on the "one thing" you see as critical to success, if you're not absolutely clear about what it is. Switch off for a while rather than immerse yourself in another task. Give yourself some time and space to do nothing apart from think about what ultimately you're trying to achieve.

Undertake **task triage**:

- tasks that do not have significant impact whether you do them or not; these are unimportant and can be set aside
- tasks that will succeed whether you do them or not; your participation is not essential so these can be parked
- tasks that will have a significant impact if you complete them on time; these are important, although not necessarily urgent, and must be dealt with. You can leave involvement in the first two categories to enable you to concentrate all your efforts on these tasks

The **don'ts** of time management:

- do all the easy stuff first because you can do it quickly; start with the most important task even though it may be difficult
- believe all your work has to be perfect instead of "good enough" to keep making progress
- start your day without a plan of action; it is too easy to become bogged down in the first email you look at

- make mental excuses, e.g. "I'll do it tomorrow". Overcome procrastination
- spend time with time wasters, whether they're friends or not; you have your priorities. Don't let others run your life
- think doing something "practical", like tidying your desk, is a substitute for what needs to be done. It's displacement activity to avoid getting on with the job

"Do you have time management skills?" at Queendom.com

"8 ways to pitch perfectionism" Margarita Tartakovsky at PsychCentral.com

"How to develop your sense of time" at WikiHow

"How to stop procrastinating: 7 timeless tips" Henrik Edberg at PositivityBlog.com

"How to effectively manage your time" at Mahalo.com

"10 tips for time management in a multi-tasking world" at Penelope trunk's Brazen Careerist

PRESENT

HOW TO CUT DOWN ON TV TIME

If it weren't for the fact that the TV set and the refrigerator are so far apart, some of us wouldn't get any exercise at all.

JOEY ADAMS

TV now offers a bewildering array of options, not to mention iPlayer, DVDs, everything from mainstream entertainment, comedy and drama to the more niche channels for those who enjoy 1970s prog rock, Canadian ice hockey or past episodes of Family Guy. But it can consume significant amounts of our time.

- **keep a TV diary**. Do you know how much time you spend watching TV? How much of this time is useful, keeping up to date with the news vs. checking out repeats because you want a bit of "couch potato time"?
- **start small**. Try not watching TV for just one day a week. How easy or difficult would that be? Don't just stop watching TV, start something else that is enjoyable and rewarding
- **use your ex TV time productively**. If you've been spending 25 hours a week glued to the tube, think about how much you could accomplish if you redirected that time towards something else!
- **record to take control**. Only watch recorded shows. This puts you in control over your schedule and encourage you to be more selective about what you watch
- **turn off and unplug the television**. See what happens

"How to quit watching TV" at Wikihow.com

WHY TIME MANAGEMENT DOESN'T WORK FOR ALL OF US

The genuinely successful are not, on the whole, the kind of people who keep glancing shiftily at their watches or making small lists entitled "to do".

BARBARA EHRENREICH

Most time management programmes can be summarised as:

- set goals
- prioritise and make lists
- start on the top priority tasks
- don't procrastinate

Ralph Keyes asks: "are these approaches to time management more part of the problem than solution?"

Time can't be managed. Time is ....time, and not something that is in our control to manage. We can manage our attitudes to time and how we deploy our energies to optimise our productivity. But we can't do much about time itself.

The problem is that most time management systems make us even more aware of the tick of the clock. We become caught up in a world of calendars, schedules and personal organisers, attempting to squeeze more and more into an already hectic life. Instead of controlling our lives, time continues to control us.

Effective time management is generally regarded as working to a great system. But it's our overall attitude to time that is far more important than any system. Indeed, for many of us, systems just don't work. The system - goal setting, list making and personal organisation procedures - becomes another management activity.

Since energy is a more limited resource than time, concentrating on managing our energy makes more sense than attempts to manage time. Some of the major obstacles to achieving maximum effectiveness such as procrastination, lack of enthusiasm, low motivation and fatigue are energy problems and won't be overcome by any rigid time management system.

"Manage your energy, not your time" Tony Schwartz and Catherine McCarthy, Harvard Business Review

WHO WAS THE TIME MANAGEMENT HYPOCRITE

We've taken Franklin's advice when we should have followed his example.

RALPH KEYES

In his "Poor Richard's Almanack" Benjamin Franklin shares his wisdom in a series of aphorisms and proverbs, typically extolling the virtues of hard work and the stewardship of time:

- If time be of all things most precious, wasting time must be the greatest prodigality, since lost time is never found again
- Early to bed and early to rise, makes a man healthy, wealthy and wise
- Never leave that till tomorrow which you can do today
- Leisure is time for doing something useful

In Franklin's world, time is running out, and we should look to optimise every moment in productive activity.

Franklin himself never took this advice too seriously.

Anyone who writes an essay "Fart Proudly" with a call to "fart for freedom, fart for liberty... and fart proudly!" is unlikely to be too po-faced about time management. Indeed, Franklin was something of a hypocrite who himself liked to stay up late, playing chess or chatting with friends, and would spend hours tinkering with gadgets or enjoying long soaks in the bath.

It's good to treat time with respect. It's also good to remember the "breadth of our life as well as its length."

WHY WE SHOULD KNOW OUR PEAK HOURS TO IMPROVE OUR PRODUCTIVITY

Time management is looking at what type of person you are. A lot of it depends on your peak hours.

ROBERT STOKES

The difference between your peak and low hours is quite marked, the equivalent of drinking three to four glasses of wine.

STEFAN KLEIN

Winston Churchill awoke about 7:30 am and remained in bed for a substantial breakfast to read his mail and the newspapers. For the next couple of hours, still in bed, he worked, dictating to his secretaries. At 11:00 am he arose, bathed, and took a walk around the garden, before returning to his study with a weak whisky and soda.

At 1:00 he joined guests and family for a three-course lunch. His wife Clementine drank claret, Winston champagne, port and brandy. With lunch over at 3:30 pm he returned to his study to work, or supervised work on his estate, or played back-gammon with Clementine.

At 5:00, after another weak whisky and soda, he went to bed for an hour and a half. A habit he learned in Cuba, Churchill thought it allowed him to work 1 1/2 days in every 24 hours. At 6:30 he awoke, bathed again, and dressed for dinner at 8:00. Sometimes, depending on the company, drinks and cigars, dinner would extend to after midnight. With his guests retired, Churchill went back to his study for another hour or so of work.

Churchill found a working routine that worked for him.

The trick is to recognise our personal peak hours, the times in the day when we are at our most productive. For some, the peak hours will be early within the morning. For others, it can be late at midnight, when everybody else has gone to sleep.

Check if you are an early bird or night owl and identify your personal "peak hours". Allocate your time to utilise your peak hours for the key tasks of the day.

"Early birds and night owls" at NewsBBC.co.uk
"How writers, artists, and other interesting people organise their days" at DailyRoutines.Typepad.com

HOW TO SLEEP

Sleep...the harder you try, the less likely you are to get to sleep. The trick is to try really hard at what it is you do during the day. This has the double benefit of tiring you out and lessening whatever you generally worry about.

GUY BROWNING

The London Times reported that Tony Wright of the UK recently stayed awake for 266 hours. He was attempting to break the world record of 264 hours awake set by Randy Gardner of the US in 1964. Wright was also attempting to demonstrate that, thanks to his "caveman diet" of raw food, he was able to "train his mind in such a way as to stay awake for 11 days and remain coherent and aware of what was going on around him."

Unfortunately Tony had some bad news. "The Guinness previous record was in fact for 276 hours, set by Toimi Soini of Finland. The Guinness Book of Records stopped recording attempts at sleep deprivation on the grounds they are harmful to health.

To sleep well:

- **improve your daytime habits**. Maintain a regular exercise programme, but don't work out last thing at night. Avoid the foods (cheese, meats, spicy, etc) that disrupt sleeping. Alcohol and caffeine don't help
- **create a better sleep environment**. Check that your bed is large enough, your mattress isn't more than 10 years old, and invest in high quality pillows and bedding. Your room should be quiet, dark and at a comfortable temperature and ventilation
- **prepare for sleep** by keeping a regular bedtime schedule, including weekends. And watch your evening food intake. Avoid eating a large meal within two hours of bed. But a turkey salad sandwich with a glass of milk might help. Take a warm bath (but not immediately before bed) and find a wind-down strategy that works for you
- **reserve your bed for sleeping**. Don't nap during the day, or watch TV in bed

Overcome middle of the night worries. If worry keeps you tossing and turning at night, sit up and ask yourself:

- is this an issue that will be less important in the morning? (almost certainly yes). Forget it and do your best to get back to sleep

- is this an issue I can do something about right now? If yes, get up and do something about it (but don't make a habit of it). If no, then go back to bed. In the morning things will look much more positive and the solutions much clearer
- in a year's time, will this issue bother me? If the answer is no, the chances are you're letting small problems escalate. If yes, then ensure you sit down the next day to clarify your life goals and priorities and conduct a review of your life style. But don't attempt to do it in the middle of the night when your life energies are at their lowest

"Sheep dash to check how well rested you are" at BBC.co.uk

"How to Sleep Better" at HelpGuide.org

"How to get a good night's sleep" Tom Weede, 2003 at FindArticles.com

"Waking up early" at HowToWakeUpEarly.com

"Alarm clocks are bad" Vincent Cheung at Veenix. Blogpot.com

HOW TO CONCENTRATE FOR FLOW

Nothing interferes with my concentration. You could put on an orgy in my office and I wouldn't look up. Well, maybe once.

ISAAC ASIMOV

Entropy is the normal state of consciousness - a condition that is neither useful nor enjoyable.

MIHALY CSIKSZENTMIHALYI

Achieve **"Flow"**. Flow is the **Fascination** with what we're doing; becoming **Lost** in what we're doing; at **One** with what we're doing; and **Wholly** involved in the task. Flow is the time when our physical and psychological energies are caught up in the task, and the moment of our optimum productivity and creativity.

Learn how to find those times of "flow". A task that can be completed within 10 minutes of concentrated power will take an hour of divided attention.

- **know why you are doing the task**. Even the most boring activity can be energising if it is part of a bigger purpose. Ask how the task is helping you advance your goals. If it isn't, don't do it. **Remind yourself of the purpose and objectives**. Know what your goal is clearly before you start
- **structure an environment** that helps keep you alert and removes any distractions. Take yourself into a work environment without newspapers, TV, etc. Clear your work area of anything that you're not currently working on
- **break the task down into chunks**. Big blobs of work that have no clear start or end point destroy focus. If you have a large project, clearly identify a path to get started working on it. If the sequence of actions isn't obvious, it will be difficult to concentrate. Taking a few minutes to plan not only your end result, but the order to complete the steps, will save hours in wasted thinking
- **set a deadline**. Deadlines have both advantages and disadvantages when trying to force concentration. A deadline can make it easier to forget the non-essential stuff and speed up your working time. But make the deadline sensible. Don't put yourself under such pressure you end up lowering your standards of quality

- look to **find out what is new and unfamiliar** in the material you are working on. Don't jump to assumptions about the task. It may seem boring at first but with a sense of curiousity, it may trigger fresh ideas. Keep alert to spot new patterns or trends

"Finding flow" Mihaly Csikszentmihalyi, 1997 at PsychologyToday.com

"How well can you focus" at Queendom.com

"10 tips for razor sharp concentration" Scott H Young at LifeHack.org

"9 steps to achieving flow" Leo Babauta, 2008 at ZenHabits.net

HOW TO BE MINDFUL

Live neither in the past nor in the future, but let each day's work absorb your entire energies, and satisfy your wildest ambition.

SIR WILLIAM OSLER

Everyone agrees it's important to live in the moment, but the problem is how.

ELLEN LANGER

Our lives can be a preoccupation with the past, either as a nostalgic desire to return to happier times, or as resentment about previous injustice. They can also be a projection into the future, played out in the fantasy of a perfect life, or as fear about emerging challenges. And whilst "decisions taken today are driven by our visions of tomorrow and based on what we learned yesterday" our life is lived in the present.

The art of now is through the mindfulness that:

- **stops thinking about ourselves**. If we're acutely aware of ourselves, our minds race off in several directions, following associations that detach us from the present. We're more likely to be mindful when we're experiencing ourselves as part of something greater rather than absorbed with our own feelings
- **knows how to savour the present**. Here we learn to enjoy what we're doing for what it is without comparing and contrasting it to related experiences in the past or our ideal of how it should be
- **keeps curious**. We don't switch off by thinking "this is stuff I already know." Instead we maintain the mindfulness that is alert to the nuances that identifies new complexities to engage our interest
- **attends to others**. Wrapped up in our ideas and feelings we disengage from the dynamics of the interpersonal situation. When we're focused on others, listening actively and questioning to understand, we're more likely to be in the now
- **becomes absorbed in an interesting task**. This is the state of absorption of when we're engaged in an activity that's challenging but attainable. In flow we are clear about our goals and concentrating our energies and creativity on the task, getting feedback that we're making progress

- **accepts the unpleasant stuff**. When faced with the painful and difficult problems, our mind goes into avoidance to block out any unpleasant sensations, feelings and thoughts. Maybe we should accept the emotion for what it is. This isn't passive resignation, but it is to take control of our emotions to avoid the rumination that obsesses
- **watches out for the autopilot moments**. This is the mindlessness in which we become so lost in our thoughts that we aren't registering life. The solution is to develop the habit of novelty, an alertness to notice what is new and different

As Jay Dixit observes: "we live in the age of distraction. Yet one of life's sharpest paradoxes is that your brightest future hinges on your ability to pay attention to the present." Our personal and professional lives will be enhanced by developing the mindfulness that attends to now.

"The Art of Now" Jay Dixit, 2008 at Psychology Today

"The Art of Work" Ann Marsh 2005 at FastCompany.com

"The Mindful Manifesto" Dr Jonty Heaversedge and Ed Halliwell

"Deliberate focus: A quick selection of simple mindfulness exercises" Michael D. Anestis, 2009 at Psychotherapybrownbag.com/

"Ellen Langer and the social psychology of mindlessness" Carrie McLaren at Ibiblio.org

HOW TO BE LESS ABSENT MINDED

I am not absent minded. It is the presence of mind that makes me unaware of everything else. G.K. CHESTERTON

The true art of memory is the art of attention. SAMUEL JOHNSON

The genius, Norbert Wiener, awarded the National Medal of Science for "marvellously versatile contributions, profoundly original, ranging within pure and applied mathematics, and penetrating boldly into the engineering and biological sciences" had a memory problem.

"When he and his family moved to a new house a few blocks away, his wife gave him written directions on how to reach it, since she knew he was absent-minded. But when he was leaving his office at the end of the day, he couldn't remember where he put her note, and he couldn't remember where the new house was. So he drove to his old neighbourhood instead. He saw a young child and asked her, "Little girl, can you tell me where the Wieners moved?"

"Yes, Daddy," came the reply, "Mommy said you'd probably be here, so she sent me to show you the way home".

Learning to drive a car, like any complex activity, requires our full attention to each element of the task. We start with full concentration, and as our skill improves with practice, we direct less attention to accommodate other tasks. This is a huge positive. When we operate on automatic pilot cognitive resources are available for additional tasks. But this automation comes at a price; we sometimes don't notice what we're doing.

That's probably manageable for the mundane stuff of life. Here we have to accept the occasional misplaced wallet, keys or spectacles because we didn't register where we put them. The problem starts when the automatic pilot begins to live our lives.

- when we wake up we miss the sunrise because we're focusing on today's pressures
- at work, we forget to enjoy ourselves because we're preoccupied with tomorrow's priorities

- at the end of the day we can't relax because we're reminding ourselves of the things we forgot today

When our attention is divided, we simply don't encode any new information. It's not that we forgot, we never remembered in the first place.

"Absentminded, here's what you need to know and do" Bonnie, 2007 at CodeForLiving.com

WHY SLOWING IT DOWN BUILDS TRUST

What is this life if, full of care,
We have no time to stand and stare?

No time to stand beneath the boughs,
And stare as long as sheep and cows:

No time to see, when woods we pass,
Where squirrels hide their nuts in grass:

No time to see, in broad daylight,
Streams full of stars, like skies at night:

A poor life this if, full of care,
We have no time to stand and stare.

W H DAVIES

Psychologist Robert Levine studied the "pace of life", his research team going to cities across the world to measure walking speed, clock accuracy, and day to day transactions (e.g. buying stamps at the Post Office).

Armed with his metrics, Levine was able to rank order countries and cities in "pace of life". Western European countries "lead" the world, with Switzerland at the top. Developing countries are generally at the bottom of the list, with Mexico at the bottom.

In addition, Levine looked at "helping behaviour", assessing the likelihood that someone would, for example, return a pen that had been dropped, helping a blind person across the street, or post a lost letter. The cities with the fastest pace of life were also the least helpful.

If we're finding it difficult to engage others in our ideas and gain their commitment to our plans, maybe we should slow down and move to a pace that helps build trust.

"A Geography of Time: On Tempo, Culture, and the Pace of Life" Robert N. Levine

PRESENT

WHY HAPPINESS IS DECEPTIVELY SIMPLE

The way to cultivate greater happiness is deceptively simple.

HARRY MILLS

Pretend that you are.

The traits associated with happy people are:

- **self esteem** and a sense of self worth and belief in personal competence
- **personal control** and the willingness to take charge of our personal destiny
- **optimism** and the belief that positive events are more likely than negative events
- **sociability** and the enjoyment of others' company

Some personality traits predispose us to happiness; others to more unhappiness. But rather than attempt a full personality make over, we can shift to a strategy in which we pretend to display these trait behaviours. Here we begin to see happiness not as the fortunate circumstance of good things happening to us, but as a habit and a way of operating.

And if we reinforce this habit, demonstrating and practising the behaviours of happiness, we may find ourselves becoming happier.

"Resilience: happiness" Harry Mills, 2005 at MentalHelp.net

"101 happiness strategies" Michele Connolly at HappinessStrategies.com

BUT WHY WE SHOULDN'T EXPECT A DEFINITIVE SOLUTION TO HAPPINESS

The purpose of the happiness programme in the human mind is not to increase human happiness; it is to keep us striving.

DANIEL NETTLE

Robert Nozick presents a thought experiment in which we are asked to imagine scientists have invented an Experience Machine. This machine stimulates our brain to induce whatever desirable or pleasurable experiences we could ever possibly want.

The happiness machine is so clever we can choose the experiences we want before we enter the machine, but the machine also senses and gives us whatever it is that we most value and enjoy, even if we don't fully know what that is. Even better, hooked up to the machine we don't know we're in it (although we can remember our previous life unless we choose to forget it). The machine will not break or malfunction, cause us to die prematurely, or produce any untoward side effects.

Nozick asks us: if we were given the choice, would we choose the machine over real life? Few of us it appears would sign up to the machine option.

The problem with the happiness machine and a life of pleasant experience is that deep in our consciousness is the sense that happiness needs to be earned. Happy outputs without the activity of inputs seem fake and inauthentic. Somehow we need the difficulty of striving to make happiness worthwhile.

The mastermind behind the evolutionary force was smart. Any solution to happiness that was easy or definitive would soon become counter-productive.

Like the Lotus Eaters of Homer's Odyssey, the islanders whose diet brought on a haze of happiness and a sleepy languor, and a loss of interest in the world around them, complete happiness would jeopardise that curiousity that keeps us advancing in life.

"Happiness: The Science Behind Your Smile" Daniel Nettle

PRESENT

HOW TO LIGHTEN UP TO LAUGH

Laugh at yourself first, before anyone else can. ELSA MAXWELL

It's good to believe in what we believe. But it's also good to accept that we may get it wrong from time to time. Humour at our expense may be a sign that we're taking ourselves too seriously. And if we're responding badly to others' humour we may need to loosen up.

Are we taking life too seriously all the time?

- **stop assuming we know everything**. Nobody knows everything, not even in their own fields of specialisation. As soon as we assume we know everything, we shut ourselves off to others' ideas and we begin to sound arrogant and uncaring about others' feelings
- **stop exaggerating**. Exaggerating about our abilities, qualifications, knowledge, hobbies etc. is soon tiresome to those around us. Eventually people start to work out the difference between authentic and artificial. In creating a larger-than-life real us, we get caught up heavily in our own self-importance and we lose a sense of reality
- **let go of things**. It's OK to lose an argument. And it's OK to make mistakes. What matters is learning from the loss and failures of life. Nobody is perfect is a life lesson better learnt sooner rather than later
- **think of others**. When we are pompous, the only person we are really focused upon is - us. Instead we should shift our perspective to listen and attend to others' opinions. Even if we are a genius, it's good to hear the voice of someone else
- **laugh**. When was the last time we laughed? What made us laugh?
- **preferences aren't principles**. We become dogmatic when we see each and every issue as a matter of important principle. It may be principle or it may be a difference of preferred operating style

"How to lighten up" at WikiHow.com
"How to be serious" Guy Browning, 2008 Guardian

HOW TO IDLE

The happiest part of a person's life is what they pass lying in bed awake in the morning.
SAMUEL JOHNSON

It may well be that the years observers described as "wasted" will prove to have been the most productive of insights which will keep you going.
JAMES MICHENER

There's a revolution brewing, and the great thing is that to join it all you have to do is absolutely nothing.
TOM HODGKINSON

Our culture extols the virtue of hard work. Surveys show that the number one attribute organisations value in an employee is the willingness to work hard. It is the individual who goes beyond the call of duty, who works longer and makes sacrifices who is praised and promoted. Industrious persistency is viewed as a key dynamic of success in life.

And of course it is...for some. As Carl Jung pointed out, "the shoe that fits one pinches another." For those who define success as financial security and organisational power, hard work is a prerequisite (unless they are very lucky). For those who value other goals in life, hard work may be the route to less, not more life satisfaction. After all, Americans have a collective 415 million unused vacation days in a year but more than 50% report job dissatisfaction.

Is hard work all it's cracked up to be?
Tom Hodgkinson, editor of "The Idler" and author of "How to be Idle" promotes the idea that idleness can be a lifestyle choice. He believes we should have the freedom to do other things by shrinking our working week and promotes the idler's golden rule: we create in inverse proportion to the time we spend working.

Laziness is viewed as a bad thing but idleness is seen as part of the creative process. Just as Bertrand Russell and Oscar Wilde, early idlers who Hodgkinson admires, achieved success in the absence of a work ethic and weren't guilty about it, Hodgkinson suggests this is the way to a happier and more productive life.

Maybe. The life of the idler may not be the optimum strategy for all. Indeed, Tom Hodgkinson's ideal - doing work you want to do when you want to do it - may be a fine life game plan for the privileged but less realistic for most.

However the point is valid: hard work can constrain creativity, and we should discover the joys of sometimes stopping to do nothing. And if we can't stop, maybe we're developing the workaholism that will be damaging to our health and well being.

"How To Be Idle" Tom Hodgkinson
"How to stop and do nothing" Sally Lever at HolisticLocal.co.uk

IS THE JOY IN THE JOURNEY OR DESTINATION

Things won are done: joy's soul lies in the doing.

WILLIAM SHAKESPEARE

Don't hurry the journey at all. Better if it lasts for many years.

C P CAVAFT

Enjoy the journey.

The positive feelings we typically experience are often less about the final achievement; our successes are surprisingly short-lived.

Our satisfaction typically lies in the progress we make in moving closer to our aims. Focus on your end-point but ensure you take pleasure and pride at each step on the way.

"Why the journey is the destination" John Sherry, 2010 at DiscoveringPurpose.co.uk

WHAT WAS IVAN ILYICH'S REALISATION

Real life is found only in the present. If people tell you you should live your life preparing for the future do not believe them. We live in this life and we know this life only.

LEO TOLSTOY

Tolstoy's novella, "The Death of Ivan Ilyich" begins with a gathering of relatives, friends and colleagues to mark the passing of Ivan, secretly thankful that they are not Ivan and pondering how his death might personally benefit them.

The story then goes back in time to Ivan as a law student, determinedly progressing his career and climbing the social ladder to become a judge. "His life ran its course as he believed life should do: easily, pleasantly and decorously." Achieving life success, Ivan starts to decorate the large house he has bought. Hanging the curtains he bangs his side, triggering the illness that will eventually kill him.

Angry at his incapacity and struggling to come to terms with his death, Ivan finds himself confiding in the peasant Garasim. Whilst his family suspect Ivan is a malingerer or a nuisance, Garisim's kindness and honesty help Ivan reappraise his life and the meaning of success.

"And in imagination he began to recall the best moments of his pleasant life. But strange to say that none of those best moments of his pleasant life now seemed at all what they had then seemed - none of them except the first recollections of his childhood. But the child who had experienced that happiness existed no longer; it was like the reminiscences of somebody else. And the further he departed from childhood, the more worthless and doubtful were the joys."

Ivan recognises he has lived an artificial life caught up in self interest. Garasim has reminded him of the authentic life of sympathy and care. Ivan is brought into the presence of a bright white light. Although he knows his mourners, caught up in the ephemeral, do not understand what is important in life, he feels compassion for them. With a sigh, Ivan dies having found joy at last in an authentic life.

It's telling to note the parallels between Ivan Ilyich, the literary creation and Leo Tolstoy, the author. Like Ilyich, Tolstoy took his work seriously, lived a comfortable life and was admired by his peers. Like Ilyich, Tolstoy had a breakdown that forced him to question his achievements. And quite some achievements; his masterpieces, "War and Peace" and "Anna Karenina" are ranked in the best three novels of all time.

In his search for meaning, Tolstoy abandoned the life of the artist to begin writing on religion and politics, attacking greed and hypocrisy to advocate a life style of simple authenticity.

That was Tolstoy's life decision to decide who he was and what he wanted to become. We all have to make our own choices in life - as expressed by Ivan Ilyich in the differences between an artificial and authentic life, and decide what that means for us personally. For Ivan, the authentic life arrived late.

"The Death of Ivan Ilyich and Other Stories" Leo Tolstoy

PRESENT

WHY WE SHOULDN'T HAVE TO WAIT FOR THE FIRING SQUAD

Someone condemned to death says or thinks, an hour before his death, that if he had to live on some high rock, on such a narrow ledge that he'd only room to stand, and the ocean, everlasting darkness, everlasting solitude, everlasting tempest around him, if he had to remain standing on a square yard of space all his life, a thousand years, eternity, it were better to live so than to die at once! Only to live, to live and live! Life, whatever it may be!

FYODOR DOSTOEVSKY

In mid nineteenth Russia, Dostoevsky began writing in an appeal for democratic reform, an illegal and dangerous undertaking. An unsympathetic government ensured that Dostoevsky and other writers were arrested, tried, and convicted as traitors to the tsar.

Condemned to death before a firing squad, Dostoevsky and his companions were brought forward. The order was given to present arms. Members of the execution squad followed the next commands: Ready! Aim!

Then...silence...as the prisoners...waited. But the order to 'Fire!' never came. Instead someone excitedly announced the Tsar's "last minute pardon". Dostoevsky was to be sent to prison camp in Siberia.

Later, Dostoevsky observed that all the misery he endured was exactly what he had needed to make him the writer he ultimately became. The concentration on his imminent death seemed to be filled with the fullness and richness of life. From then on he relished each "now" as if it were sufficient in itself.

Why do we need the immanency of the risk and threat of danger and death to remind us of the wonder of life?

AVOIDING PRESSING REALITIES

I have spent my days stringing and unstringing my instrument, while the song I came to sing remains unsung.

TAGORE

Sometimes life seems too much. It's not just about the sheer amount of stuff we have to tackle. It's the mix of different demands. At work we multi-task to juggle the competing expectations of our boss, colleagues and team, fretting that the balls are about to fall at any time. Our home and social lives are a frenetic game of catch up.

Exhausted by Sunday evening, we remember why we're dreading Monday's meeting.

This section reviews the different coping tactics we use, several of which are helpful in the short term and others which have long-term drawbacks. Here it's useful to examine the psychology of how our minds work and why we don't do what we know we should do, and how we can trick our brains to overcome procrastination and manage our priorities to turn plans into practical action.

PRESENT

WHAT IS THE FIRST RULE OF HOLES

First law on holes - when you're in one, stop digging!

DENIS HEALEY

In trying to scramble out of a hole, it sometimes digs it deeper.

WELLINGTON MARA

Have you ever been in a hole? Are you in one now? We've all been (or will be) in one at some point in our lives. The hole might be about financial difficulties, family disagreements, work conflicts, bad relationships. Whatever the reason, the hole is an awful life adversity and we feel powerless and helpless.

It's true that holes are typically the outcome of a mix of life circumstances. But sometimes (maybe often), we are the ones digging the holes we get into. Sometimes we might be digging with a trowel and it takes a while for the hole to open up. Other times, armed with a large shovel, the hole quickly becomes a massive pit and it seems there is no way out.

One of life's harsh realities is that it can take a relatively short time to dig a hole, but a long time to get out of it.

The first rule: stop digging. Ask yourself, "Why?" What got you into a hole? Was it due to some mistake? If so, what was the mistake? What led up to it? We stop digging when we realise we're in a hole and stop making it bigger.

Once you identify what got you into a hole, you must learn the lesson so you don't repeat it in the future. Revisit these lessons often so you never forget them. Holes come with a price, and sometimes a high price, especially if we don't learn from the experience.

Now that you have stopped digging, you must set yourself to the business of backfilling the hole and climbing out. Getting out of a hole requires some creative problem solving. Try the following I.D.D.I. method in your backfilling efforts:

- **identify the problem**. Identify exactly why you are in a hole and what led up to it
- **dissect the problem**. Explore the cause, by asking why? Was it some mistake? Inexperience? Fear? Greed? Write the reasons down on paper for clarity

- **define possible solutions**. Outline all the options. It's difficult to be creative when we're under pressure, but the hole will demand your highest levels of creativity. And take time to think through the opposite of what you think the solution is. Confide in a trusted friend to help explore alternative solutions
- **implement** your best solution. Reassess and adjust course along the way Don't assume your solution will get you out of the hole immediately. You will need to improvise as you go

"The first rule of holes" Doug Kelley at Enhanced-Healing.com

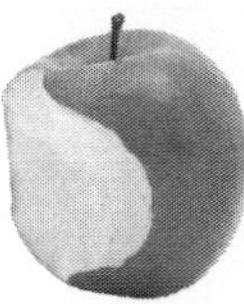

HOW THE CRAZY ZEST OF COOL HAND LUKE WAS ENERGISING

Use that shovel like a spoon.

DRAGNET

Paul Newman, the prisoner Cool Hand Luke, is working on a chain gang in a Southern US prison. Faced with the task of spreading sand on a road that is being tarred, Cool Hand Luke rejects the normal pattern of go slow. Instead he throws himself into the task with a crazy zest.

Spreading the sand like a demon, Luke's fellow prisoners are energised and begin to copy him. "Like men demented, the convicts work so frantically they eventually run out of road to cover", much to the dissatisfaction of their brutal prison guards. While the guards rage, the prisoners laugh hysterically.

The prisoners know they have discovered an important truth.

When we refuse to accept our situation, and instead of allowing our energies to sink in the face of adversity we find ways of raising them, we discover that our sense of freedom expands.

IS OUR MOJO RISIN

Mojo is that positive spirit toward what we are doing now that starts from the inside and radiates to the future.

MARSHALL GOLDSMITH

When Muddy sang "I got my Mojo working" he was highlighting the impact of purposeful energy in life meaning and success (amongst other things!) For Marshall Goldsmith, Mojo is:

- our **identity** and how we define who we are. "Without a firm handle on our identity we may never be able to understand why we gain or lose our Mojo." If we don't know who we are, what matters to us and our life purpose, it's always going to be difficult to capture the spirit of Mojo
- our **achievements** and the accomplishments that have meaning and impact. In summarising our achievements it's useful to ask: what did we bring to the task and what did the task give us? If we don't know the value of our accomplishments, gaining and expressing our Mojo may not be easy
- our **reputation** and others evaluation of who we are and what we've done. "Your reputation is a scorecard kept by others." How we maintain and improve our reputation has a huge impact on our Mojo
- **acceptance** and the understanding of what we can change and what is beyond our control. We gain or restore our Mojo when we recognise the way life is and avoid the frustrations of taking on problems we can't solve but are willing to take on the challenges where we can make a difference

If we're struggling with our Mojo, check Marshall Goldsmith's tool kit.

"Mojo: How to Get It, How to Keep It, How to Get It Back When You Lose It" Marshall Goldsmith

HOW TO AVOID MOJO KILLERS

I've lost my mojo.

AUSTIN POWERS

Mojo is that energy that arises when we are on top of our game, overcoming barriers to make progress, and engaged in the challenges we face. But our Mojo is at risk when we:

- **over commit**. We're making a positive impact and others value our contribution. Our talents are in increasing demand and we respond to this popularity by over extending ourselves, taking on too many additional responsibilities or tasks outside our circle of competence. Here we find it difficult to maintain that zest which initially made us successful
- **wait for the facts to change**. Even when our Mojo is firing on all cylinders, set backs will happen. Shifting customer expectations, changing competitor dynamics, an economic down turn, etc all incorporate potential risks. At first we don't recognise the significance of the change. And for some, used to drawing on the positive energy of Mojo, they assume that the situation will go back to the previous reality. It won't
- **look for logic in the wrong places**. In a logical world, brilliance shines, results are rewarded and talent progresses and is promoted. But organisations don't necessarily run on orderly logical lines. Our Mojo will become exhausted unless we recognise the impact of ego and emotion, interpersonal sensitivities and political gamesmanship on organisational decision making. We maintain our Mojo when we adapt to the pragmatics of organisational life rather than rely on being smart against an assumption of rational logic
- **bashing the boss**. It's easy to criticise and complain about the shortcomings and failings of our manager. Our manager is a convenient lightening rod to focus our annoyances and frustrations with organisational life. And while this criticism may - in the short-term - release negative feelings, it's difficult to see how productive this strategy can be in maintaining our Mojo
- **confusing the mode**. There are two modes: professional and relaxed. In either state we can operate with Mojo. But it's important to know the difference between the two states. In relaxation mode, when we talk freely to express our candid views, we assume others know we've moved out of professional mode. The reality is we let down our guard when we shoot the breeze with humour and sarcasm, and others begin to question our judgement and diplomacy

WHY OVERCOMING THE SMALL ADVERSITIES MATTERS

All the adversity I've had in my life, all my troubles and obstacles, have strengthened me.

WALT DISNEY

Adversity spans a spectrum, from the mild disappointment that a project is past its schedule, to the hardship of the loss of a major customer, to the awful catastrophe of a safety failure in which lives are lost.

And in dealing with maturity with the big adversities of life it helps if we've experienced and managed the smaller adversities. This is a strategy of building resilience by testing ourselves by climbing the smaller peaks to prepare for the major ascent.

If we lose the plot with the small stuff, we may lack that sense of perspective that responds coolly and calmly to the big stuff.

When we experience the small setbacks, it's worth checking our thought processes. Margolis and Stoltz suggest the following prompts:

1. **Specific** questions to identify the difference we can make. These are the types of question that ground the adversity in practicalities.
   - what aspects of the situation can I personally influence to respond to this situation?
   - what can I do to make an immediate impact on this situation?
   - what could I do to mitigate the effects of this adverse event?
   - right now, what do I need to do to make a start?

2. **Visualising** questions shift our attention from the adversity towards a positive outcome. These questions move us from the current problem to the future solution.
   - what would a person I admire do in this situation?
   - what strengths and resources will I develop in dealing with this event?
   - what will life look like after this adversity has been overcome?

3. **Collaborating** questions identify how we can reach out to others for joint problem solving. These questions help us avoid the personal heroics of the lone leader to draw on others' talents and energies.
   - who in our team could help us?
   - how can we mobilise the efforts and skills of those who need encouragement or are holding back?
   - what as a team will see us through this phase of hardship?

"How to bounce back from adversity" Margolis & Stoltz, 2010 Harvard Business Review

WHAT TOM SAWYER DISCOVERED ABOUT TIME AND HUMAN NATURE

Tom appeared on the sidewalk with a bucket of whitewash and a long-handled brush. He surveyed the fence, and all gladness left him and a deep melancholy settled down upon his spirit. Thirty yards of board fence nine feet high. Life to him seemed hollow, and existence but a burden.

MARK TWAIN

But because Tom is smart he starts work on the fence by whistling loudly and seeming to enjoy the painting as his friends congregate to watch him at work. Soon his friends, curious at his efforts, want a turn at painting. Indeed they are so keen to help they give Tom a series of gifts for the privilege. "He had a nice, good idle time all the while - and the fence had three coats of whitewash on it. If he hadn't run out of whitewash he would have bankrupted every boy in the village."

If Tom had simply asked his friends if they would help him paint the fence as a favour, they would have refused. But as they watched Tom, who initially declines their help, they want to help and they in fact enjoy the task.

An activity we have to do can be a tedious burden. It seems like hard work. But the same activity - viewed with a different mindset - can be reframed as a pleasant and fun experience.

HOW TO SPOT WHEN STRESS LEVELS ARE RISING

Over the years your bodies become walking autobiographies, telling friends and strangers alike of the minor and major stresses of your lives.

MARILYN FERGUSON

Signs include:

- **excess**: eating or drinking too much, spending extravagantly
- **denial**: refusing to accept what everyone else can see, used to tell us but have stopped because we are no longer listening
- **rationalisation**: finding "reasons" to explain our actions and "justify" our behaviour
- **retreat**: avoiding certain situations and spending increasing amounts of time on our own

We need to be honest in our appraisal to acknowledge when negative life patterns are creating problems, not just for the immediate term but are stockpiling difficulties for our long-term well being.

And we should be prepared to ask for help if our situation is getting out of control.

"Stress can help us convert problems into solutions" Maynard Brusman at WorkingResources.com

"Stress management techniques" at MindTools.com

IS OUR SPOON IN A POT THAT ISN'T BOILING

Do not put your spoon into the pot which does not boil for you.

ROMANIAN PROVERB

Know what career pot will boil for you and which won't. Don't go against the grain of your skills and motivations to pursue a role that isn't drawing on your deep-seated talents. Select your vocation wisely. And if your job in your current organisation isn't working for you, find another "pot".

Ask:

- do I enjoy what I do?
- does it allow me to utilise my strengths?
- do I have the opportunity to make a difference?
- when I perform well can I see the impact?
- if the organisation performs well, do I personally gain?

If the answer to any of these questions is no, we're avoiding the reality of our career and well being. And we need to find a role which allows us greater fulfilment and autonomy.

ARE WE TIME LOCKED

When traffic grows so congested that it can no longer move, engineers say it's reaching a state of gridlock. Many of us are in a state of time lock.

RALPH KEYES

Time lock is the condition when:

- demands on our time are making it impossible to "wring one more second out of a crowded calendar"
- after prioritising, we can't even get to the "must do's" on our lists
- we shift our definition of success from thriving to keeping up and making do
- we abandon our personal productivity and time management systems - they're not working anymore

In time lock:

- we often feel overwhelmed by the number of choices we have and struggle to make decisions
- we feel we are always rushing and have no "down time"
- our thoughts are always on what we've still to do
- our concentration wanders to the next meeting when we're speaking to people
- former pastimes and interests are neglected as we no longer have the time because we're so busy

If we're experiencing time lock - the traffic of life is so dense we feel stuck and trapped - then we need a major rethink.

Instead of viewing ourselves as another frantic driver looking for a short-cut to get out of the traffic, we should view ourselves as a traffic planner, prepared to redesign our lives to open up free space and move faster.

"Time Lock" Ralph Keyes
"Where Did Time Fly" John Swift

WHAT ARE THE ONLY 3 SOLUTIONS TO PERSONAL PRODUCTIVITY

Plans are only good intentions unless they immediately degenerate into hard work.

PETER DRUCKER

If we're struggling to get on top of life and manage "stuff", there are only three solutions.

- **increase our efficiency** in getting through our work-load
- **reduce the amount of work** that we have
- **increase the amount of time** we have available for work

This is it.

We can only pick one of the three solutions. There aren't any more options. If we can't reduce our workload and we don't want to work even longer hours, then we need to increase our efficiency.

Take a day out to get organised. Schedule a day in your diary next month to conduct a fundamental review of your systems in personal organisation and time management. It's time to sharpen the saw.

"10 quick tips for getting organised" Leslie Jacobs 2006 at Entrepreneur.com

WHY 4 Ds MAKE LIFE BETTER

Do it, Delegate it, Delay it or Dump it.

Use the Four Ds of time management and personal organisation to control your time and space. Either tackle the issue now, pass it on to someone else, schedule time in future when you will personally deal with it, or throw it in the bin. And if any doubt, then dump it.

Don't allow the "clutter of life" build up around you.

Keep on top of the necessary chores to give you the time and space to keep ahead of the game. Don't spend life on the "back foot"; looking for important documents, checking meeting times, scanning for lost emails. Establish control over the flow of information into your life.

"4 Ds of organisation" Jeff Herring at Ezinearticles.com

HOW TO EAT AN ELEPHANT AND SWALLOW A FROG

Don't try to eat an elephant for lunch. CHRIS BRADFORD

Theories pass. The frog remains. JEAN ROSTAND

We feel overwhelmed by the scale and size of the challenge facing us. It all seems too much and because we don't know where to start we don't.

"How do you eat an elephant?" It won't be in one big gulp; bite size chunks might make it easier.

Stand back from the difficult and demanding projects in life, and first break them down to identify the specific tasks to be completed. Make the big assignments manageable by breaking them into a sequence of discrete activities.

"If you know you have to swallow a frog, swallow it first thing in the morning. If there are two frogs, swallow the big one first" advised Mark Twain. We begin by doing the difficult thing first.

But we shouldn't look at the frog for too long! Get it done and out of the way before you take on more enjoyable and interesting activities. Don't start the day with the easy stuff hoping to get into the "swing of things". Do the tough thing first. You'll be surprised by how good it makes you feel and how much quicker you complete the other tasks of the day.

"How to eat an elephant" Hunter Nuttall at PickTheBrain.com

"When to swallow your daily frog" Charlie Gilkey, 2008 at ProductiveFlourishing.com

PRESENT

HOW TO SPOT THE TIME WASTERS

In a Microsoft study done in 2005, more than 38,000 people in 200 countries were asked about their individual productivity. It turned out that though they were arriving at work five days a week, they were only usefully using three days.

WHAKATE.COM

Time wasters are not necessarily the idlers of life, individuals with nothing else to do but take up our time with their petty problems and grievances. These individuals are obvious.

The most dangerous time wasters are the superficially busy, those with an inflated sense of their own importance who burden us with pointless and non-productive activity, activity with no likelihood of meaningful outcomes.

Manage the time wasters by checking:

- their **level of authority** to set your priorities; what power do they really have?
- the **clarity of their proposals** and the outcomes of their plans; do they know what they really want and why it matters?
- their **efficiency levels** to get things done quickly; can they make it happen?

If colleagues and friends prevaricate when we challenge the specifics of why and what, the chances are they will waste our time. Don't get caught up in half-baked plans with the potential to distract you from what is important.

"Eliminate timewasters" at ExcitingFutures.com

PRESENT

HOW TO MANAGE THE INTERRUPTIONS OF LIFE

Circumstances may cause interruptions and delays, but never lose sight of your goal.

MARIO ANDRETTI

Unless we are Jack Nicholson working hard on our novel in "The Shining" or living the life of a hermit we will be interrupted. Interruptions are good when:

- our children want to show us their painting after the first day at nursery
- our partner points out we've been working too long and need to take a break
- a colleague asks us for our creative input on a key project they're tackling
- a customer wants to use us as a sounding board for their ideas

The individual who always has a shut door displaying "No Interruptions" is cutting themselves off from the full flow and vibrancy of life. But there are interruptions and interruptions. The bad interruptions are:

- a sales call that pretends to be from an old friend
- a team member asks for help on a decision they can make easily, if only we'd delegated properly
- a colleague who drifts by to complain about her boss
- a boss who dumps work on us at 5pm on Friday for a presentation on Monday morning

There are times when uninterrupted activity to focus on a specific activity is key. These are the times of intense concentration for maximum productivity to complete a task. And we need to master the art of managing interruptions, with charm and grace, but also with conviction and assertiveness.

The number one rule of interruptions: if the interruption is obviously something more important and urgent than what we are currently doing, Yes is the only response. If it isn't, say: Yes But Not Now, or No.

"11 tips for managing interruptions" Paulette Ensign at DayTimer.com

HOW TO SAY NO

Learn to say "no". It will be of more use to you than to be able to read Latin.

CHARLES H. SPURGEON

Know the power of "no": don't catch every ball that others throw towards you.

We put ourselves under pressure to accommodate every demand that others make of us.

Assert your own expectations and demands. Be clear about what you want and what is important to you.

Don't let others exploit your good nature or let your relationships become one-sided in which others advance at your expense. As experienced negotiators know, don't use the "no" word, even when the answer is no. The "no" word triggers conflict and retaliation.

But know how to refuse others' requests gracefully but assertively.

"Why you can't say no, " Hara Estroff Marano, 2005 Psychology Today

"8 Essential Strategies to Saying No" Leo Babauta at FreelanceSwitch.com

WHY IN THE WORLD OF EVERYTHING IS POSSIBLE NOTHING GETS DONE

I learned that we can do anything, but we can't do everything... at least not at the same time. So think of your priorities not in terms of what activities you do, but when you do them. Timing is everything.

DAN MILLMAN

If Pareto was right - 80% of our results come from 20% of our efforts - it's worth checking where we're directing our efforts. Do we know which 20% of our efforts are generating the 80% of our returns?

Which 3 key goals are fundamentally important to you and your success? Which three objectives will make a significant impact?

Identify the 80-20 key points of leverage. How much time and effort are you directing towards them vs. other more peripheral issues? What do you need to do to redirect and refocus your energies?

"Understanding the Pareto Principle" Kalid Azad at BetterExplained.com

"Prioritisation" at TimeThoughts.com

HOW TO MAKE PARKINSON'S LAW WORK IN REVERSE

There need be little relationship between the work to be done and the size of staff to which it may be assigned. Hence Parkinson's Law: "work expands so as to fill the time available for its completion".

C. Northcote Parkinson, the British historian, observed that even though the British navy was in decline, as an administrative bureaucracy it was still expanding in complexity and staff. The number of ships and the number of officers and men was decreasing in the Royal Navy. But the number of dockyard workers and officials, and the number of admiralty officials, was increasing, and sometimes increasing dramatically.

We increase our productivity by completing work in shrinking time.

If a task normally takes 2 hours, we can try giving ourselves only one hour to complete it. Here we shouldn't be slap-dash and sloppy, but perform the task well. But if we set the clock to give ourselves less time to force us to complete it with full concentration we may be surprised by how much we can complete in less time.

"The 5 unspoken laws of Parkinson's Law" Mohamad Zaki at LessonsInLife.com

WHY THE TRIVIAL TAKES MORE TIME THAN THE IMPORTANT

Relentlessly the trivial squeezes out the non-trivial.

OLIVER BURKEMAN

The time spent on any item of the [meeting] agenda will be in inverse proportion to the sum involved. Thus a £10 million-project may be approved in two-and-one-half minutes, while an expenditure of £2,350 - a much easier sum to comprehend for a much smaller item, something easier to visualise - will be debated for an hour and a quarter.

FROM "THE UNWRITTEN LAWS OF LIFE

C. Northcote Parkinson, as well as outlining Parkinson's Law, also proposed the Law of Triviality: the time spent on any item will be in inverse proportion to its importance and cost. Whereas a Board meeting to discuss an atomic reactor - a complex, high risk and expensive project - will be wrapped up in two and a half minutes, the discussion about the colour of the company bike shed will "be debated for an hour then deferred for a decision at the next meeting."

Parkinson makes the point that the least important things, the most inconsequential, the trivial, command the attention of everyone. We all have views on what doesn't matter that much. For the complex and important issues, we defer to the experts and specialists. Attempting to participate in the risk analysis of building a new atomic reactor would simply expose our ignorance.

It's worth checking how we're spending our time, allowing others to tangle us in the trivial or focusing on what is genuinely important.

"Why trivia is so important" Oliver Burkeman 2010 The Guardian

"The Unwritten Laws of Life" at LawsofLife.co.uk

WHY WE PROCRASTINATE

The greatest amount of wasted time is the time not getting started.

DAWSON TROTMAN

24% of people identify themselves as procrastinators. Presumably this figure under-estimates the scale of the problem given that it can only be based on people who completed the questionnaires on time.

RICHARD WISEMAN

Why do we procrastinate:

- do we need to get every decision, right, every time: the perfectionist?
- do we, deep down, like the adrenalin rush of burning the midnight oil to meet deadlines at the last minute: the crisis-maker?
- are we uncertain of what we need to do and hope that by putting off the task a solution will somehow present itself: the dreamer?
- are we easily distracted, allowing more interesting activities to redirect our attention: the butterfly?
- do we fear the consequences and responsibility of success; the reluctant?
- do we resist any attempt by others to do what they ask: the rebel?

Take the time to understand why you specifically procrastinate. Pinpointing the reason will help you find the specific solution to manage procrastination.

"The most dangerous word in the world" Scott Dinsmore, 2010 at ReadingForYourSuccess.com

"Good and bad procrastination" Paul Graham at PaulGraham.com

"Choices and consequences" Dustin Wax at LifeHacks.org

WHAT 3 THINGS WILL OVERCOME OUR PROCRASTINATION

If you want to make an easy job seem mighty hard, just keep putting off doing it.

OLIN MILLER

Give up on yourself. Begin taking action now, while being neurotic or imperfect, or a procrastinator, or unhealthy, or lazy, or any other label by which you inaccurately describe yourself. Go ahead and be the best imperfect person you can be and get started on those things you want to accomplish before you die.

SHOMA MORITA

Oliver Burkeman spent much time procrastinating as he planned to write on the theme of procrastination. Given the number of books, articles and blogs on the topic, there was every opportunity to use further research as a tactic of procrastination before putting pen to paper. His discovery; there are three genuine insights about how we overcome procrastination:

1. **Motivation follows action**. We assume that we need to get into the right mind-set before we can tackle a particular task. We wait for that sense of purpose to give us the energy to make a start. The reality is in beginning the task - however listless we feel at the time - we build momentum and a sense of progress and achievement. Our motivation then is triggered to complete the activity

2. **Resistance is a sign post**. Assuming the task is a meaningful activity, our resistance to get on with a job is a signal that it is important to us. Rearranging our desk might provide the illusion of a short burst of productivity. But it's easy and it's not advancing our long-term goals. If the project plan needs to be updated but we're becoming anxious at the prospect, the chances are it's an important activity we need to tackle. Keeping alert to our emotions will highlight what we really need to do and avoid throwing ourselves into the busyness of the easy but trivial stuff.

3. **Schedule leisure not work**. Procrastination is like a difficult teenager who can only react by saying no to any reasonable request. We know what we

should do but the teenager in us is looking to rebel. Burkeman recommends the tactic of "unschedule":

- do not work more than twenty hours a week on this project.
- do not work more than five hours a day on this project.
- you must exercise, play, dance at least one hour a day.
- you must take at least one day a week off from any work.
- aim for only thirty minutes of quality work.
- make plans for leisure activities, don't schedule in work tasks
- record hours of work only after you've completed chunks of the task

Unschedule is a smart tactic to out-manoeuvre our rebellious teenager and ensure we make a start and get going.

"Pro-active procrastination" Oliver Burkeman, 2007 The Guardian

"Confronting procrastination and getting things done" Maynard Brusman at WorkingResources.com

"Structured Procrastination" John Perry at StructuredProcrastination.com

"Now" Matt Vance at MindZone Wikipedia

WHY WE SHOULD BUY A KITCHEN TIMER

Life hack refers to productivity tricks that programmers devise and employ to cut through information overload and organise their data. In more recent times, it has been expanded to any sort of trick, shortcut, skill, or novelty method to increase productivity and efficiency, in all walks of life. Or, in other words, anything that solves an everyday problem in a clever or non-obvious way might be called a life hack.

A key tool for the life hackers is the kitchen timer. We can use it to:

- **get started**. Set the timer for five minutes (five minutes doesn't seem too bad) to start work on a big project. After the five minutes, stop. We will be surprised at our progress and how motivated we are to keep going
- **speed things up**. No one wants to do the chores, the stuff of life that isn't productive, but if neglected will eventually undermine our productivity. If we set the timer for a time that will make us move fast, we make an impact on the chore
- **get a grip on life**. As Parkinson reminds us "work expands quickly to occupy the available time". The beep of the kitchen timer in the office, home, coffee house is a good reminder that "it's time to stop and switch tasks". The Pomodoro technique encourages us to optimise productivity through a combination of short bursts of activity and breaks
- **reinforce our self discipline**. Why do we need a timer? Why can't we simply apply will power to work on a difficult task for a concentrated period? If we can, we don't need the kitchen timer. But for most of us, the timer is a good trick to fool our brains into thinking: this isn't so bad, we can get this done

"The Pomodoro technique" at Wikipedia
"Is the Pomodoro technique all that it's cracked up to be?" Amr Elssamadisy, 2010 at InfoQ.com

WHY WE SHOULD SWEAT THE SMALL STUFF

Elephants don't bite. It is the mosquitoes of life that cause the most trouble.

DAVID LIEBERMAN

Keep alert to the little upsets, setbacks and minor annoyances of working life. They are not all trivia to be ignored.

At some point in our life, one niggle will trigger a major crisis. This isn't to give the minor "rubbish of life" a significance it doesn't deserve. But it is to keep on top of the small stuff to spot the issues that need our personal attention. Over time, allowed to build, the cumulative impact of the small stuff can create big stress.

Don't let problems escalate to the "tipping point", that zone beyond which the problem becomes uncontrollable. And there are ways to make things worse.

Some stratagems seem destined to add fuel to a burning fire. Be alert to those counter-productive tactics that can only make things worse.

"Eight ways to make things worse than they are" Bob Weinstein at TheBeachBootCamp.net

"How to do chores" Guy Browning, 2007 The Guardian

"101 Ways to Make Things Worse" Drew Cangelosi

HOW TO MEET THE IMPOSSIBLE DEADLINE

Time is nature's way of keeping everything from happening at once.

HENRI BERGSON

We've put it off and put it off again, until now.

Now we have no choice but to work flat out to get work completed at the last minute. It won't be a pleasant experience, but it is one we should remember whenever we procrastinate again.

- mentally prepare yourself for a long session. It won't be nice, but think how you'll feel when you've completed the task
- top up on supplies, the refreshments, drinks and food that will sustain your energy levels
- shut yourself off from any distractions. Be a hermit for a while
- take mini breaks, 5-10 minutes every hour and move to a different environment, preferably outside
- track your progress and congratulate yourself as each sub-task is completed

"How to beat an impossible deadline" Paul at LifeHackery.com

WHY 5 MINUTES MORE WORKS

You can always find a distraction if you're looking for one.

TOM KITE

If we find ourselves getting restless, wanting to stop a task and wander off to chat to a colleague, pick up a newspaper, or check our emails, then we should make a commitment to work for another five minutes.

Not another five minutes of restless and distracted clock watching activity, but five minutes of productive concentration. Then take a break.

"Five minutes more" allows us to manage that momentary annoyance or frustration - "I'm fed up with this" - and re-establishes our momentum.

WHY BOREDOM IS SO BORING AND WHAT TO DO ABOUT IT

When the cafe emptied, his head emptied too. JEAN PAUL SARTRE

Boredom is the feeling that everything is a waste of time; serenity, that nothing is. THOMAS SZASZ

The cure for boredom is curiosity. There is no cure for curiosity. ELLEN PARR

Why is:

- standing in a queue
- sitting in a conference while the presenter drones on
- waiting for a delayed flight
- listening to a friend recount the detail of their cousin's holiday

just so boring? Of course, these moments of life are boring. But why is boredom so unpleasant?

Some situations in life are intrinsically boring. They are boring because we are conscious of time dragging. And they're boring because we feel the frustration that we're wasting precious time. We also feel annoyed because we seem powerless to control events. And the tension of uncertainty - "just how much longer?" - makes us anxious.

For intrinsically boring situations the only sensible strategy is one of mind management, to accept the delay and uncertainty and use the down time in more productive ways.

As well as situational boredom - the boredom we all experience in specific situations - there is chronic boredom. This is the kind of boredom which is less about the situation and more about us as individuals. If we're:

- often drowsy and listless
- wrapped up in ourselves and our preoccupations

- finding that time goes very slowly
- reluctant to commit to plans and goals
- more alert to what's wrong and feelings of discontent than with what is going well

we're moving into a state of chronic boredom. And it's an unpleasant and distressing way to live.

If we're sinking into a chronic state of boredom we're at risk of shrinking our lives. We can shake ourselves out of boredom by the tactics of distraction to gain more stimulation (alcohol, gambling, and pornography being the most frequently deployed stratagems). Alternatively we can rethink our life outlook by asking:

- what is my **purpose** in life? What do I want to accomplish? What can I do with my life, not just for me, but for others?
- are my **attitudes part of the problem**? Am I expecting life to provide me with happiness? Or do I think I need to create my own purpose, meaning and happiness?
- is my **daily routine becoming stale**? What could I do to introduce more variety into life?
- are my **surroundings reinforcing my sense of boredom**? How could I change my physical and social scenery to freshen things up?
- how am I **spending my time**? Absorbed in myself and feelings about my current situation, or looking outwards to keep curious about others and life

"How to kill time" at WikiHow
"How to overcome boredom" at WikiHow

WHY OUR BLIND SPOT KEEPS US BLIND

There are only two people who can tell you the truth about yourself: an enemy who has lost his temper and a friend who loves you dearly.

ANTISTHENES

Trucker Sing Li drove more than 500 miles on a motorway, with a cardboard windscreen. Li refused to replace his van's glass screen after it was shattered by a stone. So he taped thick cardboard to the frame to keep out the wind and then drove by sticking his head out of the driver's window to see where he was going.

By the time police arrested him in Henan, eastern China, for dangerous driving Li's head had turned blue from the cold and one of his eyes was frozen shut.

"I didn't want to fall behind in my delivery schedule and I couldn't afford a repair," he told a court before losing his license.

We all have our blind spots - those aspects of our behaviour and impact that everyone sees but we don't recognise - and are blocking our view of reality.

And if we think we're not seeing reality as it is, we should remove the cardboard from our windscreen.

"Getting good at getting feedback" David Maister at DavidMaister.com

LIVING FOR THE MOMENT

Enjoy present pleasures in such a way as not to injure future ones.

SENECA

Time is short and every moment has to be lived to the full. In this section we highlight the opportunities and risks of that attitude to time which extracts enjoyment and pleasure from the day but also blocks out neglected problems from yesterday or ignores the looming challenges of tomorrow.

When the dominant outlook is "only the moment" there are hazards. This is life lived as the pursuit of the immediate thrill. At best, it is an exhilarating life to get caught up in "the now". At worst it is a reckless abandon that makes choices today that have damaging consequences for the future.

We explore the paradox of happiness. Why is it in attempting to optimise our happiness we usually fail? And why do we achieve it often in spite of ourselves?

When we slow down from the rush of life experience we may discover something important about how our expectations explain happiness. We may also avoid the "stupid stuff" of life that might win a Darwin Award.

PRESENT

WHY FREDDIE MERCURY WAS WRONG AND WE SHOULD WAIT FOR TWO MARSHMALLOWS

I want it all, I want it all, I want it all, and I want it now.

FREDDIE MERCURY

In 1970, researcher Walter Mischel presented four year old children with a marshmallow on a plate. He then explained he had to leave the room. However if the marshmallow was still there on his return the child would be rewarded with two marshmallows instead of one.

A third of the children ate the marshmallow immediately. Another third tried to resist the temptation but eventually succumbed. The final third held out and received the reward of the two marshmallows.

Fifteen years later, Mischel tracked down the marshmallow children to discover that the third who had held out for two turned out to be "more successful in every way, educationally and personally". The third that just couldn't stop themselves snaffling the first marshmallow hadn't done so well. They were the low achievers of life.

Freddie Mercury was wrong. We can't have it all right now. Worse still, immediate gratification may be damaging to our long-term interests. Too much too soon, as Diana Barrymore recounted, is hazardous.

If we think we can't resist the one marshmallow of life rather than wait for two, it's worth checking the tactics of the children who held out for two.

"Instead of getting obsessed with the marshmallow the patient children distracted themselves by covering their eyes, pretending to play hide-and-seek underneath the desk, or singing songs from "Sesame Street." Their desire wasn't defeated. It was merely forgotten. If you're thinking about the marshmallow and how delicious it is, then you're going to eat it. The key is to avoid thinking about it in the first place."

Four year old children know things we sometimes forget in life.

"The secret of self-control" Jonah Lehrer, 2009 The New Yorker

WHY WE DO STUPID STUFF

You only have to do a very few things right in your life so long as you don't do too many things wrong.
WARREN BUFFETT

Never do anything that you wouldn't want to explain to the paramedics.

(ANON)

Sometimes we are the architects of our own downfall.

Aspiring U.S. Presidential candidate Gary Hart offered a challenge to reporters asking questions about his track record of philandering: "Follow me around...If anybody wants to put a tail on me, go ahead. They'd be very bored." One reporter did take up the offer and wasn't bored. Gary was soon discovered with a lovely young woman, and it wasn't his wife.

His presidential campaign faltered.

We do the stupid stuff when:

- our emotions overcome logic
- we act without thinking
- our confidence becomes arrogance
- we focus on what we want now
- fear is in the driving seat and we over-react
- we don't listen to good advice

"Why do smart people do stupid things sometimes", 2007 at EnhanceLife

"Why we do dumb or irrational things", 2007 at PsyBlog

PRESENT

WHAT TO DO TO WIN A DARWIN AWARD

In the spirit of Charles Darwin, the Darwin Awards commemorate individuals who protect our gene pool by making the ultimate sacrifice of their own lives. Darwin Award winners eliminate themselves in an extraordinarily idiotic manner, thereby improving our species' chances of long-term survival.

A deceased male was brought to two Austrian pathologists for a post mortem. He had suffered severe head trauma. According to police reports, the man wanted to see how a German World War II hand grenade was constructed. His curiosity led him to clamp the grenade in a vice, and cut a thin band around the centre with a circular saw, so that he would be able to crack open the two halves. Unfortunately, the man cut a little too deep, and detonated the grenade. The pathologists stated that the man had very little brain material when he was brought to them; however, they were not sure if that was a result of the explosion.

The Darwin Awards "salute the improvement of the human genome by honouring those who remove themselves from it. Of necessity, this honour is generally bestowed posthumously." Other Darwin awards include:

- the terrorist who mailed a letter bomb with insufficient postage and blew himself up opening the returned package
- jumping out of a plane to film skydivers while not wearing a parachute
- using a lighter to illuminate a fuel tank to make sure it contains nothing flammable
- heating a lava lamp on top of a stove
- the fisherman who threw a lit stick of dynamite for his faithful golden retriever to fetch and return to him
- petting sharks during their feeding frenzy on a dead whale

In life there are some idiotic ways to behave (e.g. drink driving) that can only have disastrous consequences for others as well as us personally. Before we do the clever stuff we should check we're not planning to do any stupid stuff.

"The Darwin Awards" at www.darwinawards.com
"Stop self-destructive behaviour" Norman Rosenthal at StrengthForCaring.com

WHY WARREN BUFFETT'S GENIE WAS WISE

If I'd known I was going to live this long, I'd have taken better care of myself.

EUBIE BLAKE

"Let's say when I turned 16, a genie had appeared to me. And that genie said, "Warren I'm going to give you the car of your choice. ..Having heard all the genie stories I would say, "what's the catch?"

And the genie would answer, "There's only one catch. This is the last car you're ever going to get in your life. It's got to last a lifetime."

"I would have picked out that car. But, can you imagine, knowing it had to last a lifetime, what would I do with it?"

"That's exactly the position you are in concerning your mind and body. You only get one mind and one body. And it's got to last a lifetime."

"Leading a healthy life" at the BBC

WHY AWARENESS MAKES SENSE OF EXPERIENCE

The word experience comes from the Latin to 'try' whereas the word aware comes from the Greek to 'see'. Experience implies participation in an event whereas awareness implies observation of an event.

DANIEL GILBERT

We can throw ourselves into life's adventure to experience its events to the full. But without the moments of reflection we are players in a game without working out which game we're in, never mind what the score might be. It is awareness that gives us experience of our own experience.

And the kind of awareness that knows the rules of the game but never joins in is to live life on the sidelines. We need experience and awareness to work together.

We distil experience into awareness into wisdom when we:

- **stop to think**. Here it can be helpful to summarise our reflections of the events of the day, week and month into some kind of log or diary
- **share our experiences with others**. The act of story-telling and the willingness to listen to others' reactions to our stories will help us make sense of events
- **take the long view**. Sometimes we need the distance of time to give us the perspective that helps us understand what happened, why and what it meant in our lives

The motivation to experience life to the full is an important life dynamic. It also helps if we have the awareness to make sense of that experience.

WHAT IS THE BIG RUSH

Half our life is spent trying to find something to do with the time we have rushed through life trying to save.

WILL ROGERS

Don't hurry. Don't worry. You're only here for a short visit. So don't forget to stop and smell the roses.

WALTER HAGEN

Do you tend to:

- get upset when you have to wait?
- eat quickly?
- experience a feeling of pressure as the end of the regular work day approaches?
- experience a sense of time pressure all the time?

Our responses to these four questions may be an important diagnostic of our future health.

Often called "hurry sickness," excessive time-urgency is slavery to the clock, and trying to do too many things at once. By doing things too fast or taking on too much, we risk reducing our effectiveness. The signs that we may have "hurry sickness":

- we typically drive over the speed limit and hurry everywhere
- we interrupt others and finish their sentences
- we get impatient in meetings when someone goes off on a tangent
- we become tense if we have to wait over a few minutes for service in a shop or restaurant
- we pride ourselves on getting things done on time, rather than worry about the pride of our craftsmanship
- we often rush or hurry our partner

Excessive time-urgency is not conducive to managing our stress levels; our body is kept at a constant state of high anxiety. Researchers at Northwestern University tracked young adults ages 18 to 30 for 15 years and found that those with high TUI (time urgency/impatience syndrome) had nearly double the risk of developing high blood pressure than those with the lowest levels of impatience.

If you're suffering from "hurry sickness" start treating yourself:

- as you plan each day and look ahead to the week, plan windows of time to go off the clock
- plan time to do nothing. Enjoy day dreaming, doodling, snoozing, or coasting
- when you evaluate your day, week or month, reward yourself for creating a balance of doing and relaxing, accomplishing work and smelling the coffee, being efficient and being aware of what's happening around you
- purposely slow down. Check when you're feeling impatient. Get your partner to bring your impatience to your attention

"Time Urgency And Impatience Can Get Out Of Hand" Vijai Sharma, 2004 at MindPub.com

"Reign in Rage by Beating Hurry Sickness" Julie Christiansen at Evancarmichael.com

WHY WE WANT TO GROW UP QUICKLY AND THEN WANT LIFE TO SLOW DOWN

When I turned two I was really anxious, because I'd doubled my age in a year. I thought, if this keeps up, by the time I'm six I'll be ninety.

STEVEN WRIGHT

We're ten years old and we're impatient. Our birthday next month seems years away. And Christmas, only two months on, is an eternity to wait. And we're desperate for life to speed up to experience those things that adults enjoy.

Forty years later and we wonder where our lives went. Why did the drag of time in our early years become the accelerated rush of our middle and later life? And is there anything we can do about it?

The clock may tick at a regular rate in objective time. In the subjective time we experience, it speeds up as we age. As children we want life to race on; we're desperate for events to unfold. In our middle and old age, we're keen to slow down the party of life. Why?

- **our estimates of time shift**. As we get older we get worse at estimating lengths of time. Specifically older people under-estimate the passage of time. Asked to close their eyes and estimate 1 minute, someone in their twenties gets close, to within 5 seconds. A 60 year old however typically waits until 70-80 seconds has passed. Expand this phenomenon over a day, the weeks and months, and time will seem to go faster

- **learning slows things down**. As children we are constantly having new experiences, experiences that focus our attention to learn and which also slow down time. As we get older, the "been there, done that" factor reduces our attention. Time begins to pass by without us noticing life. Unlike children awakening to a new day and curious about its events and ready to learn, the days, weeks and months blend into our minds as we age. It's not so much that time speeds up; it's more that we blank out the experiences of events

- **the percentage game**. When we are 3 years old, a year is a third of our total experience. That third is a big deal because it's a big slice of our life experience. When we're 30, another year passes, and that year is only 3% of our life experience; not such a big deal. As we get older, and the percentages of life become smaller and we give them less importance, our memory gives them less priority. And of course time seems to rush faster

The research continues. In the meantime it seems likely that we have to find our own ways of slowing down time as we age. It helps if we:

- **focus on the small packets of time**. This is the recognition that each day is its own day and its experiences should be enjoyed and relished rather than allow events to rush us or be driven by habits
- **keep making life remarkable**. When we measure time against key events rather than the clock and calendar, time begins to slow down
- **maintain a learning programme**. Time will disappear in the mist of the known and familiar. Time slows down in the sunlight of new life events that makes us stop, think and learn

WHAT ARE WE BUSY ABOUT

It's not enough to be busy, so are the ants. The question is, what are we busy about?

HENRY DAVID THOREAU

There are many pressures to maintain existing commitments and initiate new activities.

Before we plan out additional activities, establish what needs to give before we embark on more tasks. "Stops" are difficult but critical. They represent a break with the past. But they also open up new opportunities to "start" doing new and more important things.

At the end of this week, ask: "what have I done I shouldn't have done?" Which pointless or counter-productive activities have wasted my time?

"Creating a stop do list" Hugh Culver, 2010 at ArticlesBase.com

WHY NIKE IS WRONG

Half of the troubles of this life can be traced to saying yes too quickly and not saying no soon enough.

JOSH BILLINGS

Nike's "just do it" slogan may not be the best advice. Sometimes don't do it may make life more productive. Don't:

- answer unrecognised phone calls; always call back
- e-mail first thing in the morning or last thing at night
- agree to meetings or calls with no clear agenda or end time
- let people ramble; forget "how's it going?" and ask "what's up?"
- check e-mail constantly; "batch" and check at set times only
- over-communicate with low-impact, high-maintenance colleagues; avoid them
- work more to overcome a bigger work load; prioritise to cut back on low impact activity
- carry a mobile or Blackberry 24/7
- work every evening and weekends on catch up; we'll only develop unproductive habits
- expect work to fill a void that non-work relationships and activities should

"The Not-To-Do List: Bad Habits to Stop Now" Judi Sohn, 20007 at GigaOm.com

HOW TO MULTI TASK

Multi tasking may seem more efficient on the surface, but may actually take more time in the end.

J RUBINSTEIN, JOURNAL OF EXPERIMENTAL PSYCHOLOGY

The word "multitasking" was first used in the 1960s with the advent of the computer age, describing the capability of a computer to perform several tasks at the same time. Multi tasking seemed to promise a quantum leap in our personal productivity allowing us to juggle more and more activity with greater efficiency. Perhaps we could have it all.

The reality unfortunately is that we cannot effectively multitask. Of course we can do several different things at once. We're not all like President Ford who was criticised for his inability to walk and chew gum at the same time. The issue is about the nature of the tasks, and specifically how the brain works to attend to different types of activities.

Although we can't do two things at once, or at least do things that require attention and complex cognitive processing, we can however improve the way we manage multiple tasks:

- **prioritise to put tasks into sequence**. Before we throw ourselves into a range of tasks we can work through, identify which tasks are more important and need the greatest productivity
- get on with the immediate task to give it our full attention but **know when to take a break**
- **develop a schedule that outlines how we intend to allocate our time** for the day. Here we map out time slots for the different tasks. Rather than begin the day with a "to do list" which we have to slog through, we set a timer to alert us when we need to shift tasks
- we combine **"one action that impacts in multiple ways."** Multi tasking works when we take a 30 minute walk into work. Apart from the space to anticipate the day's events, we save money on travel, and we get exercise to improve our physical and mental well being

"How to Multitask", Catherine Bush, 2001 at DualTask.org

"How to Multitask - When You Have To" Ali Luke 2010 at ProductiveFlourishing.com

PRESENT

WHY MARCUS BUCKINGHAM IS WRONG ABOUT THE ONE THING

There is no one big push, it is a succession of small pushes.

JIM COLLINS

Marcus Buckingham in “The One Thing You Need to Know” outlines an overarching life strategy that will out-perform any other approach. It goes like this: “understand your and others’ strengths and capitalise on that strength by making it even stronger and utilising it as much as possible. Everyone should focus on the strengths, not weaknesses.”

A compelling message which incorporates an important truth. We gain a lot of leverage in life by knowing what we’re truly good at, and developing that talent to turn it into a source of excellence.

But like all simple messages, one that in the process of simplification, exaggerates and distorts the complexity of human nature and life. (The one thing of the “strengths-based movement” is now seen as a major fault line in the way organisations are developing their leaders).

We become disillusioned when we expect that “the one thing” will resolve everything. There is no “one thing.”

There is no one big idea. There are lots of different ideas, each with relevance to different problems and situations. Indeed, we should be nervous of the fanaticism of the “one thing thinking” of our colleagues. Neither is there any one big breakthrough strategic programme that will deliver organisational success. And there is no one thing that will be a game changer in our personal lives.

Instead, life is a series of “lots of things”. When we become wedded to the one big idea, philosophy or project we may be disappointed. Flexibility, versatility and adaptability of tactics may be more useful attributes than any reliance on a “one thing”.

“Did our strengths lead us to this point of weakness” Randall White, Business Leadership Review, 2009

CAN ANYONE WORK A 4 HOUR WORK WEEK

You better slow down. Don't dance so fast. Time is short. The music won't last.

DAVID L. WEATHERFORD

I want to say, in all seriousness, that a great deal of harm is being done in the modern world by belief in the virtuousness of work, and that the road to happiness and prosperity lies in an organised diminution of work.

BERTRAND RUSSELL

Bertrand Russell's 1932 essay "in Praise of Idleness" extolled the benefits of a four hour working day. This wasn't simply the personal preference of a privileged philosopher. Russell thought a four hour working day would be perfectly suitable for society as a whole, allowing everyone more time for that "idle speculation from which most intellectual and creative discoveries emerge."

70 years later and Tim Ferriss in the "Four Hour Work Week" pushes Bertrand Russell's idea further: we only have to work 4 hours a week. His premise: the value of our life isn't determined by "some arbitrary number in our bank account", but instead on the experiences we live and the time we have available for those experiences.

Ferriss uses the acronym **DEAL: D**efinition, **E**limination, **A**utomation, and **L**iberation to outline the strategies to move to a four hour work week:

- **Definition** means to figure out what we need to do to get over our fears and see beyond society's "expectations" of success to work out what it will really cost us to get where we want to go
- **Elimination** is about time management. This is achieved by applying the Pareto principle to focus only on those tasks that yield most benefit, and using Parkinson's Law to limit the amount of actual time spent working
- **Automation** is about building a sustainable, automated source of income. This includes building on-line businesses and outsourcing work
- **Liberation** is dedicated to successfully automating your lifestyle and freeing yourself from a geographical location and job

At best this strategy is shrewd advice for a budding entrepreneur who wants a full and rewarding life and also has the smarts to deploy on line innovation within a sustainable business model. (Although it's probably also the same thinking behind the various pyramid selling scams on the internet).

At worst, it's of no relevance to the nurses, police officers and teachers, and others whose professional skills, vocational choices and passions make the four hour work week a non starter.

The four hour week is an exercise in life fantasy for 99.5% of the working population. However, if Ferris's formula helps us rethink and raise our expectations of the kind of life we want and the role that work plays within it, then no bad thing for that.

"The Lie of The Four Hour Work Week", 2009 at IlluminatedMind.net

"5 Time management tricks I learned from years of hating Tim Ferriss" Penelope Trunck, 2009 at Brazen Careerist

IS OUR HAPPINESS ABOUT COMFORT OR ZEST

I believe unhappiness to be very largely due to mistaken views of the world, mistaken ethics, mistaken habits of life.

BERTRAND RUSSELL

Without zest, what is life?

OSHO

Comforts are those improvements in our lives, which pleasant as they are, we adapt to quickly and take for granted. Like air conditioning, lifts or dish washers they make our lives better and their loss would make us less happy. But we don't wake up each day to marvel at the happiness of our comforts.

The zests of life however represent that component of happiness that is fun and enjoyable (the excitement of sex, the satisfaction of a good meal, the adventure of a holiday to a new place). Zests are also associated with personal expression in which we use our talents to become absorbed in a meaningful and challenging project, and can take pride in our achievements.

A world of zests without comforts runs the risk of a personal intensity that can't stop to enjoy the simple and straightforward things of life that provide security and convenience. But a life of comforts without zest would lack a certain life zing.

It's worth checking how much of our life effort is based on achieving the possessions that provide comforts or enjoying the experiences that add zest.

"Experiences Make People Happier Than Material Goods" 2004, ScienceDaily.com

WHAT WILL OUR FUTURE SELF THINK ABOUT OUR CURRENT SELF

Best of all we can be happy in the flow of time whilst simultaneously creating memories we can look back on later.

DAVID MCRANEY

We want to be happy and we organise our lives to optimise our happiness. But we sometimes forget that our future self will be different to our current self. What makes for a happy current self may reduce the likelihood of a future happy life.

This is obvious. We know that what feels good right now (e.g. munching snacks as we slump watching hours of TV each evening) may undermine our future health and well being. But things get even more complicated.

Daniel Kahneman suggests a thought experiment. Imagine we are heading off on a two week holiday, but at the end of the holiday all our memories of the holiday will be deleted. How would we spend our holiday?

Our current self that experiences the present can throw itself into the moment for maximum pleasure. That's it; great fun while it lasted, but forgotten. If our memories won't be deleted, we might plan and organise our holiday differently. Knowing that our future self will gain enjoyment from the memories of our experience we may spend the two weeks engaged in different activities.

This is a key tension in life. Our current self is happy when we're doing nice and fun things right now. Our future self that looks back feels happiest when we can "pull up plenty of positive memories".

Life happiness is complex. We can adopt a game plan that maximises our happiness today but in ways that reduce our future happiness. Or we can "grind away today, postponing happiness for later in life.

"The riddle of experience vs. memory" Daniel Kahneman at Ted.com

WHY THRILL NEEDS WILL

Happiness... it lies in the joy of achievement, in the thrill of creative effort.

VINCENT VAN GOGH

Plan to be spontaneous tomorrow.

STEVEN WRIGHT

Spontaneity to operate with freedom and flexibility is a positive attribute in life. It keeps us open to possibilities and willing to take on new activities. But impulsivity - the kind that lacks control over our emotions and wants to do immediately what feels best right now - can be the dynamic of reckless decision making that is damaging to our long-term interests.

It's true life can be over-planned. Here our schedule becomes the focus, and we forget it's a means - not an end - to greater happiness and success. When we're more interested in the calendar and clock rather than what we're doing with our time, the thrill soon goes.

Life, for the most part, is best lived when we balance freshness, variety and novelty in our activities with a degree of planning and coordination. Here time organisation before and reflection after will optimise the thrill of living.

"How to live" Guy Browning, 2009 The Guardian

"Six Principles to Best Manage Impulses to Maximize Life Satisfaction and Success" Thomas Plante, 2010 Psychology Today

"7 Essential Steps to Mastering Temptation" Jeff Wise, 2010, Psychology Today

PRESENT

WHY DEEP DOWN WE ENJOY CRISES EVEN THOUGH WE SAY WE DON'T

Next week there can't be any crisis. My schedule is already full.

HENRY KISSINGER

We like crises because they:

- are **exciting and dramatic**. Unlike calm and detached planning - which frankly can be a bit dull - the pressure of a sudden problem arouses our sense of purpose and raises our energies
- **make us feel valued and important**. It's satisfying to be part of the cavalry charge coming over the hill to resolve a difficult issue. Our effectiveness as trouble shooters is appreciated and rewarded
- **help us avoid the hard work of thinking**. Thinking about the underlying reasons for recurring problems is tougher than dealing with the symptoms as they arise. Far easier to fire fight than formulate a strategy to identify and eliminate the causes of the fires

When our working days are a series of crises (unless we work for one of the emergency services) it may be useful to stop and check if this pattern can be sustained for the long term.

Short-term crises can be thrilling; they can also be a highly frustrating and exhausting way to live.

"Stop fighting fires" Hilary Briggs, 2010

HOW TO WORK BACKWARDS BUT ONLY AFTER WE'VE DEFINED SUCCESS

Don't draw the bull's eye after the arrow has struck. DAVID MYERS

To laugh often and much; to win the respect of intelligent people and the affection of children; to earn the appreciation of honest critics and endure the betrayal of false friends; to appreciate beauty; to find the best in others; to leave the world a bit better whether by a healthy child, a garden patch, or a redeemed social condition; to know even one life has breathed easier because you lived. This is to have succeeded. RALPH WALDO EMERSON

We can make it up as we go along, shifting our criteria of success depending on what in fact we achieved. Or we can work backwards to define the outcomes of success in advance. Here we pinpoint the key metrics that will define success or failure.

It's worth checking what success means for us. If our ideas about success - its causes and consequences - are misplaced, we may devote time and energy unproductively for little meaningful outcome.

- **ordinary success** is that level of all round achievement which attains a degree of financial reward, status, work satisfaction, positive relationships and physical well being in life. It sounds ordinary. It isn't. But it highlights the fact that this kind of success still leaves many dissatisfied, and a feeling that somehow we've missed out somewhere in life

- **exceptional success** is that form of success characterised by outstanding achievement in one domain of life. It may be financial fortune, spectacular career advancement, a distinctive creative accomplishment. Or it may be a major contribution to public life. But it is success in one domain of life only. Other aspects of life may be disastrous. This is the caricature of the

high powered executive who is too tired in the evenings and weekends to do anything else in life; the creative pioneer, obsessed with her project, who never has time to spend with her family; the politician who implements radical social change whilst living a life of deceit

- **the success of a flourishing life** is that kind of success that incorporates achievement across different domains of life. This is the form of success that the ancient Greeks called the "good life" - "eudaimonia" - that life of happiness, insight and virtue, and a way of living that is fulfilling and authentic. Ultimate success is success through active engagement across the range of life challenges

If we think long and hard about how we choose to define success we may be smarter in our strategies and tactics to ensure our arrow hits the bull's eye.

WHY ENOUGH IS NOT ENOUGH

Youth is not enough. And love is not enough. And success is not enough. And, if we could achieve it, enough would not be enough.

MIGNON MCLAUGHLIN

We chase the false rabbits of success; we too often bow down at the altar of the transitory and finally meaningless and fail to cherish what is beyond calculation, indeed eternal.

JOHN BOGLE, FOUNDER OF VANGUARD MUTUAL FUND GROUP

"The world is not enough", the motto of Sir Thomas Bond, also the nineteenth film in the James Bond series, suggests the world is not enough because however much we achieve, we will never be satisfied by what the world can give us. We will always want more, and the world can never give us enough.

At a party given by a billionaire, novelist Kurt Vonnegut informs his pal, Joseph Heller, that their host a hedge fund manager, had made more money in a single day than Heller had earned from his wildly popular novel, Catch 22 over its whole history.

Heller responds:

Yes, but I have something he will never have....enough.

Do we know what enough means?

"Enough: Breaking free from the world of more"
John Naish

WHY HAPPINESS IS LIKE A CAT

Happiness is like a cat, If you try to coax it or call it, it will avoid you; it will never come. But if you pay no attention to it and go about your business, you'll find it rubbing against your legs and jumping into your lap.

WILLIAM BENNETT

We want to live the good life, experience life to the full, and be happy. And we chase the cat of happiness. And we wonder why we're still not happy. The happiness cat isn't responding to our call.

Perhaps the problem is that we see happiness as something to be pursued. We will be happy when we attain specific goals (eg get promoted, find the perfectly matched partner, lose weight). Having achieved our goals we then wonder why we're not that much happier.

Maybe John Stuart Mill got it right when he said, "Ask yourself whether you are happy, and you cease to be so."

Or as Nikolaus Lenus observed,

Many search for happiness as we look for a hat we wear on our heads.

"Be happy now" Michelle Connolly, 2007 at HappinessStrategies.com

"Stop trying to be happy" Jennifer Smith, 2010 at FreeStyleMind

ARE THE WINDOWS BROKEN

Ignoring the little problems - graffiti, litter, shattered glass - creates a sense of irreversible decline.

JAMES WILSON

How did New York go from the crime capital of the USA to the safest large city in the country?

New York implemented the "broken windows" theory."

If the first window in a building is not repaired, then people who like breaking windows will assume that no one cares about the building and more windows will be broken. Soon the building will have no windows.

Repair the broken windows within a short time and the vandals are much less likely to break more windows and do further damage. Problems do not escalate and the respectable residents don't flee a neighbourhood.

Broken windows is based on the simple idea that we have to pay attention to the small things, otherwise they get out of control and become much worse.

In our rush to achieve the big things we can forget the small stuff. Look out for the small things that can escalate to a "tipping point" of failure and decline.

ARE WE THINLY SPREAD

Beware of dissipating your powers; strive constantly to concentrate them.

GOETHE

Are we involved in so many different activities that we can make little impact in any? If we've got ten priorities, we don't have any priorities.

Work through the range of your commitments and list out those that represent genuine priorities, activities where the ratio of effort to outcome works in your favour.

Be selective in choosing those activities where you need to concentrate your efforts and direct your energies with maximum force.

Don't choose the easy stuff you enjoy but are irrelevant or unproductive. And look out for those conflicting goals that pull you in opposing directions. Apart from being a highly stressful way to operate, competing priorities will dissipate your energies.

WHY WE SHOULDN'T RUSH TO DO 100 THINGS BEFORE WE DIE

This life is a short journey. How can you make sure you fill it with the most fun and that you visit all the coolest places on earth before you pack those bags for the very last time?

DAVE FREEMAN

The most radical thing you can do is stay at home.

BEAT POET GARY SNYDER

After seeing the second plane hit the World Trade Centre on the September 11 2001, advertising executive Dave Freeman had an epiphany: he wanted to pack as much experience into his life as possible. His "100 Things To Do Before You Die" was a guide to trips to unusual and exotic locations, including running with the bulls at Pamplona, taking a voodoo pilgrimage in Haiti and participating in the World Bog Snorkelling Championships in a Welsh peat bog.

His own favourites were the night nude surfing contest on Bondi Beach in Sydney, Australia, and "land diving," the original bungee jumping, on the Pacific islands of Vanuatu, using only vines attached to your ankles to break your fall.

Inspired by the idea, waves of new lists emerged: movies to watch, books to read, music to hear. As Oliver Burkeman notes, there is even the recommended "50 places to play golf before you die". The 2007 Hollywood movie The Bucket List in which two terminally ill men set out to fulfil their fantasies before they "kick the bucket" owed much to Freeman's adventure.

We prioritise our life style around these listings, determined to cram in as many of the good things in life as possible.

But here we're living a life of someone else's "must do's". And if we know anything about fun, enjoyment and happiness we know they don't happen when carefully scripted and stage-managed; they emerge spontaneously and authentically.

Neil Teplica, Freeman's co-author, commenting on Dave's death said:

> *the book was about living every day like it would be your last, and there's not that many people who do. It's a credit to Dave he didn't have enough days, but he lived them like he should have.*

Dave Freeman did his own thing to walk his own path to find fulfilment on his terms. Maybe it's better to live life the same way.

"100 Things To Do Before You Die" Dave Freeman
"Author of '100 Things to Do Before You Die' is killed in fall" Annette Witheridge, 2008 The Daily Mail
"This column will change your life" Oliver Burkeman , 2009 The Guardian

HOW TO STOP BREATHLESS HASTE

Most people pursue pleasure with such breathless haste that they hurry past it.
SOREN KIERKEGAARD

Success is not the place one arrives, but rather the spirit with which one undertakes and continues the journey.
ALEX NOBLE

Everything is a rush. The alarm clock goes off to trigger the daily routine of a rapid breakfast and the rush of a commute. The day comprises a series of hurried briefings, meetings and conference calls. And it ends - fatigued - when we crash out to watch TV, or to fret about the next day's schedule as we check our emails.

We don't even have the time to ask: are we enjoying life? Our breathless haste rushes us on because:

- we confuse **busyness of activity** rather than assessing life's outcomes and their impact
- **we don't know what is important** and matters but think if we do lots of stuff something positive might emerge
- we're **worried we're running out of time** and need to pack more stuff into our schedule

In our breathless haste we hurry past the things that might actually make us happy.

"Don't Hurry", 2010 at ALifeOfBecoming

HOW TO SLOW DOWN

As I make my slow pilgrimage through the world, a certain sense of beautiful mystery seems to gather and grow.

A. C. BENSON

Slow down and enjoy life. It's not only the scenery you miss by going too fast - you also miss the sense of where you are going and why.

EDDIE CANTOR

The greatest choice we have is to think before we act and then take action towards our life goals every day. Our problems result not only from our lack of actions, but from our actions without thought.

DENIS WAITLEY

Leo Babuata suggests we can slow down by:

- **doing less**. When we've over extended our commitments we rush in the attempt to get everything done. Of course, everything is never done. Here we have to stand back to rethink our priorities against our fundamental goals
- **being present**. This is the mindfulness that focuses on the moment rather than worry about the last task or anticipate the next activity in our schedule
- **disconnecting**. We don't always have to be available to everyone. It's OK to switch off the Blackberry or put our email on to auto-respond
- **focusing on people**. When we listen – really listen actively – to our family, friends and colleagues, time slows down. We don't anticipate the conversation, finish others' sentences or mentally plan our next comment. Instead we simply listen to understand
- **appreciating nature**. Time slows down when we step outside, take a deep breath and enjoy the scenery
- **eating slower**. Our meals have become the interval in which we gulp our food to get on to the next thing. When we stop to savour the flavours and textures of our meals we make eating part of life's experience rather than a refuelling stop to keep us going
- **driving slower**. We can't enjoy the journey or even think if our foot is flat on the accelerator and our knuckles are white on the steering wheel
- **finding pleasure in anything**. Rather than seeing the chores of life as interruptions to be rushed, we view them as experiences to be enjoyed in their own right

- **single tasking**. Here we accept that multi-tasking, apart from being unproductive, is a highly stressful way to operate. One thing at a time allows us to focus
- **breathing**. Our breathing reflects the pace of our life. If we want to slow things down we can pause and take a deep breath

"The 10 Essential Rules for Slowing Down and Enjoying Life More" Leo Babauta at ZenHabits

HOW TO MEDITATE

Meditation is the discovery that the point of life is always arrived at in the immediate moment.

ALAN WATTS

Meditation, with its associations of the "ohm" of hippydom or contorted body positions, gets a bit of bad press. In fact science is beginning to discover major benefits for those who practise meditation.

Tips for successful meditation:

- in the first instance try for mental detachment rather than complete absence of thinking. An excellent example of mental detachment occurs in the few moments just before falling asleep. Thoughts may be going through your mind, but they appear distant and you can feeling them floating away
- avoid following up on your thoughts. Watch the thoughts pass by as if they were ships sailing on the horizon
- concentrate intensely on an object, either a physical object or a mental image. Attempt to observe each detail of the object from every perspective
- say a brief phrase or sound over and over again. You can do this to yourself or out loud if you prefer. Experiment with guttural sounds such as ahhh and ohmm, or any calming words or brief phrases
- take a walk in a park or the countryside, attentively observing each plant, tree, or wildlife, but avoiding thinking about your daily problems
- imagine a flickering candle flame, stare at it for a time, and then mentally blow it out. Repeat as necessary
- be patient. Meditation won't create an overnight solution to improved concentration or stillness. Consistency is the key to success in meditation

"Meditation techniques from across the world"
Richard Ebbs at FeedbackNildram

HOW TO SIT STILL

All men's miseries derive from not being able to sit in a quiet room alone.

BLAISE PASCAL

I live in that solitude which is painful in youth, but delicious in the years of maturity.

ALBERT EINSTEIN

Sitting still and doing nothing should be easy. After all, what should be easier than not doing anything? The problem is we're all creatures of habit used to rushing around everywhere and surrounding ourselves with people and noise.

At first glance, solitude and loneliness can look alike. Both involve being on our own. Loneliness is a negative condition, characterised by a sense of isolation when we feel that something is missing from our life. Loneliness is imposed on us; solitude is something we choose.

Sitting still in solitude is time that can be used for reflection, inner searching or creative thinking. Choosing to spend time in solitude away from the sound of television, radio, background chatter and mobile phones should leave us feeling renewed and full of vigour.

Starting to spend time sitting still and doing nothing can be overwhelming for many people.

Start small. Concentrate on 5-10 minutes at a time in a comfortable place such as your home, not at your desk at work or in a busy public place.

As we begin to feel comfortable and extend our periods of solitude we will begin to feel that we are driving our own life, rather than having it dictated to by schedules and external demands.

"The lost art of solitude" Leo Babauta at ZenHabits

PRESENT

WHY IT'S SMART TO BE PATIENT

It's not that I'm so smart, it's just that I stay with problems longer.

ALBERT EINSTEIN

If I have ever made any valuable discoveries, it has been owing more to patient attention, than to any other talent.

ISAAC NEWTON

We may be lucky.

But probably not. In life, there are very few big and quick wins. Most of the time there is a set of small gains, none of which may seem significant in themselves, but when moving in the right direction at once will make a big difference over the long run.

Know when to wait to allow events to unfold and when you need to push to take advantage of the momentum of your previous efforts. But keep disciplined in "nudging" each of your different plans forward.

"Be patient with yourself" Steve Pavlina, 2005 at StevePavlina.com

WHY TIMING IS EVERYTHING

I am aware that success is more than a good idea. It is timing too.

ANITA RODDICK

Some ideas fail because they are just bad ideas, ideas that will never work. Other ideas don't work because they are badly planned and implemented.

And other ideas fail because the timing is wrong.

Don't abandon a good idea because the timing is wrong. Be patient in waiting for a future moment when you can reposition the concept for a more favourable moment.

HOW TO HAVE A GOOD HOLIDAY: THE SCIENCE

I find it fascinating that most people plan their vacations with better care than they plan their lives. Perhaps that is because escape is easier than change.

JIM ROHN

No person needs a vacation so much as the person who has just had one.

ELBERT HUBBARD

On a long vacation, day seven is less good than day one because it's not as exciting. That's why in general, going away four times [a year] provides more benefit than you would expect, and going away for one week provides less benefit than you would expect.

DAN ARIELY

We book our two week summer break. And we anticipate the delights that lie ahead. Apart from the pleasures of a new place and the opportunity to do different things, we value our holidays as the chance to re-energise and recharge our life batteries.

So why on the first day back after the holiday fortnight do we feel tired and not a little down about the experience? And what should we do to organise future holidays for greater happiness?

Dan Ariely identifies the three elements to optimise our holiday: "anticipating, experiencing and remembering". The best holidays work on all three levels: looking forward, enjoying the moment, and reminiscing with enjoyment.

It helps then if we:

- take **more shorter trips** than one long one. This strategy only works however if we avoid the hassle of getting to and back from our destination

- **break up holidays** with a spot of work. Paradoxically this tactic delays the adaptation process in which our holiday speeds up as we do the same thing in the same place
- **vary the pattern** of our holiday. Disruption seems to prolong the intensity and duration of the holiday experience
- **end on a high**. This is the "peak-end rule" that suggests that endings are key to our memories of an experience

"The best vacation ever" Drake Bennett, 2010 The Boston Globe

HOW TO LAUGH OUT LOUD

The human race has only one really effective weapon and that is laughter.

MARK TWAIN

We appear to have forgotten how to laugh and have become more miserable. A study by German psychologist Dr. Michael Titze found that in the 1950's people use to laugh an average of 18 minutes a day. Today, that's down to 4 - 6 minutes a day.

Research from Stanford University also found that the average kindergarten pupil laughed 300 times a day. Yet, adults average just 17 laughs a day. We start out laughing a lot then go into a downward spiral.

Are we becoming so bogged down with life's pressures that we can no longer enjoy ourselves fully? We don't stop laughing because we're growing old; we start appearing older because we stop laughing.

Laughter is a uniquely human attribute which is now seen as a therapy in the treatment of certain chronic ailments.

We can start self-medicating by smiling more, counting our blessings, gravitating towards laughter, spending time with upbeat humorous people and taking ourselves a bit less seriously.

"The power of laughter" Anand Chulani, at LOLWorld

HOW TO THINK ZEN TO THINK CLEARLY

A man travelling across a field encountered a tiger. He fled; the tiger ran after him. Coming to a precipice, he caught hold of the root of a wild vine and swung himself down over the edge. The tiger sniffed at him from above. Trembling, the man looked down to where, far below, another tiger was waiting to eat him. Only the vine sustained him. Two mice, one white and one black, little by little started to gnaw away the vine. The man saw a luscious strawberry near him. Grasping the vine with one hand, he plucked the strawberry with the other. How sweet it tasted!

Zen is more than a religion. Zen is that approach to life that emphasises calmness, a lack of stress, and a mind free from intrusive and negative thoughts. Zen living means:

- **one thing at a time**. Life as single not multi-tasking
- **nice and easy does it.** Life lived slowly and deliberately rather than rushing randomly
- **do it completely.** Finish what you start before moving on to the next job
- **do less**. Focus on the essentials and do them well
- **put space between things**. Don't allow your schedule to get too full. Allow time to re-group and prepare
- **rituals help**. Giving moments of life (preparing and eating food, sitting down to study, etc) a significance
- **to every thing there is a season**. Keep certain times for certain activities
- **sit still to meditate**
- **smile and serve others**. Look for opportunities to help
- **eliminate what is unnecessary**. Knowing what is essential to the "good life"
- **live simply**. Get rid of the clutter of life

The slow and simple life isn't just for the hermit or monk. Zen is the elimination of unnecessary pace and complexity from our lives.

"10 Zen Principles to Help You Live Life Better" Wayne Allen at PhoenixCentre.com

"How to Stimulate Your Creative Thinking" John Rocheleau at ZenMoments

PREPARING FOR FUTURE CHALLENGES

The vast possibilities of our great future will become realities only if we make ourselves responsible for that future. GIFFORD PINCHOT

This is the mature outlook on time that walks a difficult tightrope to the future. On the one hand, fear of what lies ahead makes us cautious of the dangers. On the other hand, fantasy about what is possible makes us bound on with confidence.

A mature stance to the future incorporates an understanding of the nature of uncertainty and complexity to evaluate what is knowable and what is unknowable. Here the strategies and tactics we deploy - our ends and means - are based more on flexible opportunism than any predetermined blueprint to map out the detail of our future lives.

This section suggests that we build for the future when we accept what we can't predict and control but are still willing to seize the initiative.

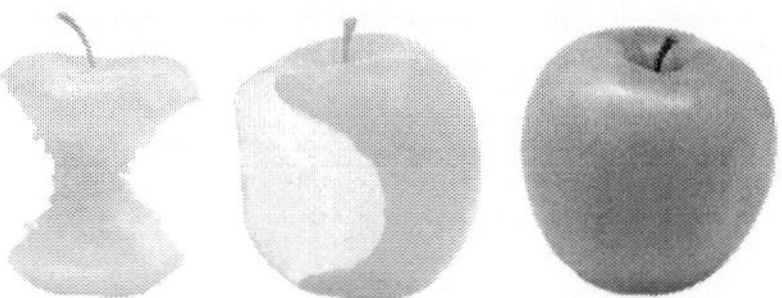

HOW WE THINK ABOUT THE FUTURE MATTERS

The future belongs to those who prepare for it today. MALCOLM X

Edward Banfield, of Harvard University, looking for the reasons that some people moved up economically from one generation to the next, while others did not, concluded that "success" is based on a person's attitude toward time.

Banfield called this the **"time perspective"**. He found that people who became successful invariably had a long time perspective. They took the long term into consideration when they planned their daily, weekly and monthly activities. They thought 5 years into the future. They allocated their resources and made their decisions based on how these choices would affect where they wanted to be several years from now.

Keeping track of our time horizons. Where are we spending most of our thinking time: in the past, present or future?

It's easy to allow our past to become our future in which we rewind past experiences to relive previous hurts or grievances. We should appreciate what is good about our upbringing, our early life experiences, school years, relationships, and so on. And if it wasn't so good, we should put it behind us.

And it's easy to get caught up in the priorities and pressures of the present, becoming so busy we forget why we're busy.

We must live in the present, drawing from the experiences of the past and enjoying the flow of our current life. But we also need to **prepare for the future**. This isn't life as conducting "if only" thought experiments in which we live out our life within a fantasy scenario. It is the courage to look ahead at future challenges and put in place grounded plans to move from where we are to where we might be.

"Long-time perspective" 2006 at Leadership Perspective

WHY NODDY HOLDER KNOWS THE FUTURE NOW HAS JUST BEGUN

Look to the future now, it's only just begun. NODDY HOLDER

Britain in 1973 is in recession. The miners are on strike, and TV goes off at 10pm because there is no electricity. The country is in turmoil. And on Tops of the Pops, an implausibly dressed and strange looking band strike up: "Are you hanging up your stockings on the wall."

With classic riffs and the immortal line, "does your granny always tell you that the old ones are the best", "Merry Christmas Everybody" by Slade hit the 1973 Christmas number one slot, was the fastest selling single in the UK, stayed in the charts remarkably until February 1974, and went on to sell over one million copies, thanks to re-releases each decade.

In a 2007 poll, "Merry Xmas Everybody" was voted the UK's most popular Christmas song. Slade's Noddy Holder reminiscing says: "You had to look to the future and hope things were going to get better because they couldn't get much worse. I think that's valid now."

Over 30 years later, what was the future of the four members of the band who gave us our best-loved seasonal hit?

Dave Hill, guitarist, has gone from the silver Lurex suits, mirrored top hats and stack-sole boots of stage to become a practising Jehovah's Witness

Drummer Don Powell suffered a car accident that killed his girl friend and damaged his brain, leaving him with long-term amnesia and permanent loss of his senses of taste and smell. Powell now lives quietly in Bexhill-on-Sea, East Sussex, when he is not touring in Slade 2.

Jim Lea, bass player, the creative force behind Slade sank into a state of depression when the band's popularity waned. Impressed by his programme of psychotherapy, he began studying for a psychology degree. His "admitted vices are a weakness for his native West Country beer and collecting antiques."

Noddy Holder, lead vocalist, has become one of Britain's Great National Treasures, appearing in sitcoms, DJing a golden oldies show, and appearing in many TV adverts, and no doubt enjoying the arrival of his royalties each year.

The man who once wrote: "Look to the future now, it's only just begun. . ." says he is enjoying this latest chapter in his life.

ARE WE PART OF SOMEONE ELSE'S LIFE GAME PLAN

If you don't have a strategy, you're part of someone else's strategy.

ALVIN TOFFLER

In 1970, America was gripped by Alvin Toffler's book "Future Shock". For Toffler, life was changing at a faster and faster rate, everything from technology to family structures to politics. The result was a kind of culture shock of the future: "too much change in too short a period of time".

In FutureShock "the future arrives too soon and in the wrong order."

Toffler got it completely wrong in many of his forecasts. We still await the huge amounts of leisure time Toffler predicted over 40 years ago that we would be enjoying now.

But Toffler got it exactly right when he suggested that we can let the future happen to us, or we can seize the initiative to take control of our own personal destiny. Or as Jim Rohn suggested: "If you don't design your own life plan, chances are you'll fall into someone else's plan. And guess what they have planned for you? Not much."

This isn't the folly of formulating a life strategy with the clear expectation of how the future will unfold in detail. But it is to recognise that although the future seems a far away place it will happen. And it will help if we're clear about:

- what kind of person we want to be in future
- what kind of life style we want to be living
- what kind of activities and interests will be the focus of our life energies
- how we want to be remembered

If we don't know the answers, the chances are that we'll end up as part of someone else's life strategy.

"FutureShock Reassessed", Richard Slaughter, 2002 at MetFuture.org

FUTURE

WHY NINA SIMONE IS FEELING GOOD

It's a new dawn. It's a new day. It's a new life. For me. And I'm feeling good.

NINA SIMONE

Make time for yourself each day.

It might be late at night or early in the morning but develop a pattern in which you find time for yourself, not to plan work activity but time to think your own thoughts. This is extra time you've created for yourself.

Use it for yourself - to reflect, meditate, pray, dream - whatever it is that helps you get in touch with that aspect of yourself you want to develop further.

And don't rush in the morning. Each day is a new day in your life so take time to get ready for it and prepare yourself for its challenges.

"Five Hints to Reclaim Time for Yourself" Shane Magee at StepCase LifeHack

WHY WE GET THE FUTURE WRONG AND WHAT TO DO ABOUT IT

The mistakes we make when we try to imagine our personal future are lawful, regular and systematic. They have a pattern that tells us about the powers and limits of foresight in much the same way that optical illusions tell us about the powers and limits of eyesight.

DANIEL GILBERT

Classic goal setting assumes our current self knows what our future self wants and what will make us happy. What if what we think will make us happy doesn't?

We get the future wrong because:

- we buy into a culture that reinforces **flawed assumptions about the dynamics of happiness and success**. Consumerism has little to do with the factors that determine genuine well being. We think our future life will be much happier if we have a much bigger salary, house, car, and more and better holidays. The evidence suggests they won't make anything like as much difference as we think and expect
- we **over-estimate the impact of positive events**. This is us imagining a happier future self if our circumstances changed; if our partner was younger and better looking, or if we moved to a house in a better neighbourhood. The reality is that a shift to a more positive life situation doesn't result in more positive feelings that sustain. Yes they do make us feel better - but not for as long as we think. We simply get used to our new life circumstances. (The good news here is that we also get used to more negative life events. We don't feel as bad about a down turn in our circumstances than we might expect)
- we don't simply compare our future happiness against our current happiness and look at absolute levels of how much happier we've become. Instead the **comparisons we make when we get to the future are relative to others**. This is Gore Vidal's maxim that "It is not enough to succeed. Others must fail." And it explains why people would rather earn a salary of £89,000 if their colleagues are paid £83,000 than £94,000 if others earn £100,000

Daniel Gilbert suggests a way forward to compensate for the failings of our minds to think about the future. And it's quite simple.

Look at people who either are experiencing what you will either experience or want to experience.

How they feel is a better guide to your future feelings than how you currently think you will think! This is a little counter-intuitive. After all we like to think we're unique in our life situation. Others have their experience and we have our own distinctive life experience. The reality is that we can discover more about what will make us genuinely happy from others who have experienced what we now hope will make us happy.

Dan Gilbert on our mistaken expectations at Ted.com

WHY WE SHOULD COMPARE OUR PLANS AGAINST POSSIBILITY RATHER THAN THE PAST

People are always prophesying what will happen next; and they are always falling into the folly of making it merely the same as what happened last.

G K CHESTERTON

At one level we know our future will be different to our present. But caught up in the immediacy of today, our extrapolations of tomorrow are largely a continuation of the present. We hope the future will be better but we don't envisage how radically different it might be.

Business planners look back at last year and how well they did this year, and their forecasts are an extension of this history.

Similarly the objectives we set ourselves for our personal and professional lives are for the most part a bit more and better than how we think we're currently doing. And we lock ourselves into a mindset of incremental improvement rather than identify opportunities for a major leap forward.

We open our horizons when our view of the future is based, not on a comparison with the past, but a comparison against what is possible.

When we think possibility rather than past, we move into a trajectory that can take us from good to great.

"Good to Great" Jim Collins, 2001 at JimCollins.com

FUTURE

WHAT GOT US HERE WON'T GET US THERE

Something always goes wrong when things are going right.

MATT JOHNSON

The drivers of our past success will not guarantee our future success.

"More of the same" will not be enough to succeed in our next role and through the next phase of our development. Success may require us to abandon previous skills and operating styles, not just acquire new skills.

Review your outlook to identify the shift in priorities and where you may need to stop doing old things before you begin to do new things.

"The Success Delusion" Marshall Goldsmith, 2007
The Conference Board Review

WHY ENDS MATTER MORE THAN MEANS

If you're not sure what to do with the ball, just pop it in the net and we'll discuss your options afterwards.

BILL SHANKLEY, FORMER LIVERPOOL FC MANAGER ON TACTICS

Success is best achieved when you are clear about the goal but flexible about the process of getting there.

B TRACY

Steve Pavlina points out our **end goals** are the life outcomes that matter; these are our overarching goals that are fundamental to our values and aspirations. Here there is no compromise. **Means goals** define our options, and we can select which of many paths will move us towards our end goals.

The problem arises when we confuse the two types of goals. Here we become so caught up in means goals that we lose sight of the bigger picture, persevering with a set of tactics that aren't advancing our long-term aims. Frustrated by a lack of progress we assume more time and effort is the solution and we work harder and longer to attain our means goals (confusing them for our end goals).

Instead we need to shift tactics to find a new set of means goals. Of course if we don't know our end goals we're in serious difficulty.

As Sun Tzu, the great strategist, observed: "Strategy without tactics is the slowest route to victory. Tactics without strategy is the noise before defeat."

We make progress in life when a smart life strategy is aligned with clever tactics. We need our means goals to work for our end goals (not become the focus in themselves). And if the means goals aren't working we should accept we need to replace them with better tactics.

"End Goals vs. Means Goals" Steve Pavlina 2005 by at StevePavlina.com

WHY WE CAN GET WHAT WE WANT BUT LOSE WHAT WE HAD

He got what he wanted but lost what he had.

LITTLE RICHARD SPEAKING OF ELVIS PRESLEY

We realise our dream and wonder why it now feels like a nightmare.

DAVID BYRNE

Don't attempt to attain success at any and all costs, the price may prove too high.

JOSEPH MARTINO

He is no fool who gives what he cannot keep to gain what he cannot lose.

JIM ELLIOT

It's not clear that Elvis Presley did know what he wanted. But his final days weren't so wonderful.

We can achieve our long-term goals but the result may come with a cost. The cost may be our time, money, friendships, happiness; success can be expensive.

When we plan our future and set ourselves goals it's worth remembering:

The means **we deploy to attain these ends will change us**. Machiavelli was wrong for all sorts of reasons when he said: "the means justify the ends." The means we deploy to reach our goals will change us, and not always in ways that are conducive to our long-term happiness. If we're wondering why, having achieved our original goal we still aren't happy, it may because the means we selected turned us into a different person.

The achievement **of these goals will have consequences**. We think if only...if only we attain A, B and C, life will be so much better. But our thought processes often don't work through what it means to achieve A, B and C. A, B and C seem to create a set of consequences of X, Y and Z that we didn't anticipate and are now constraining our enjoyment of our original aims.

When we're thinking about our future success, it might be useful to think through what price we're paying for achieving that success and the cost of the consequences.

WHY FUTUROLOGISTS SHOULD BE IGNORED MOST OF THE TIME

Forecasting is not a respectable human activity and not worthwhile beyond the shortest of periods.

PETER DRUCKER

The predictors have claim to be the second oldest profession. 5,000 years ago the diviners forecast the future by "seeing patterns and clues in everything from animal entrails to celestial patterns." As Isaac Asimov observed in his book Future Days "such was the eagerness of people to believe these augurs that they had great power and could usually count on being well supported by a grateful, or fearful, public."

We have a deep-seated need to avoid the anxiety of uncertainty. We want to know what will happen next. And because certainty provides us with a sense of control, we admire and will pay large amounts of money to those who have seen our future.

In 2011 the prediction business is a multibillion-dollar industry, everything from the psychics, astrologists and paranormalists, to the weather forecasters and climate change trackers, market research analysts, strategic planners, economists and business gurus, and newspaper columnists, share tipsters and betting pundits.

We shouldn't waste too much time on these forecasts. Prediction might be the world's second oldest profession but its track record remains appallingly bad. In, for example, an important prediction that affects our future, that of financial management, blindfolded investors throwing darts at a list of stocks did as well as professional stockbrokers.

When we think about our future, it may be better to live with uncertainty than place our bets on the predictions of the professional forecasters.

"Top 87 Bad Predictions about the Future" 2006 at 2Spare.com

Arthur C Clarke's three laws of prediction at Wikipedia

"2011 predictions for 2050" Tim Leberecht at PFSK.com

"Randomness as Meaning: how people see coincidence as destiny" Paul Lutus, 2010 at Ararchnoid.com

HOW INK BLOTS, CRYSTAL BALLS, PALM READING AND PERSONALITY TESTS PREDICT OUR FUTURE

Disciplined and self-controlled outside, you tend to be worrisome and insecure inside. At times you have serious doubts as to whether you have made the right decision or done the right thing. You prefer a certain amount of change and variety and become dissatisfied when hemmed in by restrictions and limitations.

BERTRAM FORER

Professional astrologers now outnumber astronomers.

MARTIN GARDNER

Overall, the review committee concluded that the Myers Briggs Type Indicator has not demonstrated adequate validity although its popularity and use has been steadily increasing.

THE NATIONAL ACADEMY OF SCIENCES

Because we want to know what lies ahead we look to those who can forecast our futures. The Rorschach ink blot test, crystal ball, reading of palms and personality profiles all provide an insight into our psyche to predict what is likely to happen to us next in life.

All these methods manage the art of prediction through the stratagems of:

- **ambiguity**. This is the trick of the vague forecast that can be interpreted or re-interpreted depending on how subsequent events unfold
- **inconsistency and contradiction**. If our predictions maintain an element of "on the one hand, but on the other" they possess compelling truths but with an exit door of "but"
- **stating the blindingly obvious** to predict important truths that apply to everyone. Given a positive but slightly vague description of ourselves we are impressed by the accuracy with which our personality is revealed

We can predict the future when our forecast of events are: ambiguous, incorporate enough uncertainties to allow for different interpretations after the event, or simply state the obvious, but wrap it up in impressive but vague vocabulary.

Faced with the futurologists and their claims to know what will happen, we should ask what specifically is being predicted. This is the detail of the what and when to pinpoint the exact forecast. If the answer is vague and ambiguous it's probably not a prediction we should factor into our plans.

"The Forer effect" at Skeptic's Dictionary

"The Rorschach Inkblot Test, Fortune Tellers, and Cold Reading" James Wood 2003 at Skeptical Inquirer

WHY WARREN BUFFETT ACCEPTS UNCERTAINTY RATHER THE CONSENSUS OF CERTAINTY

The price for rejecting easy answers is that we must be willing to tolerate ambiguity and accept one's own ignorance.

RICHARD FEYNMAN

We take a test to indicate if we have a dangerous genetic defect.

1. The test is conclusive: we don't have it
2. The test is inconclusive: we may or may not have it
3. The test is conclusive: we have it

Which of these three scenarios would make us most and least happy? We feel unhappiest when the test is inconclusive.

Human nature can withstand lots of things but uncertainty isn't among them. Uncertainty keeps us in a state of anxiety, and our mental software is not well equipped to deal with it.

We want to know what happened and why it happened. We also want to know what will happen in future. Religion, philosophy and science have been the big explainers (the causes of the way things are) and predictors (the way things will be) to help us eliminate uncertainty and anxiety and establish greater control over our lives.

The problem arises when, in our need to avoid the anxiety of uncertainty, we accept faulty explanations and dodgy predictions for greater certainty. Here we just need to know that there was a reason why something happened and that we can forecast what will happen. We just need to know something, anything that makes sense of our past, present and future.

Alternatively we can accept that sometimes stuff in life happens and maybe there is no obvious reason. And we can acknowledge that we don't know always what will happen in future.

Warren Buffett, as an investor, makes the point:

> *The future is never clear; you pay a very high price in the stock market for a cheery consensus. Uncertainty actually is the friend of the buyer of long-term values.*

This is the acceptance of what we know and don't know, and investing well in what is knowable rather than the pursuit of the unknowable.

If we can make uncertainty our friend (rather than a source of ongoing anxiety), reject the cheery consensus of flawed explanations and flaky forecasts, but still maintain our sense of curiousity then we might be on to a winning strategy.

"The Power of Curiosity" Todd Kashdan 2010 at ExperienceLife

HOW WE CAN SEE THE DETAIL OF THE FUTURE

Seeing in time is like seeing in space.

DANIEL GILBERT

Planning is bringing the future into the present so that you can do something about it now.

ALAN LAKEIN

Of course, the future is distant, uncertain and unclear. But those who see clearly into the future have an advantage over those whose horizons are limited to the pressing realities of the moment.

ANON

When we look around, it is the objects that are closest that appear most detailed, and those furthest away, the fuzziest. This is obvious. Similarly with time. Tomorrow is finely textured in its detail. Next week clear but a bit blurred. And next year is a complete abstraction we can't quite envision.

Just as we can use binoculars to see objects far away, we make the future clearer when:

- we **recognise the fundamentals that won't change**. These are the timeless principles of human nature, social interaction and life success that endure. As Jeff Bezos of Amazon notes: "There's a question that comes up very commonly: "What's going to change in the next five to ten years?" But I very rarely get asked, "What's not going to change in the next five to ten years?" Somethings don't change that much

- we know the **difference between the unknowns and unknowables**. Donald Rumsfeld was roundly mocked by media and public alike for his unknown unknowns statement. But he made an important point. Maybe Warren Buffett put it better: "Everybody's got a different circle of competence. The important thing is not how big the circle is. The important thing is staying inside the circle." If we know what we know, are smart in finding what is unknown before others, and don't worry too much about the unknowables, maybe we'll get ahead of the game

- **we remember that what is easy to say today may be difficult to do tomorrow.** Here we need to monitor the commitments we make. They're easily made, but lots of commitments create a future problem. The small elephant on the horizon quickly becomes large when it is charging at us

- **we make the future as immediate as we can.** Rather than operate with the strategy of "it'll be all right on the night" we are clear about our objectives, the options and their consequences. It's true that not everything can and should be planned to the nth degree, but we may as well think through the implications of our commitments now rather than work them out later

Master Oogway in Kung Fu Panda was right: "tomorrow is a mystery", but it doesn't always have to be a complete surprise if we think clearly.

WHY SOME IS NOT A NUMBER, SOON IS NOT A TIME

On the 14th December 2004, Don Berwick, CEO of the Institute for Healthcare Improvement, in a conference presentation to health care administrators said:

> *Here is what I think we should do. I think we should save 100,000 lives. And I think we should do it by June 14th, 2006.*

Berwick's Institute for Healthcare Improvement had amassed evidence that the "defect" rate in healthcare was as high in 1 in 10, and that a high defect rate "meant tens of thousands of patients were dying every year, unnecessarily." The Institute proposed six specific interventions that would save lives.

Every hospital of course wants to save lives. But Berwick's path to change was filled with obstacles. First of all, no one wanted to admit that patients were dying needless deaths. "Hospital lawyers were not keen to put this admission on record." Second, adopting the proposals required hospitals to overcome decades' worth of routines and habits.

But progress was made in signing hospitals up to the campaign. Early adopters shared their successes and supported hospitals that later joined the enterprise.

Eighteen months later, Berwick announced, "Hospitals enrolled in the 100,000 Lives campaign, have collectively prevented an estimated 122,300 avoidable deaths."

When the destination is crystal clear and "some" begins 100,000 and "soon" is June 14th, 2006, and there is a clear focus - only six interventions - big change can happen.

When we know what can be achieved, and put in place the specifics to ground this future in the practicalities of a grounded action plan rather than talk in the generalities of what is possible, we may surprise ourselves.

WHY WE SHOULD KNOW THE DIFFERENCE BETWEEN SIMPLE, COMPLICATED AND COMPLEX PROBLEMS

Make everything as simple as possible, but not simpler.

ALBERT EINSTEIN

There are three kinds of problems. And knowing the difference is critical to our effectiveness in thinking about the issues and implementing solutions to optimise our time and realise our goals.

1. **Simple** problems are those that follow a recipe. Like baking a cake from a packet, there are clear instructions which in combination with a few basic skills will produce a successful outcome.
2. **Complicated** problems, like sending someone to the moon, have no standard recipe. Solution requires multiple people in different teams, drawing on a range of specialist expertise. Complex problems can be broken down into a series of simpler chunks; sequencing and coordinating are therefore key to successful outcomes.
3. **Complex** problems are complicated and more. Once we've sent someone to the moon, we can repeat the process and keep perfecting it. In complex problems, like bringing up a child, experience may be useful but doesn't guarantee success. Because each child is unique, there is a level of uncertainty that remains.

We get ourselves in a decision making tangle when we confuse the three types of problem and the confusion wastes time.

Simple problems are about speed and efficiency of solutions. But when we apply the mind set of speed and efficiency to complicated and complex problems, we run into difficulties.

Complicated problems can and should be simplified, but not until we've drawn on the learning to work out the key steps, ironed out the wrinkles and established robust process. For complex problems we need curiousity to keep exploring the full range of issues, wisdom to recognise the level of uncertainty and judgement to trade off the pros and cons.

Premature attempts to simplify the genuinely complex can only generate simplistic solutions with damaging long-term consequences. Conversely, elaborate and convoluted responses to what are essentially simple issues are time-consuming and inefficient.

Our future is a mix of the simple, complicated and complex. If we know the difference we'll get to where we want to be faster.

WHY STRAIGHT UP IS THE BEST WAY TO LIVE

Straight up is a way of serving a drink. It is also a way to climb a mountain and of living a life.

JAMES RAMSEY ULLMAN

"Straight Up" is the account of the young mountain climber John Harlin, who at thirty years of age, died trying to climb the Eiger "diretissima", straight up.

Straight up is a difficult and demanding way to live. And it's risky.

But it's also authentic and rewarding. In our response to challenge, it helps if we are adaptable and flexible. It also helps if we avoid unnecessary posturing and gamesmanship to keep things simple and direct.

Of course from time to time we will have to "zig zag". But "straight up" might be the best overall strategy that maintains our integrity and ensures our short term means don't change our overall ends.

ARE WE SELLING SUGARED WATER OR CHANGING THE WORLD

Do you want to spend the rest of your life selling sugared water or do you want a chance to change the world?

STEVE JOBS IN HIS PITCH TO PERSUADE JOHN SCULLEY OF PEPSI TO JOIN APPLE

We can't all change the world in the way that Steve Jobs' pioneering innovation has. But we can find a role in life that is personally fulfilling, rewarding and authentic.

And it helps if we know what we have to offer the world. Everyone is in the sales business so know what you are selling and why others might want to buy it.

Imagine stepping into an elevator with a person you are attempting to influence, someone with the power to implement your ideas. But first, they need to buy your concept. From the time between stepping into the elevator to arriving at the 10th floor for their next meeting, you have to summarise your message, in 30 seconds.

What would you say?
Can you condense down the "pitch of your proposition" into a vivid and compelling statement? Know what you need to say. If you don't, then keep working it through until you can boil down your ideas into a 30 second summary. Rehearse it and perfect it into a clear expression of what you're selling.

"How to Craft a Killer Elevator Pitch" K. Stone 2007 at Life Learning Today

WHY WE NEED TO WORK THROUGH THREE PHASES

I like to tell people that all of our products and business will go through three phases. There's vision, patience, and execution.

STEVE BALLMER, CEO MICROSOFT

Vision is clarity of purpose. But our vision is not necessarily the vision of others. Our vision needs to be communicated, debated and explained.

Patience is the process we must work through to ensure others understand our vision, not at an intellectual level, but emotionally to become committed.

Execution is when we press the button of implementation to move ideas into plans.

Misjudging this sequence of phases is the number one reason why organisations lose their way, becoming frustrated that implementation has failed to deliver the initial promise of imaginative ideas.

It is also the reason why at a personal level we get ourselves in a tangle.

We have a vision of our future lives but we become frustrated when it isn't realised. It's often because our impatience moves us into action too quickly before others engage with our vision.

HOW TO PUT FIRST THINGS FIRST

Set priorities for your goals....put first things first. Indeed, the reason most major goals are not achieved is that we spend our time doing second things first.

STEPHEN COVEY

What is the best way to motivate yourself for your daily work? Obviously, enjoying your work and having a clear vision are very important, but I don't believe they are the most important things for keeping going during the daily grind. On the contrary, I believe that what gives us the most energy is the feeling of being totally on top of our work.

MARK FORSTER

It's best to prioritise by our goals not by others' urgency.

Urgency is emergency and if we are in the emergency business, we need to get organised to respond with immediacy. But most urgent items are only urgent because they haven't been done when they could/should have been, or when our manager's sense of urgency conflicts with our priorities of importance.

Put in place the planning systems and work disciplines to avoid urgency. Urgency is disruptive (though some people seem to like it) and encourages a reactive operating style that is prone to bad judgement calls.

Establish control over your life by reducing urgency wherever you can through the introduction of better systems to control and coordinate your work flow.

"Time Management is Dead" Michael Linenberger at Ezine articles

"Do it Tomorrow and Other Secrets of Time Management" Mark Forster

WHY PROJECT CHICKEN IS ONE REASON FOR PROJECT FAILURE

To estimate a project, work out how long it would take one person to do it then multiply that by the number of people on the project.

(ANON)

At the project team meeting, each member is eyeing their colleagues nervously. The chair asks everyone for an update. The first project team member says, "Yes, their part of the project is making good progress". This is a response in hope, the hope that someone else in the project team will admit they're behind and that the deadline needs to be extended.

The updates work their way around the table. The first person to lose their nerve is the "project chicken". Once that individual has indicated they have a problem with time-scales, everyone else in the project breathes more easily. They are "safe", benefiting from the new extended deadline.

At "best", Project Chicken creates more slippage time and the breakdown of the disciplines of execution. At worst, if no one blinks, but most of the project team have failed to meet their commitments: major project failure threatens product and service delivery.

When we forget to factor in the realities of human nature and the dynamics of social interaction into our project plans, we can be confident about the likelihood of project failure.

"Reasons Why Projects Fail" Tom Carlos at ProjectSmart

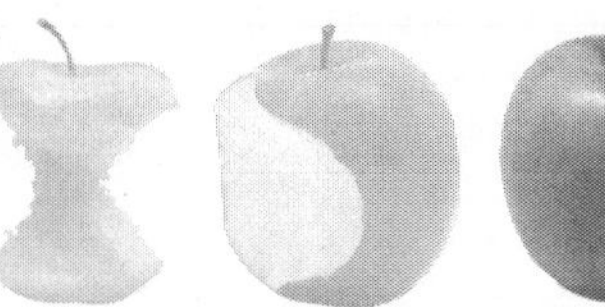

FUTURE

WHY BIG RESULTS EMERGE FROM SMALL IDEAS

It's the little details that are vital. Little things make big things happen.

JOHN WOODEN

The best ideas usually start out as little ones.

We pursue the big initiative, that one big programme of action that will transform the organisation or will make a major difference to our personal lives.

Big ideas get lots of attention; they also consume massive amounts of energy, time and money. And they require complex coordination. One breakdown in the process and the big idea can become quickly unstuck.

Encourage and nurture the small ideas with the potential to grow and make a practical business impact. Take time out to talk informally with colleagues from other functions at other levels and ask:

- what are you working on at the moment?
- what do you see as our key challenges, our strengths, our weaknesses?
- what's getting in the way of you doing a good job?
- if you had a bit more time, what would you spend it on?
- if you were the CEO, what would you focus on? What would you do? What would you stop?

Keep asking and listening. And the "small ideas" will emerge.

"How to Nurture New Ideas" Brian Libby 2007 at Bnet.com

WHY MURPHY'S LAW APPLIES

If something can go wrong then it will. And Murphy was an optimist.

Natural enthusiasm and curiousity to respond positively to new ideas drives us to take on different challenges. But if something can go wrong, it will.

We shouldn't assume the worst but it helps if we anticipate there will be problems on the way.

Think through the implementation of your ideas in detail to anticipate what might go wrong and how you will respond.

"Origins of Murphy's Law" Joe Smith at Murphy'sLaws.com

"The Unwritten Laws of Life: Unofficial Rules Handed Down by Murphy and Other Sages" Hugh Rawson

AND WHY IT'S GOOD TO HAVE A BACK UP PLAN

Keep climbing. If you can't fly, run. If you can't run, walk. If you can't walk, crawl. But by all means, keep moving!

MARTIN LUTHER KING JR.

Think "what if."

Always have a fall back plan.

The drive to plan and coordinate activity is admirable. It can also result in misguided and wasted effort when attempting to implement an unworkable plan.

Build contingency plans into your projects. This isn't the assumption of failure but it is the recognition of knowing what to do if things don't work out as we intended. Here we know what will trigger the decision to "pull the plug" and stop a project that isn't working.

Formulate "plan A" and be committed to its execution but know the point at which it will be replaced by "plan B".

WHY WE SHOULD REMEMBER THE 10,000 HOUR RULE

If people knew how hard I had to work to gain my mastery, it wouldn't seem wonderful at all.

MICHELANGELO

The 10,000 Hour Rule:" the key to success in any field, is simply a matter of practicing a specific task that can be accomplished with 20 hours of work a week for 10 years.

MALCOLM GLADWELL

Ten thousand hours is equivalent to roughly three hours a day, or 20 hours a week, of practice over 10 years... No one has yet found a case in which true world-class expertise was accomplished in less time. It seems that it takes the brain this long to assimilate all that it needs to know to achieve true mastery.

DANIEL LEVITIN

Learning chess is difficult. It takes a while to learn the basic moves and rules, then longer to work out the patterns of play to develop the strategies and tactics for reasonable proficiency. And acquiring the status of grand master requires dedicated practice over an extended period.

If we're serious about developing our personal and professional effectiveness, we should accept the realities that hold for any field of endeavour. It helps if we:

- **love what we're doing.** It's difficult to maintain discipline about a programme of practice for exceptional proficiency if we don't enjoy the task
- **experiment** with different methods to spot what is enhancing or detracting from improved performance
- **get feedback** on our performance to identify the specific ways in which we improve
- **put in the hours**. Malcolm Gladwell describes the 10,000 hours needed for exceptional performance. But this isn't the mindless treadmill of non-stop hours. It is practice when the mind is alert and concentration is focused

Our confidence and capability will take time to develop. Gladwell's rule of the 10,000 hours is of course simplistic. There is no final point of mastery, but it will help if:

- we see it as a priority, not as an unavoidable nuisance but as an intrinsic and enjoyable aspect of our work
- we feel comfortable facing new situations and tackling unusual problems
- we ask "how am I doing?" to find out what is and isn't working and listen to the answers
- we keep learning, asking for feedback and enhancing our effectiveness over time

"Success is all in the mind" Shelley Gare, 2009 The Australian

"Malcolm Gladwell says that if you want to shine, put in 10,000 hours" Steven Swinford 2008 The Sunday Times

"The Grandmaster in the Corner Office" 2010 at StudyHacks

HOW TO RECOVER PERFORMANCE BETWEEN POINTS

With confidence, you can reach truly amazing heights; without confidence, even the simplest accomplishments are beyond your grasp.

JIM LOEHR

After watching thousands of hours of tennis matches, attempting to identify what the top players did that distinguished them from the others, Jim Loehr found nothing. Then he noticed what players did between points.

The top players had a better way of relaxing after each point in preparing for the next one. During breaks, the less successful players dragged their rackets, muttered under their breaths, dropped their heads and shoulders, looked around at the crowd distractedly, or even threw fits. Giving vent to energy-draining emotions like anger and fear, they looked either demoralized or tense.

The top players, on the other hand, kept their heads high even when they'd lost a point, maintaining a confident posture that telegraphed no big deal. The top players would concentrate their gazes on their rackets or touch the strings with their fingers and stroll toward the backcourt, focusing, avoiding distraction, relaxing, and effectively letting the past go. After this mini-meditation, they'd turn back toward the net, bounce on their toes, and visualize playing the next point.

Our effectiveness hinges on consistency of performance. And consistency comes from knowing how to revitalise ourselves to prepare for the next set of challenges.

"Preparing Mentally for the Leadership Challenge"
George Ambler 2006 at ThePracticeOfLeadership.net

WHAT WAS ANDREW CARNEGIE'S GLITTER OF THE GOLD

Do your duty and a little more and the future will take care of itself.

ANDREW CARNEGIE

When journalist Napoleon Hill met Andrew Carnegie, the industrialist was in his prime. From a poor weaver's cottage in Scotland, then life as a bobbin boy in a cotton factory, the steel magnate was the wealthiest person in the United States. Carnegie began to share his wisdom on success, wealth and happiness.

Carnegie attributed much of his success to his ability to delegate, his belief in others and the desire to give of himself. "People are developed the same way gold is mined. Several tons of dirt must be moved to get an ounce of gold. But you don't go into the mine looking for dirt, you go in looking for gold." Among the 43 millionaires he created, labourer Charles Schwab became president of the United States Steel Corporation.

For Carnegie the "glitter of the gold" was evident in the "extra mile", the extent to which individuals put in effort over and above the call of duty to perform more and better service.

No one will praise us for doing our job. But we will be admired and rewarded for the "extra mile", the additional stuff that gets us noticed.

We should get on top of the basics of the role without getting bogged down in the maintenance activities. But if we want to stand out from our peers, we need to keep pushing the boundaries to take on those activities that go "the extra mile".

"The habits of going the extra mile" Keith Ready at AgiftOfInspiration.com

WHY PERSEVERANCE LOSES GOLDEN OPPORTUNITIES

Sometimes persevering turns out to be glorious stupidity, and not giving up can lead to the loss of a golden opportunity. PAUL PEARSALL

Determination and persistency are valued qualities. But sometimes they take us down a route that is unproductive. We think "one more push" when the reality is that we should walk away from the door we're attempting to open.

Investment in a misguided course of action misses opportunities to direct our time and energies more productively.

If we're relying only on the power of persistency to achieve our goals, maybe we should rethink our goals. Persistency in a flawed endeavour can only frustrate. Even worse it stops us from embarking on more productive activities.

As W C Fields wryly suggested: "If at first you don't succeed, try, try, again. Then quit. No use being a damned fool about it."

WHY PLANS ARE USELESS

Planning is indispensable but plans are useless.

DWIGHT EISENHOWER

When General Eisenhower led the D Day invasion on the beaches of Normandy, his first leadership task was to throw out the plan.

Although his troops wouldn't have reached the beaches without a plan, faced with a new reality, improvisation would be the guiding force.

The planning process provides important thinking time. It should help clarify long-term objectives, evaluate the pros and cons of different options, and identify potential risks and hazards.

But we shouldn't get too fixated on the "plan", allowing our efforts to be driven by a map of implementation that has outlived its usefulness. Flexibility to adapt our approach to changing circumstances may be a better strategy.

WHY IT'S GOOD TO GET DISTRACTED (SOMETIMES)

As soon as anyone starts taking about focus, I go next door to look up the derivation of the word, and then find my eye diverted to fo'c'sle.

FERDINAND MOUNT

Focus is important in directing concentrated effort at the task at hand. But constant focus can become a blinkered life outlook that lacks curiousity about wider events, issues and ideas outside the immediate field of vision.

Sometimes it's good to follow the distractions of life.

"Over flow: The dangers of excessive focus" Andre Kibbe, 2008 at ToolsForThought.com

"The power of curiousity" Donald Latumahina at LifeOptimizer.org

WHY OPPORTUNISM MAY BE BETTER THAN OPPORTUNITY

Many have found to their horror when they leaped up that their limbs had gone to sleep and their spirit had become too heavy. It is too late, they said to themselves.

FREDRICH NIETZSCHE

One must pass through the circumference of time before arriving at the centre of opportunity.

BALTASAR GRACIAN

In 2006, Barak Obama was advised that a run for presidency would be a mistake. He was too young, lacked experience and was too much of an unknown. Ignoring their counsel, Obama entered the race. Because everything and everyone was against him, he had to compensate with a superior political strategy and campaigning tactics. Turning his negatives (inexperience) into virtues (a force for change) his opportunism won the presidential election.

We like to think that opportunity is something that exists out there in the world. If and when it comes our way we can grasp it. It might be a job offer that is the perfect match with our skill set, or a meeting with an influential individual who can change our lives. In this mind set opportunity represents that good fortune that crosses our path from time to time. The challenge is to be ready to exploit the good luck.

In fact, the psychology of good luck indicates that opportunism may be a better strategy. In opportunism every event possesses the possibility for success. Rather than passively waiting for the right constellation of events and time, we proactively look for advantages.

Opportunism follows the principles of:

- **make the most of what we have.** We always want more: a bigger budget, larger team, an extended deadline, etc before we get started. When we are forced to work with what we have, and make do, our ingenuity is called on and we develop new expertise and skills
- **turn obstacles into openings.** This is the mindset in which blockages and barriers, viewed through the lens of opportunism, energise and motivate and impart a greater urgency. Opposition to our plans focuses our minds on ways to overcome it

- **look for turning points.** It is the unexpected - sudden successes or failures - that indicates a shifting trend, a change that if we register quickly, has the potential to benefit us
- **move before we are ready.** Rather than hold back, waiting for the perfect moment (unlikely to occur), we make a start. We learn quickly what will and won't work, and we make progress, moving faster than those who are waiting for "all the ducks to line up"

Opportunity knocks often, but sometimes softly. STEPHEN SHAPIRO

"Seeing The Gorilla" Richard Wiseman 2007 at Forbes.com

HOW NOT TO PLAN OUR LIVES

The most powerful and effective way to set goals is to make choices for the future.

FREDERICK MANN

Goal obsession is the force at play when we get so wrapped up in achieving our goal that we do it at the expense of a larger mission.

MARSHALL GOLDSMITH

In 1953 researchers surveyed Yale's graduate class to determine how many of them had specific written goals for their future. The answer: 3%. Twenty years later, researchers tracked down the '53 class, and found that the 3% with goals had accumulated more personal financial wealth than the other 97% combined. An extraordinary finding and one that has been repeated in many success books and lifestyle workshops.

But this powerful story has a problem - the research was never conducted!

But like many other urban myths, the feeling is that even if the story isn't true, it should be true. So goal setting is seen as a key life skill.

Classic success thinking emphasises "big dreams and practical goals". Think big thoughts about what is possible, create a vision of what this looks like, and then set specific goals to achieve this vision. Focus is powerful; it helps us make life choices. Plans, goals and targets are highly effective in directing our time and effort around what is important.

But what if we don't know what we want. Or, if what we think we want doesn't make us happy, fulfilled and authentic in the long run? Goals help us attain our aims, but they can also be blinkers, blinding us to the unexpected and to new life possibilities. Is "purposive drift" a better life strategy?

In purposive drift, we accept that life can't be lived like a project plan. Instead we keep an open mind, alert to what is and isn't working, recognising that our values and priorities will change during the course of our lives. Right now we don't know what in 10 or 20 years will be important to us, make us happy or what will be trivial and make us miserable.

It is our willingness to live with paradox that helps square the circle. Goal setting, when we nail down the specifics of our objectives, works well in the short and medium term. Here think SCAMPI to provide discipline to your plans over the next year or so:

- **Specific**: goals that focus on the detail of what needs to be attained
- **Challenging**: goals that require the application of effort around what is possible rather than just reinforce the status quo
- **Approach**: goals that pull us towards positive outcomes rather than push us away from negative outcomes; goals that make us feel good
- **Measurable**: goals that set a target that can be tracked and evaluated; not objectives with lots of "wriggle room"
- **Proximal**: goals with relatively short time horizons are more powerful than more distant aims
- **Inspirational**: goals that we feel are important to us and consistent with our ideals and aspirations for the future

But maybe purposive drift, that mind-set that keeps open and flexible to life's opportunities and the reality that we will change, is a good meta-strategy in life.

"If Your Goal Is Success, Don't Consult These Gurus" Lawrence Tabak 1996 at FastCompany.com

"Purposive Drift: Making It Up As We Go Along" Richard Oliver 2007 at ChangeThis.com

"What will make you happy?" Eric Jaffe 2007 The Smithsonian

"The downsides of goal setting, or why Brian Tracy makes me feel ill" Oliver Burkeman 2010 at OliverBurkeman.com

SHOULD WE DISCOVER THE SECRET

This is like having the Universe as your catalogue and you flip through it and you go, "Wow", I'd like to have this experience and I'd like to have this product. It's you placing your order with the Universe.

DR JOE VITALE

Jim Carrey, the out of work actor, is sitting on Mulholland Drive, Hollywood, writing himself a cheque for $10 million. He was penniless and out of work at the time. A few years later he cashes the cheque. Jim Carey is a success and he knows the secret.

The secret is The Law of Attraction. "You become or attract what you think about the most. This isn't just an idea - this is a literal truth - it's a law. And it works every time. No exceptions. Not sometimes. It's a law, just like gravity." At $35, the DVD "The Secret" by Rhonda Byrne and other gurus, has sold over 3 million copies with the simple message: what we truly believe in our hearts and minds will come to us, good or bad.

David Schirmer, one of the experts on the DVD explained what happened when he discovered the Secret. "Every day I would get a bunch of bills in the mail. The law of attraction states that what you focus on you will get, so I got a bank statement, whited out the total and put a new total there. I thought what if I just visualized checks coming in the mail? Within just one month, things started to change. It is amazing: today I just get checks in the mail."

Mr Schirmer obviously ignored the letter from the Australian Securities and Investments Commission, investigating the loss of tens of thousands of dollars from his investors.

Of course how we think is important. And some people do "reap what they sow". Those who do the hard work often do see the benefits, and people who do dumb things receive the penalty. But "The Secret" claims something more: mysterious forces in the cosmos that can unleash "unimaginable wealth, happiness and success".

Apart from the lack of any scientific underpinning, compassion seems in short supply among proponents of "The Secret". When parts of San Diego were engulfed in flames, Joe Vitale commented that the inferno had spared the homes of his fellow contributors to "The Secret", the implication being that those less fortunate homeowners had brought the disaster on themselves. Here the "Law of Attraction" is a pitiless philosophy that blames the victim.

When we're planning ahead, and anticipating the challenges that lie ahead, it's tempting to look for a short cut, The Secret, which will help achieve our goals easily and quickly. When we discover there is no secret, but the reality of smart planning, the implementation of shrewd tactics and a fair bit of hard work, we make progress.

"The Real Secret" Michael Shermer 2007 at Forbes.com

"Positively Misguided: The Myths & Mistakes of the Positive Thinking Movement" Steve Salerno, 2009 at Skeptic.com

IS IT BETTER TO BE A REALIST OR AN OPTIMIST

I was 52 years old. I had diabetes and incipient arthritis. I had lost my gall bladder and most of my thyroid gland in earlier campaigns, but I was convinced that the best was ahead of me.

RAY KROC, FOUNDER OF MCDONALDS

One of the major biases in risky decision making is optimism. Optimism is a source of high-risk thinking.

DANIEL KAHNEMAN

Realism is best when we're making our decisions and optimism helps us when implementing our plans.

When we allow our personal enthusiasm run ahead of the game in formulating our plans we forget that our ideas will be much more difficult, take longer and cost more to implement than we think. Instead we should check our proposed solution from every possible angle to assess the up and downsides.

And once we have made up our mind and feel we have selected the best solution, we should commit, deploying our energies and resources to make it happen, operating on the assumption that the solution will be implemented.

WHY WE SHOULD THINK THE LONG NOW

Civilization is revving itself into a pathologically short attention span. The trend might be coming from the acceleration of technology, the short-horizon perspective of market-driven economics, the next-election perspective of democracies, or the distractions of personal multi-tasking. All are on the increase. Some sort of balancing corrective to the short-sightedness is needed - some mechanism or myth which encourages the long view and the taking of long-term responsibility, where 'long-term' is measured at least in centuries.

STEWART BRAND

The Long Now Foundation wants us to think more responsibly about the future of the planet and mankind. A key symbol of the Long Now Foundation is the 10,000 year clock "a clock that ticks once a year. The century hand advances once every one hundred years, and the cuckoo comes out on the millennium."

The basic principles of the clock:

- it should be able to work relatively free of regular maintenance and be accurate for the next 10,000 years
- should be simple enough to maintain if the world falls back into a time without the technology that currently exists
- a close inspection of the clock should reveal its inner workings and operating principles
- no matter what point in time someone comes upon the clock, it should be able to be improved upon
- the clock should be able to be constructed small enough to fit on a table

George Bernard Shaw observed that we "are made wise by the responsibility for our future."

The Long Now encourages us to think about the impact we will have, not just on tomorrow, next month, next year, but on future mankind in 10,000 years.

"The 10,000 Year Clock" at LongNow.org

FEAR OF THE FUTURE

Real difficulties can be overcome; it is only the imaginary ones that are unconquerable.

THEODORE N. VAIL

When we fear the future our emotions are alert to life's risks. An opportunity is interpreted as a threat, and a new possibility is the hazard of potential failure. This is our imagination working against us rather than being a positive force to anticipate and plan for emerging challenges.

This section explores the nature of fear and the psychology of anxiety to identify the strategies and tactics we can deploy to ensure our emotions are helping not hindering us. When "fear is in the driving seat" we lose our curiousity to explore, our confidence to think boldly and courage to act in the face of uncertainty.

How do we balance the gains of pessimism with the benefits of optimism to overcome the fears of today to achieve the opportunities of tomorrow?

WHY THE JONAH COMPLEX HOLDS US BACK

One day in class, Professor Abraham Maslow asked his students: 'Which of you expects to achieve greatness in your chosen field?' The class looked at him blankly. After a long silence, Maslow said: 'If not you - who then?' And they began to see his point.

Maslow called this evasion of growth to fulfil one's best talents, and "fear of one's greatness", the Jonah complex. It was Jonah, the Old Testament prophet, who asked by God to go to the city of Nineveh and inform them of God's plans, decided to evade the assignment and escape to sea.

Unfortunately for Jonah, the huge storm that battered the boat, and the decision by the crew to throw him overboard, resulted in three days and nights in a whale's belly. Reminded by God of his destiny, he went on to fulfil his assignment and his destiny.

The realities of competition mean we can't be equally successful in financial terms. But we can all be "great" in living to our best ideals and fulfilling our potential.

"The Jonah Complex" Dr. Moses Simuyemba, at CornerStone Executive & Life Coaching

HOW SHOULD WE LIVE IN EXTREMISTAN

Well, you ain't seen nothing yet. Starting at 1 AD, it took 1500 years for the amount of information in the world to double. It's now doubling at the rate of once every 2 years.

M J RYAN

We used to live in a country called Mediocristan. This was a simple country in which the range of possible events was small, and cause and effect were closely connected. In the country of Mediocristan, life was reasonably secure and certain. If the average height in Mediocristan was 5 foot, 9 inches, we expect someone of 6 foot. We don't expect our neighbour to be 9 feet tall.

We don't live in that country anymore. In the new country of Extremistan, life isn't secure, predictable or certain. In Extremistan, highly unlikely events with a massive impact occur. In Extremistan, in which global forces create massive inter-dependencies with huge consequences, we are at the mercy of "the singular, the accidental, the unseen and the unpredicted." In Extremistan, the nine foot neighbour does move in next door and changes our lives drastically.

"For most of us, uncertainty isn't fun." But it helps if we develop the kind of agility - mental and emotional - that provides the flexibility to respond with "easy grace" to respond to emerging challenges.

And our agility is developed when we:

- **accept change is a reality.** It's human nature to preserve what we have and hold on to our sense of who we are. Habits can operate as efficient life algorithms; the auto-pilots of our life habits can also resist the novel and unfamiliar
- **expand our options.** Here we reframe change. Rather than viewing change as a threat to our current position we see it as a way of opening up new life possibilities. Our brains may be hardwired to detect risk and prepare for flight. But lions aren't chasing us anymore. Our brains often get it wrong, sensing danger when we should be identifying possibilities
- **take action.** Here we develop adaptability when we switch from problems to think solutions. Problems can paralyse us, holding us back in the belief that we are stuck. Actions around solutions builds the kind of momentum that makes progress and move us forward

- **review progress.** Some of the decisions we make and the plans we implement will work. Some won't. Establishing a feedback loop to learn quickly what is and isn't working pinpoints where we need to shift course and change tactics

"The Black Swan: The Impact of the Highly Improbable" Nassim Taleb

"Why adapting is the most crucial skill we'll ever learn" M J Ryan at ChangeThis

HOW TO AVOID SAYING IF ONLY

If that plane leaves the ground and you're not with him, you'll regret it. Maybe not today. Maybe not tomorrow. But soon and for the rest of your life.

HUMPHREY BOGART IN CASABLANCA

If you decide to do something and it turns out badly, it probably won't still be haunting you in a decade down the road. You'll reframe the failure, explain it away, move on and forget it. Not so with failures to act.

NEAL ROESE

I'd rather regret the things I have done than the things that I haven't.

LUCILLE BALL

Prudence to weigh up the pros and cons of our life options, to identify their benefits and risks, and the longer-term consequences is of course a sensible tactic in life. But if prudence is that life caution and hesitancy that avoids the uncertainty of new challenges or the risk of potential mistakes, it holds us back from the decisions and actions that have the potential for greater fulfilment and happiness.

Why do we tend to regret what we didn't do rather than what we did?

Because our minds find it easier to make sense of the consequences of mistakes. After all there is hopefully some kind of experience we can learn from. If nothing else, our catastrophes and disasters make for entertaining dinner party conversation. Why are we more inclined to regret the things we didn't do? In failing to act there is no experience to review, learn from or provide an interesting conversational topic.

The next time we're contemplating a life choice, rather than just imagine the downsides of a decision option going badly, we should **think about the consequences of missing the benefits** if the option goes well.

"If Only: How to Turn Regret Into Opportunity" Neal Roese

"The biggest regret of your life" Josh Foster, 2010 Psychology Today

"Avoiding a life of regret" Scott Dinsmore, 2010 at Reading For Your Success

WHAT LINKS ANXIETY AND PLANNING

The human being is the only animal that thinks about the future.

DANIEL GILBERT

In 1848, Phineas Gage was the foreman of a work gang blasting rock on an American railroad construction. An explosion, probably due to an incorrect mix of blasting powder, went wrong, and a three and a half foot iron rod was shot through the top of Gage's skull and out of his left cheek. Amazingly, despite the destruction of the front left part of his brain, Gage, within a few minutes was speaking, and made his way to his rooms to wait for the doctor.

Within a short period, Gage was functioning like a normal person. However, his employers quickly noted a change. Once regarded as "the most efficient and capable foreman in their employ", Phineas was now described as "no longer Gage". "Obstinate, irresponsible and capricious", Gage was unable to keep his job. Despite the severe down-turn in his personality, Gage lived on for another 12 years, working and travelling, including a period in Chile and time as an exhibit in a travelling circus.

Neurologists wondered if the frontal lobes of the brain were in fact that important.

Phineas Gage was the victim of one of life's contingencies, a kind of real life experiment. In the twentieth century, surgeons advanced this experiment to find a different pattern: the frontal lobes did seem to matter, and were associated with anxiety. Portuguese surgeon, Moniz, looking for a treatment for psychotic patients, wondered if the removal of the frontal lobes, might alleviate patient symptoms of agitation and emotional distress. Frontal lobotomy arrived as a medical procedure.

At first, the signs were encouraging: the treatment produced a calming effect on patients where other therapies had failed. But further research noted the costs. Patients might report greater calmness and happiness, but they showed "severe impairments on any test that involved planning."

What links anxiety and planning? "Both are intimately connected to thinking about the future." The frontal lobes are key to going beyond the present to project ourselves into the future. But thinking about the future makes us anxious. It's not only the uncertainty of it all, it's the anticipation of what might go wrong and the potentially bad things that might happen to us.

We might be calmer if we live purely in the present. But it won't help us prepare for our future or take control of our lives. Alternatively, if we only live in the future we might find it difficult to achieve that stillness of simply enjoying the moment.

"Hello Present Me Meet Future Me" Winnie Yong, 2009,

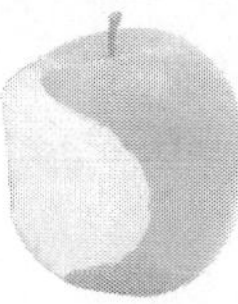

WHY THE DOG THAT DIDN'T BARK EXPLAINS WHY WE FORGET FUTURE GOOD TIMES

Is there any point to which you would wish to draw my attention?
To the curious incident of the dog in the night-time.
The dog did nothing in the night-time.
That was the curious incident.

SHERLOCK HOLMES

Sherlock Holmes in "The Silver Blaze" makes the astute observation that it is what we don't notice that didn't happen that biases our problem solving and imagination. Silver Blaze, the horse, had been stolen by stable-hands familiar to the dog, hence the absence of the dog barking.

College students were asked to predict how they would feel if their football team won or lost. One group of students - the describers - were also asked to note the detail of the events of their typical day. The other group - the non-describers - weren't. A few days on and the students were asked how happy they were. Whereas the non-describers over-estimated the impact the win or loss had, the describers were accurate in their forecasts of their happiness.

Why? Because in the act of outlining the detail of their day, the describers identified all the other stuff that goes on to influence happiness. The non-describers, on the other hand, focused on one and only one aspect of the future - winning and losing the football game - and forgot the absences that shape happiness.

We see what we expect. And we plan based on what we expect. But events outside our expectations fail to register. We spot the presences but we fail to note the absences.

If we're fearful about the future we anticipate the difficulties of the challenges that lie ahead, alert to the risks and hazards we face. What we don't do is register the reality that whatever happens in future there will be good times. We may succeed but even if we fail, other nice stuff in life will in all likelihood happen.

When we find ourselves fearing the future it's worth remembering the absences of the positives that we're forgetting right now.

"Affective forecasting" Simon Moss, 2009 at Psychlopedia.com

WHEN IS IT A GOOD TIME TO PLAN

We cannot feel good about an imaginary future when we are busy feeling bad about an actual present.

DANIEL GILBERT

The way we think and feel about the present affects how we look back to our past and how we imagine our future.

If we're feeling low we're more likely to recall moments of unpleasantness, embarrassment and adversity from our past. And the present also sets boundaries when we contemplate the future. Despite the power of our creative imagination to think outside the box, the box still manages to constrain our assumptions and options of what is possible.

If it's a bad idea to reflect back when we're in a bad mood, it's also hazardous to look forward and plan ahead when we're feeling down. When we do, the future we project will be one of challenge, difficulty and adversity.

If we wait until our mood picks up, our future becomes brighter and we're motivated to set the kind of objectives that will improve our current life situation.

But we should check our mood isn't too up-beat. When we're at our most positive and optimistic we over-estimate the likelihood of positive events and under-estimate the likelihood of negative events. Here our plan becomes an exercise in wishful thinking rather than a grounded sequence of actions to achieve our goals.

It's a good time to plan when we're feeling positive about ourselves and current situation but also prepared to work through the issues with a combination of emotional honesty and intellectual rigour.

"Kool-Aid Psychology: Realism versus Optimism"
Michael Shermer, 2009 Scientific American

WHY WE SHOULDN'T LOOK TOO FAR AHEAD

It is a mistake to look too far ahead. Only one link in the chain of destiny can be handled at a time.

WINSTON CHURCHILL

Planning is generally seen as a good thing. Planning helps us clarify our priorities, set objectives and map out the sequence of actions that will help us get from where we are to where we want to be.

But there are times when long-term thinking becomes counter-productive. When we begin to imagine every possible obstacle to our future plans and anticipate the potential risks, we become overwhelmed by the scale of the challenge we face.

Sometimes in life, it may be better to advance step by step and "cross the bridge when we come to it" rather than plot out the full sequence of manoeuvres we need to undertake.

WHEN TO MAKE IT UP AS WE GO ALONG

I have long considered it one of God's greatest mercies that the future is hidden from us. If it were not, life would surely be unbearable.

EUGENE FORSEY

There are many methods for predicting the future. For example, you can read horoscopes, tea leaves, tarot cards, or crystal balls. Collectively, these methods are known as "nutty methods." Or you can put well-researched facts into sophisticated computer models, more commonly referred to as "a complete waste of time".

SCOTT ADAMS

When the future is uncertain, and we're not sure what to do, we should try lots of different things and see what works.

Some individuals know their life destiny and purpose at an early stage. Most of us don't.

If we move to a mindset in which we accept uncertainty and the likelihood of mistakes and failures as we test and experiment and are prepared to listen and learn, maybe a life purpose emerges from:

- recognising what did and didn't work for us
- identifying our deep-seated strengths and limitations
- discovering what we like and dislike
- gauging the realities of our expectations about what is possible to achieve

This is a life strategy on the fly. It is messy and confusing. But sometimes this may be the best course of action.

IS IT BETTER TO BE ENVIED OR PITIED

A wise man owned several beautiful horses. One horse was so fast and strong that it evoked the envy of the man's neighbour. One day the horse broke free and ran into the hills. At once, the neighbour's attitude changed from envy to pity at the man's loss. But the wise man said, Who knows if I should be pitied or envied?

The next day the horse returned leading a herd of fifty magnificent wild horses. The neighbour was again filled with envy. The wise man said, "Who knows if I should be pitied or envied?"

Not long after this, his only son tried to ride one of the wild horses but was thrown off and broke his leg. Again, the neighbour's attitude shifted from envy to pity. But the wise man answered: "Who knows if I should be pitied or envied?" The following day an officer in the emperor's army came to draft the man's son for a dangerous mission. But because his leg was broken, he was relieved of a responsibility that would have almost certainly meant death. Instead, the neighbour's son was taken. As before the wise man responded, "Who knows if I should be pitied or envied?"

Sometimes we don't know if a life event has been a good or a bad thing. The bad thing we experience may turn out to be a blessing in disguise. And that moment of apparent good fortune may trigger future negative consequences.

Sometimes it may be better to let life unfold before we jump to conclusions to either feel sorry for ourselves or to congratulate ourselves with our achievements.

WHY WE SHOULD DO AT LEAST ONE SCARY THING A DAY

Do one thing every day that scares you. ELEANOR ROOSEVELT

This is good but awkward advice.

If we wait until the big frightening moments of life we might find ourselves exposed and vulnerable. We build our resilience by facing the day-to-day difficult problems, the issues that ask questions of our courage. When we start to address:

- the rudeness of a shop assistant
- the bad habits of a teenage child
- a noisy neighbour
- the appalling discriminatory humour of a colleague

we strengthen our confidence to face life. Courage of course isn't just about the conflict situations of life. We all have our own "scary things". For some of us it might be

- an apology to a colleague we have upset
- a decision to press on with a high risk project
- initiating conversation with a colleague in another work area
- saying no to a better job offer

Each day of course is different for each of us. But each day has its "one scary thing". And if we face and tackle that scary thing we may find it easier to build the courage that takes on the big and the tough life challenges.

WHAT HELPED WILLIAM JAMES RECOVER FROM A HORRIBLE MOMENT

Human beings, by changing the inner attitudes of their minds, can change the outer aspects of their lives.

WILLIAM JAMES

In a bout of pessimism and "general depression of spirits about my prospects", the famous psychologist William James, entering his dressing room one evening, suddenly had an image of a patient from the hospital he had visited earlier in the day.

"A black haired youth with greenish skin who used to sit all day, moving nothing but his eyes....That shape am I potentially. Nothing I possess can defend me from that fate if the hour should strike for me as it struck for him."

This is an acute awareness of the contingencies of life, the impact of chance and the recognition that we are not masters of our destiny. We like to think we are in control of our lives. But as William James suddenly realised: if the hour might strike for us, anything might happen. Our company has gone into bankruptcy, we find a note informing us that our partner has left us, we are a victim of a mugging, or stricken by illness.

Troubled by this thought it took William James a while to recover from his depression. It was an essay by Renouvier that jolted James' attention. Reading Renouvier's definition of free will: "the sustaining of a thought *because I choose to* when I might have other thoughts", William James determined that free will was not an illusion. "My first act of free will shall be to believe in free will."

When William James took control of his mind - "to run his own brain" - he moved from fear to freedom.

To perceive the world differently, we must be willing to change our belief system, let the past slip away, expand our sense of now, and dissolve the fear in our minds.

"You Are What You Think. What Are Cognitive Distortions?"Nancy Schimelpfening, 2007 at DepressionAbout

WHY WE GET PANIC ATTACKS AND WHAT TO DO

This collapse seems to be a sudden loss of nerve, a failure of certainty and confidence, an overwhelming feeling that I can't do this anymore.

MICHAEL FOLEY

The mid life crisis is of course a cliché. This is the life episode when, in the attempt to rediscover our youth to avoid facing the passing of the years, we embark on lots of stupid stuff.

But more common is that collapse in our energies, a sense of futility, feelings of boredom and intermittent panic attacks. Just as we feel we've built up an experience base, a repertoire of skill-sets and a certain amount of wisdom, it seems to count for nothing.

Ironically it may be that it is our experience, skill and wisdom that are part of the problem. When we were less experienced, skilled and wise, we saw life as simple and certain. Experience, skill and a degree of wisdom makes life more complex and uncertain. And faced with this new complexity and uncertainty, we become anxious and the panic attacks begin.

We can recover our equilibrium by:

- eliminating this life phase of anxiety by asking our GP to prescribe massive amounts of anti-depressants
- doing everything in our power to jettison the experience, skill and wisdom that is now making life difficult for us. This is a life strategy in which we shift to ignorance, naiveté and folly
- embarking on a programme of intense work activity to ensure we are just about coping to keep the panic attacks at bay

Or we can shift approach completely.

In the early days of aircraft design to break the sound barrier, although the engineers had "solved the aerodynamic problem", planes kept going into a steep dive and crashed. And the harder the pilot pulled on the stick, the steeper the dive. Until one day, a test pilot tried something different. "Instead of frantically trying

to pull back the stick, he tried pushing it forward - which logically ought to have made the dive steeper. Instead the plane straightened out."

If we're experiencing panic attacks, we can stop pulling away from the anxiety and fear, which only reinforces our sense of panic. Instead we can face the panic attack by "pushing the joy stick" forward to accept it and to confront it.

There is good news here. If we "hang on, things begin to look up". The panics of our mid years begin to disappear to become the detachment and calmness of our later years.

"Researchers replace midlife myths with facts" Rebecca Clay, 2003, American Psychological Association

"Is Wellbeing U-Shaped over the Life Cycle?" David Blanchflower, 2006

"The U-bend of life: Why, beyond middle age, people get happier as they get older" 2010, The Economist

"Panic attacks" Charles Linden, 2010 at KickAnxiety

HOW TO CREATE URGENCY FOR THE LONG-TERM

I have been impressed with the urgency of doing.

LEONARDO DA VINCI

Tasks can be grouped into those that are:

- not important and not urgent
- not important but urgent
- important but not urgent
- important and urgent

And, faced with a series of work demands and pressures, it is critical that we know the difference.

Unimportant tasks that aren't urgent can largely be ignored. And the important and urgent activities are obvious priorities. The tasks that jeopardise our overall impact are the important but not urgent activities. It is attention to these tasks that has the potential to optimise our personal effectiveness. But the lack of urgency means they don't receive the time and effort they deserve.

We manage our competing priorities by creating urgency for long-term important tasks. These are the tasks we keep on our radar screen, recognising the impact if they are neglected.

If we do something each day, however small, to tackle the important but not urgent tasks we build momentum and make progress.

"Time Management Matrix" at EffectiveTimeManagementStrategies
"Good and bad procrastination" Paul Graham, 2005

WHY WE SHOULD BEGIN WITH THE BRIGHT SPOTS

Asked to open a new office in Vietnam to tackle malnutrition Jerry Sternin, working for Save The Children, knew he had a problem. The Foreign Minister frostily told him: "you have six months to make a difference.

Sternin knew the realities of childhood malnutrition, a dynamic of poverty, sanitation and nutrition. But he couldn't tackle the fundamental infrastructure behind these problems in six months.

So he travelled to rural villages to meet groups of mothers, setting up teams to weigh and measure the children in the villages. His question: "do you find very poor children who are bigger and healthier than others?" met the answer "yes".

So he searched in each community for the "bright spots", the successful activities that would be worth replicating. He found practical suggestions that made a difference (e.g. "bright spot mothers" were feeding their children four times a day - using the same amount of food as other mothers but spreading it across four rather than two servings - a tactic that made it easier for children to digest the food.)

Because Sternin is a smart guy he didn't turn his findings into a manual: "The Five Rules to Fight Malnutrition". Instead he shared his results village by village, in cooking classes to allow the community to work through and implement the changes.

The program went on to reach 2.2 million Vietnamese people, with 65% of the children better nourished.

When we were faced with the need to plan ahead but don't have the answers or a budget to implement solutions, beginning with the **bright spots** is a good start.

"Switch: How to Change Things When Change Is Hard" Chip & Dan Health

ARE THERE ANY ALPS

The knife's edge that separates failure from success in life. That edge is your attitude which has the power to help shape your reality. If you view everything through the lens of fear, you tend to stay in retreat mode.

ROBERT GREENE

It is the spring of 1800 and Napoleon Bonaparte is preparing to lead his army into Italy. His Field Marshalls are warning him that the Alps are not yet passable, advising him to wait, even though waiting will spoil the chances of success.

His reply:

For Napoleon's army, there shall be no Alps.

Mounting a mule, Napoleon proceeded to lead his troops through the difficult mountain pass. His army took the enemy by surprise and defeated them.

Sometimes the advice of caution is sensible and right. Sometimes boldness based on unwavering confidence and commitment is required.

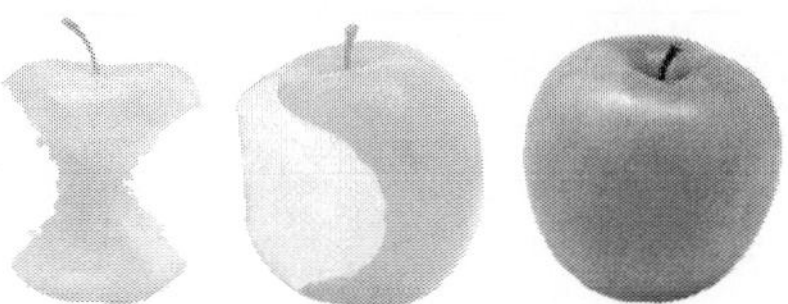

WAS THE SHORT LIFE OF FRANCIS MACOMBER HAPPY

Macomber felt a wild unreasonable happiness that he had never known before.

ERNEST HEMINGWAY

In Ernest Hemingway's short story, Francis Macomber is 35, handsome and wealthy, married to Margot, who stays with him because he is rich and likely to get even richer. Their marriage sort of works; she stays with him because of his money, and he tolerates her infidelities.

On safari in Africa, Francis Macomber disgraces himself by his cowardice in running from a wounded lion they are hunting. Disgusted, Margot decides to spend the night with the big game hunter guide.

The next day, motivated by humiliation, hatred and anger, Francis faces a buffalo head on. He shoots fearlessly as the buffalo charges. Margot in a panic shoots from the car and misses, killing her husband. Or, as some critics suggest, Margot deliberately shot to kill Francis because "he was becoming too brave, too soon. As a brave man, he would have the courage to leave her."

This is a story, full of complex emotions, not least the dynamics of courage. For Hemingway, Francis Macomber only became happy when he faced his fear.

Hemingway, ever the chest-beating narrator, is an unlikely guide to the subtleties of human psychology. But in his account of the life of Francis Macomber he raises important questions:

- can we ever be happy if we live a life of fear?
- what happens when we lose our fear?

IS FEAR IN THE DRIVING SEAT

Fear is a kind of prison that confines us within a limited range of action. The less you fear, the more power you will have.

ROBERT GREENE

What we fear doing is most usually what we need to do. A person's success in life can usually be measured by the number of uncomfortable conversations he or she is willing to have. Resolve to do one thing every day that you fear.

TIM FERRISS

From the beginnings of time fear has served a simple purpose: survival. The emotion of fear - triggered in the face of danger - motivated us to flee or defend ourselves. And an awareness of fear meant we could anticipate and avoid future danger.

This power to imagine danger and risk also had a downside: creating multiple worries and anxieties about potential threats. Fear, instead of being a powerful tactic to cope with real and specific danger, became a generalised attitude towards life.

And we live in fear; fear of expressing ourselves and offending others; fear of disagreement that might trigger conflict; fear of taking the kind of bold actions that drive change but might upset vested interests; fear of the shame of failure.

But if we can overcome our anxieties, we "forge a fearless attitude towards life" and gain control over our circumstances.

Imagine the freedom that results from:

- embarking on those actions we would naturally fear
- taking the tough decisions we have been avoiding
- confronting problems directly rather than play games
- outlining the specific changes we know need to be made rather than accept unsatisfactory compromises

"10 Life-Changing Facts About Fear" Gail Brenner, 2010 at A Flourishing Life

"How to Overcome Your Fear: 7 Tips from the Last 2200 Years" Henrik Edberg at The Positivity Blog

"The 50th Law" Robert Greene

HOW TO MANAGE THE 5 FEARS

Don't short change the future, because of fear in the present.

BARACK OBAMA

If I were asked to guess what people are generally most insecure about, I would say it is the content of the future. We worry about it constantly.

ISAAC ASIMOV

Although we should emphasise the positives of life it helps if we also recognise that much of human behaviour is driven by fear. As that wise counsellor Yoda observed: "Named must your fear be, before banish it you can."

To know the fear is to know how to provide a response that will reassure and encourage others. The five fears - universal and deep-seated within our natures - are:

1. **the fear of the stranger** and the need for community. We fear who we don't know and we like those we grew up with and know
2. **the fear of the future** and the need for clarity. The future has uncertainties which create anxieties. We value those who know the future and can provide purpose and direction
3. **the fear of chaos** and the need for authority. We fear disorder and that sense of things being out of control and we need someone to take charge
4. **the fear of insignificance** and the need for respect. We fear that we don't matter, aren't valued and no one cares about us. We look for the reassurance that we're important and a recognition that our contribution makes a difference
5. **the fear of death** and the need for security. This is a tough one. We worry about what might happen to us, our family and friends and we need to feel that sense of security that everything will be OK

If we understand what we personally fear, and can recognise what lies behind others' anxieties and concerns, we will be ready to provide that insight and compassion which reassures and comforts.

"Dealing with Fear" Geshe Kelsang at DealingWithFear

WHAT MUST WE DO

We stand on a mountain pass in the midst of whirling snow and blinding mist, through which we get glimpses now and then of paths which may be deceptive. If we stand still we shall be frozen to death. If we take the wrong road, we shall be dashed to pieces. We do not certainly know whether there is any right one. What must we do? Be strong and of good courage. Act for the best, hope for the best, and take what comes. If death ends all, we cannot meet death better.

JAMES FITZJAMES STEPHEN

This is all we can do.

We must make a choice not simply about what we want to achieve in life. We have to decide how we want to live our lives. And it seems that the "how" turns out to be as important as the "what" of our happiness and success.

If exuberant recklessness to throw ourselves into each and every opportunity in life is hazardous, then fearful caution limits our options in life. We may prefer to wait for that clarity in life to see through the "whirling snow and blinding mist" that provides the reassurance that our choices and their consequences will work out favourably. But we may find ourselves standing in the mountain pass.

"The Courage to Live Consciously" Steve Pavlina

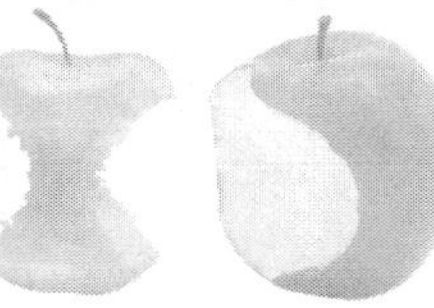

WHY WE ARE MORE RESILIENT THAN WE THINK

Man never made any material as resilient as the human spirit.

BERN WILLIAM

You all know that I have been sustained throughout my life by three saving graces - my family, my friends, and a faith in the power of resilience and hope. These graces have carried me through difficult times and they have brought more joy to the good times than I ever could have imagined.

ELIZABETH EDWARDS

At one point or another in our lives we will experience the loss of a loved one, the trauma of a serious illness, the awfulness of a major crime or the bad luck of a major car accident.

It is true and obvious that these adversities represent life tragedies. It is also true, but less obvious, that "the majority of those who survive major traumas do quite well, and a significant portion claim that their lives were enhanced by the experience."

This isn't the hard hearted view that we all should "get on with it". A significant number don't get over it to get on with their lives. For these individuals the traumatic experience is a trigger to sustained distress and chronic depression. But most of us display remarkable levels of recovery in our response to life adversity.

Just as our body possesses an immune system to defend us from illness, our minds deploy a psychological immune system to protect us from unhappiness. Our psychological immune system is adept at finding ways to make us feel better about ourselves. Its tactics are:

- **finding the facts that make us feel better** about our current situation. And one important trick is to shift the comparisons we make. Faced with a life threatening illness we are more likely to compare our situation with those in even worse shape. (The comparison factor also explains why people are happier in a less expensive house as long it is more expensive than their neighbours than living in a more expensive house but which is worth less than that of their neighbours)

- **adapting to the situation** we find ourselves in. This tactic of habituation explains why our first drive in a new car is delightful; the second drive enjoyable, but future drives deliver diminishing returns of happiness. Conversely, we become accustomed to any down turn in life, which is why lottery winners were found to be no happier than accident victims two years later

When we worry about what lies ahead it's reassuring to know that we will be more resilient than we anticipate.

"Positive Change Following Trauma and Adversity: A Review" Alex Linley & Stephen Joseph, Journal of Traumatic Stress 2004

"Can Money Buy Happiness?: Are Lottery Winners Any Happier in the Long Run?" at Psychology and Society

"A Personal Strategy for Engaging and Building Your Resilience" at UCSF

"Tips on how to build resilience" Deborah Serani, 2007 at MindFields College

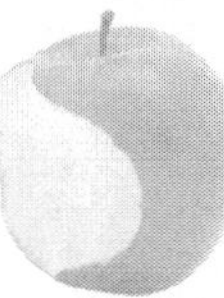

HOW TO WORRY

Worry never robs tomorrow of its sorrow; it only saps today of its strength.

A J CRONIN

Worry is a stream of fear trickling through the mind. If encouraged it cuts a channel into which all other thoughts are drained.

ARTHUR SOMERS ROCHE

"About 40% of what we worry about will never happen. Another 30% concerns old decisions we cannot change. About 12% is related to criticisms of ourselves that are not fair and made by people who feel inferior to us. Another 10% of our worrying is related to our health, and worrying only makes us sick. About 8% of our worrying is worth the effort because it can help us find a starting point for doing something about whatever it is that is worrying us." Paul Pearsall.

If we allow ourselves to be caught up in the useless 92% of worry we'll find it difficult to apply our minds productively to the 8% that needs our full attention.

Worry is fundamental to how our minds and feelings have evolved to anticipate and respond to risk. The challenge is to become more efficient in how we worry, and the ways we interpret, frame and respond to negative events. Instead of counter-productive anxiety and inaction, worry is a positive dynamic to motivate us into problem solving mode

We manage our worries by:

- **accepting worry as a life fact.** Worry helps prepare us for the future, identifying the challenges we need to overcome to make progress in life. But we should balance our worries with the positives about our present and future

- **controlling our worry time.** Rather than allow worries to invade every minute of our day, schedule in a 20 minute "worry session". Any worries that enter our consciousness outside this time should be written down and saved for review. Try to plan our "worry time" for the same time each day. But not just before we head for bed

- **talking logically to ourselves.** "If the problem can be solved then why worry? If the problem cannot be solved worrying will do us no good." Treat each worry as a problem to be solved. Translate the worry into a practical problem. How would others define this worry? Think of all the possible solutions to the problem. What has worked for you in the past when faced with a similar worry? Work through the pros and cons of different solutions and choose one that you feel can work for you. Map out the key actions you will undertake to implement the solution

- **drawing on others' support.** A problem shared is not always a problem halved. But others - family, friends, colleagues - can be an invaluable resource in helping us overcome life's problems. Don't go it alone when you can call on the experience, insights and ideas of those who have similar problems

See worry as a pre-flight schedule, the kind of checklist an airline pilot works through before take-off. What might go wrong? what will I do if the worst happens? what skills can I call on to manage the situation? what back-up plans are in place to manage the situation?

Keep your analysis practical. Airline pilots don't panic in reviewing the potential hazards. They know it makes good sense to conduct a thorough review in advance of take off to minimise risks and rehearse contingency plans if the worst does happen. Don't assume every life situation needs a full pre-flight review. But when you do feel under threat, work through the issues objectively.

We can easily manage if we will only take, each day, the burden appointed to it. But the load will be too heavy for us if we carry yesterday's burden over again today, and then add the burden of the morrow before we are required to bear it. JOHN NEWTON

"The Beethoven Factor" Paul Pearsall
"The useless emotion" Oliver Burkeman, 2007, The Guardian
"How to deal with your worry" The Daily Mind

HOW TO SCHEDULE IN WORRY TIME

We are uniquely among the earth's creatures, the worrying animal. We worry away our lives.

LEWIS THOMAS

Worrying, for the most part, is an unproductive enterprise. As with rumination we engage in this type of thought because we believe that our worry is an important problem solving tool or a key factor in preventing problematic outcomes.

This belief is reinforced by the fact that the things we worry about rarely occur, and we make the mistake of interpreting this fact as a sign that our worrying played a role in the outcome. "I worried, my feared outcome didn't happen... looks like my worrying did the job." The outcome would not have occurred even if we had not worried. And the negative reinforcement reinforces our future worry.

Paradoxical as it seems, for the major worriers, we should schedule in "worry time" every day, say 20 minutes of worry time each morning. Outside of this 20 minute window, we can acknowledge that there is something to worry about, but to delay that worry until its next appointment.

We're not ignoring the issue, but rather allotting it a specific time. The worry can sit in the waiting room until its appointment.

Worry time helps us to take control over our own thoughts and to challenge our lopsided beliefs about the importance of worry and our ability to control it. If an issue requires concern, it will still be anxiety provoking when worry time comes around. But we move into problem solving mode to work on a specific plan to respond to the worry.

"The Worry Cure: Seven Steps to Stop Worry from Stopping You" Robert Leahy

"What if?!?! - How scheduling time to worry each day can decrease how often you worry" Michael Anestis, 2009, PsychoTherapyBrownBag

HOW WE USE EXCUSES TO SELF-HANDICAP

In the long term, self handicapping may be easier to live with for some people than to know that they did their very best and failed.

DR. HIRT

It is one thing to make our excuses after we fail. It is another to create the excuses before we even start. Self handicapping is when we "hobble" ourselves in advance of undertaking an activity in which our performance will be evaluated. "The excuses come preattached: I never went to class. I was hung over at the interview. I had no idea what the application required."

The term "self-handicapping" was originally used to describe students who were given positive feedback on problem-solving tests, regardless of their actual performance. Half the subjects had been given fairly easy problems, while the others were given difficult problems. The students were then given the choice between a "performance-enhancing drug" (inert) and one which would inhibit it. Those subjects who received the difficult problems were more likely to choose the impairing drug, and subjects who faced easy problems were more likely to choose the enhancing drug. Those students presented with the hard problems, believing that their success had been due to chance, chose the inhibiting drug because they were looking for an "excuse" for their expected poor performance in future.

The self-handicapping motive isn't just the lowering of expectations as we contemplate potential failure. It is seeking out obstacles that actually undermine performance; after all, the obstacles can be attributed as the cause of failure, and our self esteem is protected.

Do we get our excuses in first to explain why we might fail in future? Even worse, are we authoring our own downfall by embarking on activities that will undermine our performance?

"Delay as a self-handicapping strategy" Timothy A Pychyl, 2008, Psychology Today

"Some Protect the Ego by Working on Their Excuses Early" Benedict Carey, 2009, New York Times

ARE THERE REASONS TO BE CHEERFUL

More than any other time in history, mankind faces a crossroads. One path leads to despair and utter hopelessness. The other, to total extinction. Let us pray we have the wisdom to choose correctly.

WOODY ALLEN

The juice of the carrot, the smile of the parrot.

IAN DURY, REASONS TO BE CHEERFUL PT 3

While there is a chance of the world getting through its troubles, I hold that a reasonable person has to behave as though they were sure of it. If at the end your cheerfulness is not justified, at any rate you will have been cheerful.

H G WELLS

We live in gloomy times. As one Amazon reviewer warns us of our future: "war, famine, death, drought, pestilence, climate catastrophe and Katie Price's next book." And, because bad news sells, the media continue to create the general impression that "we're all going to hell in a handcart", fearing the next terrorist attack, outbreak of a new flu variant, freak weather pattern and alien abduction in the process.

This isn't new. Throughout history we have been warned of a future time of "trouble and distress, wasteness and desolution and darkness." And of course the up-beat predictions of the politicians, technocrats and scientists continue to be hopelessly wrong.

But there are reasons to be cheerful. In this great adventure of life, in the last 100 years life expectancy continues to rise, real income has increased, we are better fed, child mortality rates have plummeted, many diseases have been virtually eliminated, and technology makes available the kind of life styles that a king in the nineteenth century would have envied.

This isn't the argument that we live in the best of all possible worlds. But it is to suggest that we're not quite in the handcart to hell that the doom and gloom of the media suggest, and to remind us that the dire warnings of the gloomy futurologists have been consistently wrong.

We might not live in the best of all possible worlds. But we can maintain the commitment that our curiosity, ingenuity and creativity to face and tackle new challenges will maintain progress to a better life.

"Arthur C Clarke and the end of upbeat futurology" Darragh McManus, 2009, Guardian

"An Optimist's Tour of the Future" Mark Stevenson

"The Rational Optimist: How Prosperity Evolves" Matt Ridley

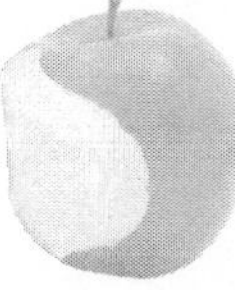

HOW TO GET FURTHER ON UP THE ROAD

But no matter, the road is life.

JACK KEROUAC

Where the way is dark and the night is cold
One sunny morning we'll rise, I know
And I'll meet you further on up the road.

BRUCE SPRINGSTEEN

"Further on up the road" has been described as a song about an individual who is:

- looking for something they can't find
- obsessed by wealth and prospecting for gold
- desperate for revenge
- confronting a dark and dangerous past life
- lonely and lost and still searching

It's probably the sign of a great song that it is capable of so many varied and complex interpretations.

But maybe "Further on up the Road" is a commitment to make it through and to persevere, choosing to put "one foot in front of another" on the path of life.

We all are on the road, and sometimes the way is dark. The song may remind us of a "sunnier morning" if we are willing to keep walking on up the road.

WHY WE NEED TO SHIFT OUR THINKING TO BE MORE OPTIMISTIC

Optimist: someone who figures that taking a step backward after taking a step forward is not a disaster, it's a cha-cha. ROBERT BRAULT

It's easy to think that we're either born optimistic, pessimistic, or somewhere in between. And of course our temperament makes an impact. But it seems that how we think is important, and specifically how we describe both the good things and the bad things that happen to us. Pessimists and optimists have a very different explanatory style in how they attribute the causes of success and failure.

Pessimists describe bad things as permanent and pervasive, i.e. any shortcomings, for example, a presentation that goes badly, reflect a fundamental lack of skill that spills over into other activities. Optimists, on the other hand, see the causes of any failings, as temporary and specific. If a presentation goes awry, it was one of those things that can happen, and no big deal.

Conversely when good things happen, pessimists describe them as temporary and specific. Success is attributed to good luck, good luck that is unlikely to be repeated. Optimists see good things as caused by permanent and pervasive factors. Passing an important examination, for example, is explained by advanced intelligence that will have a positive impact on future examinations and other activities.

If our temperament is more "glass half empty than full" then we can learn to move to greater optimism by checking how we describe events and explain the causes. When things go wrong, pessimists think:

- **me**: it must be me making a mistake
- **always**: I keep getting things wrong
- **everything**: I can't do anything right

Next time you experience a set back, shift your mind set to recognise it may be bad luck about a specific situation, and doesn't say much about you as a person.

ARE WE WILLING TO BET ON THE ODDS

Do or do not do. There is no try.

MASTER YODA

We can anticipate failure and accept defeat now.

Or we can plan for success by focusing our time and effort on those activities that will pay off and ignore those with a high risk of failure. Here we evaluate every potential opportunity by asking:

- **what is my personal involvement?** The odds of success are greater when we are personally accountable for the success or failure of the project, and closely involved in the implementation process? If we are at the mercy of others' input, the odds of success are lower?
- **can I control events?** What power and influence do we have in planning, decision making and coordination? Or are we pawns in a bigger game we can't control?
- **can I manage the complexity?** Highly complex projects, requiring an elaborate sequence of activities and coordination of a range of different inputs and interdependencies, have a high risk of failure. Prioritise those simple activities that you can manage

If we bet on those activities we are interested in and passionate about, activities we can coordinate and manage, we improve the odds of success.

SHOULD WE ALLOW THE DICE TO DECIDE

The golden rule is that the dice must be obeyed; however, you still have ultimate control, because you decide when to roll and what options go into the lists. By playing dice, you introduce random selection with a field of possible actions which are of interest to you.

DICE YOUR WAY TO MULTIPLE FUTURES

Sometimes you need to go too far in order to discover just how far you really want to go.

BEN MARSHALL

George Cockcroft, a psychology lecturer in the US in the late 1960s is becoming bored with his life and is exploring ways to break out of his "uptight habitual life". One day, faced by a decision, he lists six options and rolls the die to decide which he should follow. "I started using the dice to challenge myself to do things I didn't dare otherwise do."

Depicted in "The Dice Man", George Cockcroft becomes psychiatrist Luke Rhinehart, who despite his successful practice, attractive wife and lovely children, is having something of a mid-life crisis. He embarks on a life led by the dice. Every life decision should be decided by the throw of the die.

An initial experiment in randomness to break out of familiar habits and routines, Rhinehart soon begins pushing the boundaries to open up unusual experiences and discover new and darker facets of his personality. The novel soon becomes "an amoral rampage" as the philosophy of the dice creates "a frightening and maniac series" of events. Rhinehart's experiments result in psychotic madness rather than a life enhancing journey.

Thirty years later Cockcroft accepts that "dicing" might not be the key to life fulfilment. "Once you get somewhere you were happy you'd be stupid to shake it up any further." But Cockcroft still argues: "it is probable that just the act of listing

six things you might do on a particular day will open up possibilities you would never otherwise considered. Allowing you to replace "what must I do" with "what could I do?"

Can we become a different person by a roll of the dice to follow the random options? Cockcroft laughs: "No. But anybody can still be a lot more people than they think."

"Dice Your Way to Multiple Futures" at Wilderdom.com

"The Dice Man" Luke Rhinehart

"Dicing with life" Tim Adams, 2000, The Observer

HOW TO SAY NO TO SAY YES

Half of the troubles of this life can be traced to saying yes too quickly and not saying no soon enough.

JOSH BILLINGS

"Yes" avoids conflict. It is easy, at least in the short-term, to agree to additional demands. But lots of yes's add up to competing tasks and a lack of focus on what will give us most leverage.

When we review our various commitments over the last month, what was our yes: no ratio? If we're saying yes more than no, the chances are that we are losing clarity about our distinctive contribution.

Of course, if we have too many no's, others might begin to view us as unhelpful and obstructive.

"The Gentle Art of Saying No" Leo Babauta, 2010 at Stepcase Lifehack

DO WE NEED TO BE AS THICK-SKINNED AS JEFFREY ARCHER

In every deliberation, we must consider the impact on the seventh generation…even it requires having skin as thick as the bark of a pine.

GREAT LAW OF THE IROQUOIS

So what if you've made a fool of yourself, dust yourself down and get back on.

JEFFREY ARCHER

Archer has issued a strenuous denial – as good as a signed confession, really!

DES LYNAM

If we're serious about succeeding for the long run, resilience and fortitude to keep going when faced by adversity, ridicule and humiliation may be critical. An unshakeable confidence in our purpose combined with a thick skin seem to be major life assets if we are to survive and thrive.

But a thick skin can detach us from life's realities. And that detachment can easily become a recklessness that assumes that the rules of life don't apply. Rules that Jeffrey Archer didn't think applied.

A peer of the realm, former deputy chairman of the Conservative party, and bestselling novelist, Jeffrey began life modestly. A combination of boundless energy and imaginative CV writing led Jeffrey into the House of Commons at the age of 29. After falling victim to a fraudulent investment scheme and facing likely bankruptcy he resigned his seat and started work on his first best seller," Not a Penny More, Not a Penny Less".

Undeterred by ongoing allegations of shoplifting or plagiarism, Jeffrey advanced a highly successful writing career and then moved back into political life. His "champagne and shepherds pie" parties became legendary among the political elite.

Faced with allegations of sex with a prostitute, Archer then successfully sued the UK tabloid, the "Daily Star" for libel. Several years later, a key witness admitted that he had conspired with Archer to fabricate his alibi. On trial for perjury and perverting the course of justice, Archer was sentenced to four years imprisonment. This judgement also undermined his plans for a political comeback as Lord Mayor of London. In prison, Archer wrote "The Prisoner's Diary", a book he is publicising actively.

We need a thick skin to withstand the slings and arrows of life. But when that thick skin is blocking the kind of feedback that reminds us of our failings and weaknesses we may need to check if our arrogance is going to derail our career.

"The Thick Skinned: It's not all about you" Lybi Ma, 2004, Psychology Today

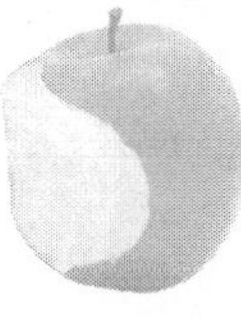

HOW TO IGNORE TBU

Summing up, it is clear the future holds great opportunities. It also holds pitfalls. The trick will be to avoid the pitfalls, seize the opportunities, and get back home by six o'clock.

WOODY ALLEN, MY SPEECH TO THE GRADUATES

In problem solving and planning some issues are relevant but outside our control to address. They are TBU: **true but useless**.

If we're planning any kind of change in life, we will be faced by an array of complex factors others highlight as potential barriers and obstacles. The implicit assumption is that we're foolish to even contemplate tackling the problem.

But just because we can't solve every aspect of the problem, it doesn't mean we can't solve some elements of the problem to make a difference.

When we ignore the "true but useless" we focus on the factors we can control and address.

WHEN TO TAKE CONTROL AND WHEN NOT TO

God, grant me the serenity to accept the things I cannot change, courage to change the things I can, and wisdom to know the difference.

REINHOLD NIEBUHR

The belief that we have control over our lives and able to influence events is important in building resilience. Without this sense that our personal efforts can make a difference we feel vulnerable and helpless. But we cannot control every aspect of life, and the attempt to, can only be a frustrating experience.

It helps if we see control as having two components:

- **Primary** control involves the ability to actually change a situation
- **Secondary** control is the ability to change how we think about a situation

In **primary control** the challenge is using our judgement and applying courage and determination to address the problem. In **secondary control,** our wisdom recognises when we can't change the situation or do much about the problem. Here we find the most positive way to think about the issues. In secondary control we choose our emotional response to the situation.

WHY SPEED IS BETTER THAN PERFECTION

Most problems have either many answers or no answer. Only a few problems have a single answer.

We shouldn't aim to make the perfect decision, all the time, every time.

A prompt decision based on a "guestimate" is often the best tactic to move quickly.

We can waste time collecting and analysing information that will at best, make a modest difference to our decision-making process and at worst, result in lost opportunities.

Speed, based on getting it right 90% of the time, is a better strategy than one that waits to get it right 100% of the time.

Accept that you will make your fair share of wrong decisions. And be ready to take advantage of good luck. Sometimes life throws up opportunities, the kind of opportunities that need to be exploited quickly.

"The loser's guide to getting lucky" Richard Wiseman, 2003, BBC

"Overcoming Perfectionism, The Pursuit of Perfect" Jerry Lopper, 2009 at Suite 101

WHY (SOMETIMES) WE SHOULD PRACTICE DELAY, CONSCIOUSLY

There's nothing to match curling up with a good book when there's a repair job to be done around the house.

JOE RYAN

The time management industry urges us to see any delay as the vice of procrastination. If we delay we are wasting precious moments as time rushes on. Alternatively, delay is the avoidance of our responsibilities. As C Northcote Parkinson admonished us: "Delay is the deadliest form of denial."

And of course, Parkinson was right; at least some of the time.

But is delay always **that bad**?

At times we feel that, although we are really busy and have no time to ourselves, we don't seem to be accomplishing anything of much value. It may be that we're working on the wrong objectives in non productive ways. Or it may be we are not practising the tactics of delay. At times the more value we want to create, the more we need to put off doing some things.

Spending time on tasks of long term importance often involves procrastinating on the short-term, trivial details. Bogged down in the short-term we drown in the details. If we stay focused on detailed to-do lists, we quickly lose sight of the big picture.

Conscious procrastination allows us to learn to become skilled at putting off the minutiae. Often these minor tasks will simply go away. Things change, and they may no longer need to be done at all. Or additional resources become available that make the task easier to complete. And when there is real time pressure we can usually complete a job faster than when time is plentiful.

Using a delaying tactic can be valuable if used consciously, but a career disaster when used unconsciously. It entails strict discipline to consciously delay some of our seemingly important tasks, but it can be a powerful way to commit time to what is really valuable.

"Good and bad procrastination" Paul Graham

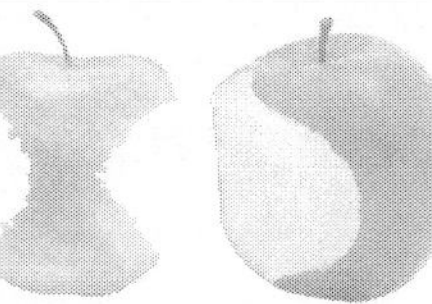

FUTURE

WHY THE 5 MINUTE ROOM RESCUE GETS US STARTED

Shine your sink.

MARLA CILLEY

We know what we need to do. And we're overwhelmed by the scale of the challenge we face. So we postpone activity until we feel more energised. Somehow we never get started and that promising idea or potentially profitable project never gets going.

Imagine a house that is cluttered, messy and dirty. We want a house that is organised, tidy and clean, and we appeal to our family to get organised to have a massive clear out and clean up. But nothing changes.

Marla Cilley, the home organising guru, suggests a different strategy.

Get a kitchen timer and set it for 5 minutes. Then go to the worst room in the house and for 5 minutes do something. 5 minutes isn't so bad. Best of all it makes an immediate impact. We see the benefits and we keep going.

Chip and Dan Heath call this "shrink the change." Break the overall task down into specific chunks and start to tackle each chunk. Rather than feeling overwhelmed by the task, and we do nothing, we make progress step by step.

As Marla Cilley notes: "Things done imperfectly still bless our lives."

"Switch: How to Change Things When Change Is Hard" Chip & Dan Heath

HOW TO MAKE THE FINISH LINE NEARER

To finish the moment, to find the journey's end in every step of the road, is wisdom.

RALPH WALDO EMERSON

When a car wash company introduced a new loyalty card programme, it tried an experiment. One group of customers received a card that after eight stamps entitled them to a free carwash. The second group got a loyalty card that required ten stamps before the free wash, but they were given a "head start". On receiving their card, two stamps had been added.

The goal was the same for both customer groups. Buy eight car washes and you get one free.

A few months later, the carwash firm evaluated their experiment. Less than a fifth of the eight stamp customers had come back for a free car wash. Over a third of the "head start" group had earned a free car wash.

We feel motivated when we feel we've made progress. And we find it difficult to motivate ourselves when we have to begin at the very start.

When we're kick starting a project, rather than focus on the novelty of the challenge, outline any progress that has already been made to indicate how near the project is to the finish line.

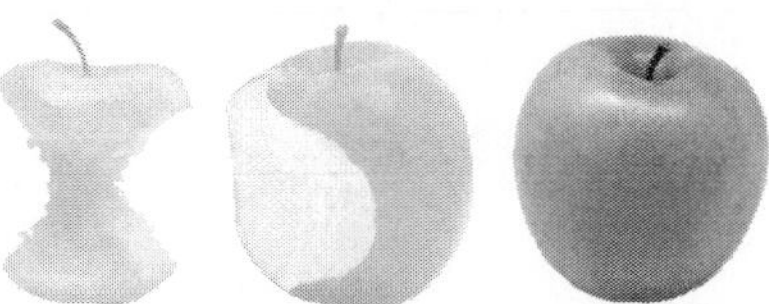

WHO MATTERS AND WHO MINDS

Be who you are and say what you feel, because those who mind don't matter and those who matter don't mind.

DR. SEUSS

We can be held back in our progress in life through an acute sensitivity to others' opinions. This is a life lived through a fear of embarrassment, ridicule and shame. Or it is the life strategy of looking to fulfil others' expectations of how we should live rather than setting our own distinctive agenda.

Others' views and feedback are of course important in providing a reality check on life. But we should be careful we're not worrying too much about the criticisms from those who "mind". In the long-run, they might not "matter".

"Criticism: Taking the Hit" Judith Sills, 2006 Psychology Today

WHY FAILURE IS NEVER FULL OR FINAL

"Henry Ford forgot to put a reverse gear in his first car."

Not every setback is a personal critique of our current effectiveness or a damning indictment of our future potential.

It might be tough but when we treat failure as a valuable teacher, it provides us with the learning to refocus our strategy and tactics.

Failure is inevitable if we attempt anything difficult. Directing our efforts on the easy and trivial won't disappoint, but it won't accomplish anything significant either.

We shouldn't allow the fear of failure deter us from pursuing ambitious goals. Instead we should accept we will experience failure at some point or another, but be sufficiently open minded to gain some important insight that will move us to greater success.

"The Tripping Point Michael McKinney, 2006 Leading Blog

FUTURE

WHY IT'S GOOD TO HAVE FAILURE PARTIES

The important question is not whether you will fail, but when, and above all, what happens next.

ED SMITH

Failure lies concealed in every success, and success in every failure.

ECKHART TOLLE

Presentations, conferences, articles and books showcase success. We all want to hear about what works, discover the reasons and apply the learning. But these success stories are highly selective.

Maybe we should be more open in our discussion of failure. Not the kind of failures that are the outcome of incompetent bungling, but the attempts at experimentation that try to do something better, but didn't work out.

If we look for failure and see it as an exercise in risk taking that is prepared to take on new challenges we might learn something important for future success.

"How failure breeds success" Jena McGregor, 2010
Bloomberg Businessweek

WHAT DO WE DO IF GODOT DOESN'T APPEAR

Yes, in this immense confusion one thing alone is clear. We are waiting for Godot to come.

SAMUEL BECKETT

In Samuel Beckett's play "Waiting for Godot", two tramps Vladimir and Estragon, are hanging around. "Too lazy and incurious to go on a journey in search for meaning", they wait for Godot. To pass time, they eat, sleep, converse, argue, sing, play games, exercise, swap hats, and contemplate suicide - anything "to hold the terrible silence at bay".

Estragon and Vladimir signify life as a period of waiting, waiting for meaning to emerge and make sense of life, and to provide purpose.

What if Godot isn't going to come - and never will? Here we have to find our own personal meaning and purpose.

We can go head long into serious absurdity. Like James Cawley we can devote 10 years of our life to building a full sized replica of the bridge of the Starship Enterprise in our garage. Or we can prove our daughter's school teacher wrong by demonstrating it is possible to write in full the numbers for one to one million (a task that took Martha Drew 5 years and 2, 473 sheets of paper.) Or in the hard-headed world of business we can sign up to a programme of "Six Thinking Hats" to discover that "a bird is different from an aeroplane, although both fly through the air."

Or we can accept life is absurd enough without making things even more ridiculous.

"The Age of Absurdity: Why Modern Life Makes it Hard to be Happy" Michael Foley

"Six big questions to answer" Paul T. P. Wong at ExistentialPsychology.Org

FUTURE

HOW TO LIVE TO BE 100

To know how to grow old is the master-work of wisdom; and one of the most difficult chapters in the great art of living.

HENRI AMIEL

In the early 2000s, the National Geographic Society sent a team of longevity experts to those four parts of the world where people are much more likely to attain the age of 100, in good health, than all other places on earth. In Sardinia, Okinawa, Costa Rica, and Loma Linda, California, Dan Buettner partnered with scientists to examine why the number of centenarians vastly exceeded the statistical average.

Longevity was found to be a function of:

- **genetics;** but only about 25% of the equation
- **diet and exercise;** another 25% of the equation. Virtually all of the centenarians were lean, active, and had a mainly plant-based diet. All ate until they were not hungry - as opposed to eating until they were full; a significant difference ... as the former involves relatively small meals. Their active lives also involved being outside in the sunshine on a daily basis
- **sociology and psychology;** 50% of the long life equation. All were "embedded in respectful, caring social networks, involving family and friendships." The long livers had spent a lifetime investing themselves in these relationships, with time, energy, and emotion. They all lived for the day; had a good sense of humour that tended toward the sardonic. All had a purposeful life, and could tell you in an instant what that purpose was. The centenarians were also spiritual; they all took time at least once a week, more commonly daily, to reflect on the gift of life, and how wondrous it can be. None prayed for a "long life," but most arose with a simple prayer each morning: "thank you God, for another day"

Success in life isn't just about its length. Breadth is important. But the factors that make for a broad and fulfilling life also seem to add to our years.

"The Nine Secrets of a Long Life" Josh Dean, 2009, National Geographic

"How to live to be 100" Dan Buettner At TedCom

"The pros and cons of increasing longevity" George Dvorsky & Anders Sandberg, 2007 at Sentient Developments

WHAT DID JANE TOMLINSON DISCOVER ABOUT THE LUXURY OF TIME

Death doesn't arrive with the prognosis.

JANE TOMLINSON

Jane, a mother of three from Leeds was diagnosed with incurable, advanced metastatic breast cancer in August 2000. The disease spread was extensive and the prognosis was for her to survive six months. Over a seven year period, Jane fought through numerous courses of chemotherapy and various drug regimes despite also developing chronic heart disease.

During the period up to her death in 2007, Jane took on a series of apparently impossible challenges for someone undergoing chemotherapy treatment. She completed:

- a full Ironman (4km swim, 180 kilometre bike ride and marathon)
- the London Marathon three times
- three London Triathlons
- three long distance bike rides, including John O' Groats to Lands End, Rome to Home and her final huge challenge, a 6782km ride across America

Jane received numerous awards for her efforts including an MBE and subsequently a CBE by the Queen, being recognised twice at the Sportswoman of the Year awards and being voted the most inspirational woman in Britain in 2003.

Jane's book "The Luxury of Time is, as one reviewer wrote: "beautifully written, painfully honest, heartbreaking at times but uplifting at others." And another: "I felt less afraid of the future and excited about getting on and doing things."

How we think about mortality and the prospects of our own death shapes the way we live now.

"The Luxury of Time" Jane Tomlinson
"I have the right to live the way I want" 2005, The Guardian

HOW TO THINK ABOUT DEATH

I'm not afraid of death. It's the stake one puts up in order to play the game of life.

JEAN GIRAUDOUX

It is not easy to die a happy death. To die a happy death, one has to live a meaningful life. To live a meaningful life, one has to realise his true worth and create values. None of us know when we will die. While we can't decide how or when we will die, we can certainly decide how we should live our lives. Since we need to die at some time, isn't it better to die knowing that we have lived a meaningful life?

DL HOH

We view death in different ways.

For T S Eliot, death is simply another fact; "birth, copulation and death; that's the facts when you get to brass tacks".

For Dylan Thomas, death is a battle to be fought; "do not go gentle into that good night".

For Marcus Aurelius, death is an acceptance of the wonder of life; "go to your rest with good grace, as an olive falls in its season with a blessing for the earth that bore it, and a thanksgiving to the tree that gave it life."

We know we will die, and the prospect creates anxiety. The fear of death is of course a healthy instinct; it's hard-wired within us to ensure our evolutionary survival. (Imagine a society in which individuals didn't worry about death). Our fear is partly:

- our worries about how we die and the fear of any distress and pain or of "being a burden" to others
- our concern for our loved ones and their future without us
- the uncertainty of the unknown. Is death really it? Or is there an after-life? If there is, what will it be like?
- the sense of loss of life's opportunities and missing out on what's going to happen next

We each think of death in our different ways. But we all like to think that when the time comes we "have a good death". And twelve principles have been identified to guide a "good death".

Perhaps the only strategy, rather than allow death to become a preoccupation, is to see a "good death" as part of a "good life." The death of a young child is especially tragic because of that huge sense of unfulfilled possibilities and the waste of potential.

If our fear of death has any value, maybe it is when it focuses us on today and tomorrow and the life we want to live to ensure it is with "good grace".

"Can we predict how we will die?" at GoToQuiz

"Twelve Principles of a Good Death" Kirsti Dyer, 2006 at DyingAbout.com

"BBC vote on the "bucket list": things to do before we die" at BeforeYouDie.com

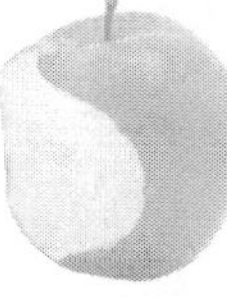

FUTURE

WHAT CAN WE LEARN FROM THE DEATHS OF PHILOSOPHERS

To philosophise is to learn how to die.

CICERO

Socrates, condemned to death, unjustly, by the Athenian democracy is forced to swallow the hemlock. But there is no rage in Socrates; he could have escaped; he chooses not to escape. He swallows the hemlock, he is thinking all the time of other people. He washes his body to save the women the trouble. He jokes kindly with his jailer, he doesn't rail against him. And he sits and accepts the loving companionship of his friends as he drinks the hemlock. There is no rage, there's a big accepting kindness. And that was not just because Socrates got a blast from God at the end, but because his whole life had been about facing the unknown, preparing for this moment, sitting loose to life and ego, and emptying himself compassionately in dialogue with other people. And that endless discipline throughout his life enabled him to face this unjust death.

KAREN ARMSTRONG

If we can learn from anyone about the meaning of life and death, maybe we should start with the lives and deaths of the big thinkers, the philosophers who devoted their lives to the analysis of life's puzzles and paradoxes, and how they ended their lives. As Montaigne argued: "My wager is that in learning how to die, we might also be taught to live."

Seneca wasn't just theorizing when he said: "they live badly who do not know how to die well". Seneca knew what he was talking about. All but banished to death by the emperor Caligula in AD 39, banished by Claudius on a charge of adultery, he was forced to commit suicide by Nero in 65.

As "The Book of Dead Philosophers", detailing the last hours of 190 philosophers, recounts: not every philosopher has died philosophically. La Mettrie died of ingestion brought on by eating a huge quantity of truffle pate. Nietzsche began his descent into oblivion after kissing a horse. Whilst some philosophers graced their last moments with dignity, others' deaths were marked by absurdity. Some died peacefully and at rest, others horribly and in delirium.

A near death experience seemed to have changed logical positivist Freddie Ayer who “died twice”. The first time after choking on a piece of salmon he told a tale of celestial cabinet ministers and a red light that rules the universe. His wife claimed “he has got so much nicer since he died”.

Death is a signal to us of our limitations. It is the most powerful prompt of life’s constraints and necessities to highlight our small place in the grander scheme of things. Unlike Caesar we do not have a slave whispering the admonition: “Remember, Caesar! Thou art mortal!” Instead we have death to remind us of the limitations of our power and influence.

To philosophise about our death is to learn humility about today and courage about tomorrow.

“The Book of Dead Philosophers” Simon Critchley
“Near Death Experiences of Atheists” at NearDeath.com

WHY WE SHOULD ATTEND THE LAST LECTURE

Never underestimate the importance of having fun. I'm dying and I'm having fun. And I'm going to keep having fun every day, because there's no other way to play it....Having fun for me is like a fish talking about the importance of water. I don't know how it is like not to have fun...

RANDY PAUSCH

"Really Achieving Your Childhood Dreams" - also known as "The Last Lecture"- was a lecture given in 2007 by Randy Pausch, a Carnegie Mellon University computer science professor. The talk was based on an ongoing series of lectures where top academics were asked to think deeply about what matters to them, and then give a hypothetical "final talk," i.e., "what wisdom would you try to impart to the world if you knew it was your last chance?"

Randy Pausch told his audience that he had been diagnosed with terminal pancreatic cancer, in all likelihood, with only three to six months left to live. On stage with slides of his CT scans displaying his tumours Randy was upbeat, energetic, often cheerfully, and darkly funny.

"The Last Lecture" discusses everything Pausch wanted his children to know after his cancer had taken his life. He constantly stresses that we should strive to have fun in everything we do in living life to its fullest because we never know when it may end.

Randy's lecture and book have become a phenomenon, celebrating the dreams we all have and how to make them a reality.

To be cliché, death is a part of life and it's going to happen to all of us. I have the blessing of getting a little bit of advance notice and I am able to optimize my use of time down the home stretch.

RANDY PAUSCH

"The Last Lecture" Randy Pausch
"Achieving your childhood dreams" at YouTube
"Chasing Daylight: How my forthcoming death transformed my life" Eugene O'Kelly

FANTASISING ABOUT POSSIBILITIES

"One of the most tragic things I know about human nature is that all of us tend to put off living. We are all dreaming of some magical rose garden over the horizon - instead of enjoying the roses blooming outside our windows today.

DALE CARNEGIE

In our minds everything is possible. The compelling message of the self help gurus is that what we think we can achieve. Here we dream of what might be to visualise the successful future me, and take "massive action" to transform our lives. The only limits to life success are the constraints of our imagination.

But what if our imagination about the future, like our memory of the past, incorporates a design flaw, and what we think will make us happy in future doesn't when we arrive there.

Fantasy has the potential to transport us from now to tomorrow to create a new world of opportunity. This is the power of the "active imagination" to translate our inner creativity into outer success. But fantasy can also be a projection of "should be's" that become the fabulist project that can only disappoint.

This section reviews the dynamics of imagination and dreams, and of expectations and entitlements to suggest that small gains today may be better than thoughts of big action tomorrow.

IS THE ANTICIPATION MACHINE WORKING PRODUCTIVELY

The human brain is an 'anticipation machine' and 'making the future' is the most important thing it does.

DANIEL DENNETT

Anticipation is a powerful asset. It allows us to look into the future and imagine "what might be". Anticipation is evolution's gift of energy and time to ensure we prepare for tomorrow's challenges.

Like most of evolution's gifts it comes with a price. Deployed positively, anticipation equips us for new life tasks. Deployed negatively, it can either:

- create unrealistic expectations of how the future will transform our current life situation
- flood us with anxiety about our capacity to cope

When we move from the joyful prospect of future happiness to expectations that won't be met (and only disappoint) or put us under fearful pressure, "the anticipation machine" is no longer working productively for us.

The trick is mind management, and to walk the line between the optimism that "things can only get better" and the pessimism that "if we don't expect much we won't be disappointed."

"Kinds of Minds: The Origins Of Consciousness" Daniel Dennett

Mind management as "Explanatory Style" at Wikipedia

"Mythbusting myths on pessimism" Titus Armand at Project Armand

WHY POSSIBILITY THINKING MAY BE COUNTER PRODUCTIVE

This is the despair of possibility. Possibility appears to the self ever greater and greater, more and more things become possible, because nothing becomes actual.

SOREN KIERKEGAARD

Under the rules of Empowerment, you were the sovereign master of your fate and could defeat any and all obstacles in life.

STEVE SALERNO

Because "we are all brilliant" we should "awaken the giant within" to unleash our inner potential to be everything we can and should be in life. This is the empowering message of the self help and actualisation movement. With a five step programme available for download at only $99, we will master the key skills to self growth to realise our latent capabilities to achieve the kind of success we deserve. Imagine the possibilities!

Kierkegaard, the gloomy Dane, suggests that a wise life balances necessity and possibility. Too much necessity - the awareness of life's constraints - and we are trapped up in the pressures of our current circumstances. But too much possibility and we embark on a fantasy life in which, in believing that anything and everything is attainable, we fail to make the practical decisions that make genuine progress.

The existentialists like to remind us that our freedom lies in choice. And in selecting some options, other life options are closed down. Everything is possible but only in the imagination of our fantasy. To live is to choose and take responsibility for our decisions and the consequences of our actions.

"SHAM: how the self help movement made America helpless" Steve Salerno

"Kierkegaard on Necessity and Possibility" Zach Sherwin at Arete

DID NAPOLEON HILL THINK AND GROW RICH

Everything your mind can conceive, you can achieve. NAPOLEON HILL

His book "Think and Grow Rich" sold 30 million copies, is the sixth best-selling business book of all time, and is still in popular demand; author Napoleon Hill pioneered the self help industry. From Norman Vincent Peale, Tony Robbins, The Secret to Paul McKenna, all have been inspired by Hill's fundamental concept.

Hill, struggling to escape an impoverished background in the Blue Ridge mountains of Virginia, entered the world of journalism, gaining access to steel magnate, Andrew Carnegie, at the time the wealthiest person in the world. Hill discovered that Carnegie believed there is a simple formula of success. "It's a shame that each new generation must find the way to success by trial and error when the principles are really clear-cut."

Impressed by his enthusiasm, Carnegie commissioned Hill to interview over 500 successful men and women, including John Rockefeller, Theodore Roosevelt, Thomas Edison, Henry Ford, FW Woolworth and William Wrigley, giants of political and business life. Hill devoted the next 20 years of his life to research "the laws of success", setting down his fifteen principles in the eight volume "Law of Success". Planning to open the world's first University of Success, the Great Depression thwarted his plans and Hill began his master work "Think and Grow Rich".

Accepting that "Think and Grow Rich", written in the late 30s, reflects the cultural mores of the time, its racism and sexism is still remarkable, not to mention the bizarre theory of sexual transmutation: "There never has been, and never will be a great leader, builder, or artist lacking in this driving force of sex."

But given the massive impact of the book, what of the man himself? Did his thinking produce great success?

Hill's own life is not one of consistent and sustained success. He covered up the death of a bellhop accidentally shot by his boss, a coal mine manager. When one of his business associates (a man with a German accent) once threatened to sue him, Hill reported him to the FBI as a suspected enemy agent. The man ended up spending most of the First World War in a detention centre. Hill's own son described him as "unscrupulous, holier-than-thou, two timing, double crossing, good for nothing".

But did he achieve his goal of financial success? He abandoned his first wife because of a lack of money, despite his wife's family money bailing him out of business failure. Marrying a younger woman, Rosa Lee Beeland, she later divorced him, taking him to the cleaners in the process. Ironically Rosa later produced her own self help book "How to Attract Men and Money"; she knew what she was writing about.

In a moment of rare humility, Hill observed: "I had spent the better portion of my life in chasing a rainbow. I had begun to place myself in the category of charlatans who offers a remedy of failure which they, themselves, cannot successfully apply."

As one observer commented, the lesson from Hill's life is: "Don't waste your time chasing a rainbow. Package it and sell it to others. Then you'll find a pot of gold"; advice that was to become the business model of the self improvement industry.

When we begin to think that there is a money making secret that will give us it all, it's worth asking what is the "all"?

"A Lifetime of Riches: the biography of Napoleon Hill" M Ritt and K Landers

WHAT ARE THE SHOULD BE'S

The 'what should be' never did exist, but people keep trying to live up to it. There is no 'what should be,' there is only what is.

LENNY BRUCE

Lenny Bruce, the edgy stand up comic of the early 1960s, based his humour on "pointing out the differences between the way things are and the way they should be." Bruce, unconstrained by what "should be", developed an improvisational style to "blow, blow, blow everything that came into his head just as it came into his head with nothing censored, nothing translated, nothing mediated."

Obsessed with attacking the hypocrisy of the gap between the "should be" and the "what is" of political, social and organisational life, Bruce pioneered a new wave of comedy.

What is your "should be"?

Our should be's typically are when we:

- attempt to fulfil our own expectations when we've forgotten where these expectations came from and why we think they will make us happier
- respond to others' expectations of who we should be and to live other people's lives for them, allowing their aspirations to become our ambitions
- operate within a moral code handed down by others when we haven't worked through what it means for us personally

It is easy for our plans for the future to become a set of "should be's". It's worth asking why they "should be" to remind ourselves of what is important to our future.

WAS WALTER MITTY AVOIDING SOME AWKWARD TRUTHS

Fantasies are more than substitutes for unpleasant reality; they are also dress rehearsals, plans. All acts performed in the world begin in the imagination.

BARBARA GRIZZUTI HARRISON

"Captain Mitty stood up and strapped on his huge Webley-Vickers automatic. "It's forty kilometres through hell, sir," said the sergeant. Mitty finished one last brandy. "After all," he said softly, "what isn't?" The pounding of the cannon increased; there was a rat-tat-tatting of machine guns, and from somewhere came the menacing pocketa-pocketapocketa of the new flame-throwers. Walter Mitty walked to the door of the dugout humming "Auprés de Ma Blonde." He turned and waved to the sergeant. "Cheerio!" he said."

The fictional character created by James Thurber is a meek, unassuming accountant who daydreams of an exciting and heroic life. In Thurber's story, which takes place over a single day, Mitty drives his wife to town for a shopping trip, while dreaming that he is a Navy pilot flying through the worst storms in 20 years. The rest of the mundane day incorporates a series of daydreams in which Mitty also fantasises that he is a famous surgeon, notorious murderer on trial for his life and a war-time general. In the final daydream, he faces a firing squad alone without a blindfold, enigmatically smoking a cigarette, "inscrutable to the last."

Thurber himself was a fantasist. Blinded in childhood in one eye by an arrow while playing with his brother, and unable to participate in games and sports, and missing out on a university degree because of his visual impairment, he found imaginative escape in his writing. But Thurber's characters (Walter Mitty wasn't the only one) indicate the potential hazard of fantasy. None of them succeeded in changing their life situation for the better.

Fantasy is a key element of the active imagination that underpins much creative achievement. Fantasy allows us to go from the day-to-day routine, stuck in today's pressures and priorities, to dream of new worlds and imagine how life can be different.

But we've all encountered those fabulists who suffer from the Walter Mitty syndrome, individuals whose fantasies allow them to escape from their day to day

lives and whose life adventures range from the extravagant tales of an aristocratic lineage, alien abductions or SAS expeditions to the more frequent exaggerations of falsified university degrees, friendship with a famous celebrity or the possession of psychic gifts.

Imaginative fantasy has power when it moves us towards purposeful action that changes us and our situation. Imaginative fantasy that remains in dreamland has the potential to keep us stuck in thinking about the entitlements of what "should be" rather than face life "as is". When fantasy hits reality it creates a sense of disillusionment and disappointment.

If we're preoccupied by what we might be rather than address the reality of what we are doing to advance our goals, we should check our Walter Mitty index.

"Faking It: People who live a lie" Andrew Wilson, The Independent, 2006

"The courage to be ourselves" at Personal Development Coach

"What makes us so special?" Mary Jaksch at Good Life Zen

DO WE KNOW WHAT WE WANT

If I'd known what it would have been like to have it all I might have been willing to settle for less.

LILY TOMLIN

Our imagination generates possibilities of what we may become and achieve in our future life. But fantasy is an "illusive will of the wisp". Our fantasy future typically includes variations of:

- greater power and influence to "call the shots"
- improved status to gain the respect and admiration of others
- higher levels of financial security and material comfort to enjoy the good things of life
- greater interpersonal attractiveness and charm to widen our popularity and improve our sex life

These are vague and idealised impressions of a future life that is in some way bigger and better than our current life situation. But until these dreams are translated into clear and grounded goals it isn't clear how they help make progress. As Mark Twain observes: "I can teach anybody how to get what they want out of life. The problem is that I can't find anybody who can tell me what they want."

Even worse, as Daniel Gilbert points out, what we think in theory might make us happier often doesn't in reality. Our current fantasy isn't in fact that good a predictor of what in fact does make us happy when we reach that future.

If our "fantasy" of the future becomes a practical programme of action, based on a realistic insight into the dynamics of our happiness and success, so much the better. But if our fantasy remains a set of wishful dreams, we may be frustrated.

"What will make you happy?" Eric Jaffe, Smithsonian 2007

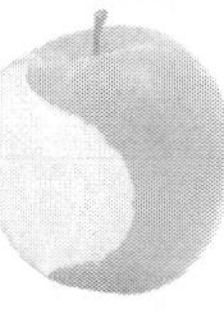

WHAT WILL IT BE LIKE IF

It's a poor sort of memory that only works backwards. LEWIS CARROLL

We plan our life future and we ask: "what will it be like if?" And we imagine different scenarios. Because we don't know if our fiancé will be a wonderful husband, whether the trip to the Great Barrier Reef will be worth the cost, or the job we see in the newspaper is a fantastic career opportunity, we have to imagine.

Of course we can do the research. We can meet our fiancé's parents, check what other visitors to the Reef said, and we can look up the recruiting company on the internet, but it won't provide a definitive answer to predict exactly how we will feel in this future.

Imagination helps us fill in the gaps in our knowledge, and is a powerful function to look into the future. But just as our memory lets us down about the past, our imagination incorporates some design flaws that make it difficult to get it right about the future. Our imagination forecasts how life will be. So why when we get there isn't it often as we anticipated?

Mark Twain shrewdly suggested: "You can't depend on your eyes when your imagination is out of focus." Our imagination has to walk a fine line between:

- the fantasy of our best expectations being fulfilled
- the fearful pessimism that nothing ever turns out how we hope

And if our eyes are out of focus today we shouldn't expect our imagination to get it right tomorrow.

"The science of happiness: a talk with Daniel Gilbert" at Edge: The Third Culture

"Strategic optimism and defensive pessimism" at www.wellesley.edu/Psychology/Norem/Quiz/quiz.html

HOW TO FANTASISE WELL

We can do, have, and be exactly what we wish. TONY ROBBINS

Classic positive thinking suggests that the major barrier to life success and fulfilment is the limit we set on our dreams and goals. Focusing on the problems that lie ahead, we constrain our options about possibilities. Instead we should use the power of our dreams to picture our future success.

Is this correct?
Researcher Gabriele Oettingen at the University of Pennsylvania examined how people faced four different challenges: finding a job, finding a partner, passing an exam and undergoing surgery.

She measured how people in each of the four different situations fantasised about a positive outcome and how much they expected a positive outcome. If fantasies reflect our hope about what will happen in future, expectations indicate our past experiences of success and failure. The researchers found that those who spent more time fantasising about a positive outcome in fact did worse in the four challenges. Those who "entertained more negative future fantasies were more likely to have achieved their goals; but only when combined with positive expectations of success."

Gabriele Oettingen proposes the different strategies we adopt when thinking about future problems:

1. **indulge**, here we imagine a positive vision of the problem being solved
2. **dwell** in which we think about the negative aspects of the current situation
3. **contrast** to first imagine a positive vision, then think about the negative aspects of reality

The contrast strategy seems to the most effective in encouraging us to take action, but only when our expectations of success are high. "There's a good reason why we need to rub our noses in the difference between fantasy and reality": we avoid bringing fantasy and reality together because it's uncomfortable.

Mental contrasting brings us out of our fantasy world to ask the difficult question: is this a goal we really want to pursue? If we only fantasise about the positive

outcomes we don't do the hard work of committing to the goals that will help us bridge the gap from our current reality to where we want to be.

If our hopes for a better future are based on big dreams, positive affirmations and a collage of fantasy photographs of success, we may need to shift to a strategy in which contrast replaces indulgence.

"Success! Why Expectations Beat Fantasies" at PsyBlog, 2011

"The Positive Side of Negative Thinking" Ken Ward at Trans4Mind

WHAT IS THE STUFF THAT DREAMS ARE MADE OF

The interpretation of dreams is the royal road to a knowledge of the unconscious activities of the mind.

SIGMUND FREUD

Dreams are answers to questions we haven't yet figured out how to ask.

X-FILES

Although dreams are bizarre and otherworldly, they are as likely to be moulded by mundane, humdrum and everyday activities as by life-changing events.

ROGER HIGHFIELD

Why do we dream? Do our dreams provide important insights that illuminate our past, indicate potential dangers in the present, or foretell our future? Or are our dreams simply the random by-product of our brains conducting a nightly back up to consolidate our memories?

In our daily lives, everything - at least for the most part - flows in an orderly and organised way. But, at night, when we sleep, our dreams conjure up images and impressions that sometimes make no sense. We are with strange people in unusual locations, doing things that defy logic. Sometimes the dreams are enjoyable excursions into a pleasant and comforting different world. Other dreams are the nightmares of danger and dread that take us into the territory of terror.

So why do we dream? The theories:

Dreams protect sleep. Even as we sleep, our sub-conscious is playing out deep-seated desires and wishes. If fully experienced we would be woken from our slumber. Dreams are the brain's ways of protecting our sleep. For Sigmund Freud, these dreams provide a big clue into the dynamics of our lives. Because nothing happens by chance, the content of our dreams is highly revealing. A dream of a lost handbag is never simply that. Through the interpretation of these dreams, important truths about our deepest fears and motivations are revealed to provide critical insights into our lives.

Dreams remind us of something important that our day to day consciousness is overlooking. This was Freud's rival, Carl Jung's view: the "issues, concerns and even dangers in our everyday experiences" are often ignored. In dreams, events that we have neglected in the day are given the opportunity to surface at night. Here, dreams are a kind of wake up call, a letter the unconscious part of our mind posts to our conscious brain to tell us something important we may be forgetting.

Dreams **help solve our problems.** When we dream our brains are busy consolidating our memories of the day, connecting them to our past experiences as well as our future aspirations to construct a narrative that helps us make sense of the issues we face. Dreams are the outcome of a process in which our brains review the day's experiences, edit the important issues and inform us of key priorities. The bizarre nature of our dreams may not feel like any specific problem has been solved, but without these dreams, we would find it difficult to keep on top of the challenges we face.

Dreams are the **outcome of random brain activity.** Our brains while we sleep don't stop working. Faced with a barrage of impulses throughout the night we have to find a way of making sense of this confusing stimuli; dreams are the weird stories we experience from the fragments our brain generates. And as a variation to this theory we **dream to forget**. To minimise any potential information overload, and the risk of combining unrelated data to make associations that might interfere with our memories, dreaming is the brain's solution to avoid making bizarre connections that would interfere with our lives the next day.

Dream theories overlap and also compete. The more intuitive of us identify with the meaning and purpose that dreams may provide. Of course some dreams are a bewildering and inexplicable series of images. But over time we feel there must be patterns that tell us something about our past, our present or even our future. Dreams seem to want to tell us something, even if we don't know what it is.

If we are in the community of hard headed scientists we are more inclined to think that dreams are little more than the "whirring" of data processing as our brains use downtime night time sleep to consolidate the day's experiences. The output may be entertaining or terrifying, and often weird, but of no significance.

As one reviewer summarised: "it's fair to say that most academic psychologists and clinicians would agree that we don't know why we dream and what our dreams mean." In the absence of a definitive view of dreams, their meaning and impact on our lives, the only sensible course of action is of course to combine critical scrutiny and open mindedness

As Freud himself observed, "Sometimes a cigar is just a cigar". Not every dream has symbolic meaning. Sometimes dreams are haphazard sequences of stuff from the physiology of a combination of too much wine, cheese and chocolate. However it would be foolish to ignore completely the patterns of our dreams.

Of course we can interpret our dreams based on our current mood to generate any explanation, but if there is a recurring theme (fear, escape, aggression) there may be reason; maybe our emotional system is creating a scenario for our rational minds to tell us something important.

"Dream theories" Joe Griffin at Why We Dream
"Freud's Approach to Dreams" at ThinkQuest
"The Jungian Method of Dream Analysis" Michael Catley, 2009, Suite 101
"How to remember our dreams" at Wikihow
"Over-interpreting our dreams" at PsyBlog, 2011

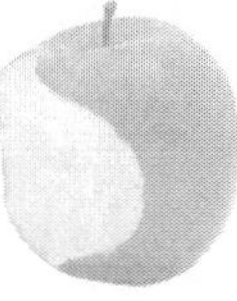

HOW JUNG USED THE POWER OF ACTIVE IMAGINATION

The great person is only an actor playing out their ideal.

FRIEDRICH NIETZSCHE

Imagination is more important than knowledge. For knowledge is limited to all we now know and understand, while imagination embraces the entire world, and all there ever will be to know and understand.

ALBERT EINSTEIN

Carl Jung, troubled and depressed by his break up with Sigmund Freud, the founder of psychoanalysis, began to engage with the impulses and images of his unconscious. Here he experienced an "incessant stream of fantasies", a drama in which he encountered visions of individuals, mysterious characters from history - Ka, Elijah, Philemon, Salome - with whom he began to converse.

I caught sight of two figures, an old man with a white beard and a beautiful young girl. I summoned up my courage and approached them as though they were real people, and listened attentively to what they told me.

Jung found himself, through this internal dialogue, asking questions and receiving wisdom that he didn't have, gaining new and creative insights and possibilities about himself and his life.

This is active imagination and the willingness to explore our interior drama in which we begin a dialogue with the intuitive aspects of our mind, those areas we rarely discover through rational analysis. This isn't self indulgent rumination in which we sit passively watching the film of our future life played out as a projection of vague dreams of who we might be. Instead it's an active process in which we are the Director of the film in constant communication with the screen play writer and actors.

Through the power of active imagination, we identify new facets of our character and personality. As Carl Jung observed: "who looks outside, dreams; who looks inside, awakes." When fantasy is based on what might be "out there", based on others' expectations, we become disillusioned. When our fantasy arises out of our own creativity we identify new possibilities in life.

"Memories, Dreams, Reflections" Carl Jung
"Jung's active imagination" Gary Lachman at Reality Sandwich
"The power of Imagining", Bernadette Lancefield, 2011 at Suite 101

FUTURE

WHY WE SHOULDN'T WORRY TOO MUCH ABOUT OUR PASSION

If there is no passion in your life, then have you really lived? Find your passion, whatever it may be. Become it, and let it become you and you will find great things happen for you, to you and because of you.

T. ALAN ARMSTRONG

The Passion Trap: the more emphasis you place on finding work you love, the more unhappy you become when you don't love every minute of the work you have.

CAL NEWPORT

The message is relentless: discover and live your passion. Our passion is that life purpose that galvanizes our time and effort. Our passion is that awesome energy which transforms our life situation from "getting by" to "thriving and flourishing".

But what if we don't know what this passion is? What if we don't even know where to start looking? And what if we suspect there isn't that much we can ever get that passionate about?

As Cal Newport points out there is pressure to find this passion, "a mysterious Platonic form waiting for us to discover." But this passion is not Steve Martin's special purpose. And the more emphasis we place on finding our passion the greater the pressure we put on ourselves to be fulfilled and happy, and the more miserable we become. This is the passion trap.

Rather than discovering our passion, perhaps we have to create it. And it is created through:

- curiousity and courage to expose ourselves to the full flow of life experience
- the hard work of "doing" to experiment and evaluate and identify what does and doesn't work for us

Passion of course matters. Enthusiastic commitment to deploy our fundamental talents and skills is of course more rewarding than the dull lethargy of half-hearted effort.

But if we're looking to "uncover some magical pursuit that unmistakably sings to our soul" we may have to wait a while. Passion isn't an energy out there we can discover. Instead it is the outcome of experience and endeavour when we connect the skills we've built to something that is worthwhile and enduring.

"The Passion Trap" Cal Newport at Study Hacks 2010

"The Minimalist's Guide to Cultivating Passion" Cal Newport at Zen Habits

"The passion for passions" Oliver Burkeman, 2009, The Guardian

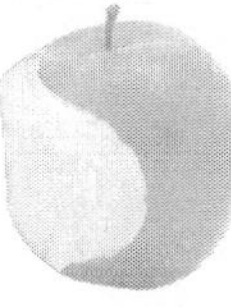

FUTURE

HOW ACCURATE ARE OUR EMOTIONAL FORECASTS

Reports of a hurricane are unfounded.

MICHAEL FISH

When we think about the future we make an "emotional forecast". In our life choices we are placing bets on what will make us more or less happy in future. And because we're rational we place bets on those options that we know will make us happier.

What if our capacity to forecast our future happiness is faulty?

As Daniel Gilbert outlines we're not very good emotional forecasters about our future selves; we consistently get it wrong.

Bizarre as it sounds we don't really know what will make our future selves happy.

It's worth checking therefore that we're not creating an imaginary future that sets expectations of a happy life that can't be fulfilled.

"Stumbling on Happiness" Daniel Gilbert

"Daniel Gilbert's views on happiness" at Positive Psychology Resources

"Is the pursuit of happiness futile?" Jon Gertner, Health and Energy, 2003

WHY IT'S GOOD TO ASK

Before we set our hearts too much on anything, let us examine how happy are those who already possess it. DUC DE LA ROCHEFOUCAULD

We can't do what we'd really like to do - namely travel through time, pay a visit to our future selves and see how happy those selves are - and so we imagine the future instead of actually going there. But we can travel in the dimensions of space, and the chances are pretty good that somewhere there is another human being who is actually experiencing the future event that we are merely thinking about.

DANIEL GILBERT

When Doris Day sang "que sera sera: the future's not ours to see" she was only half right. We don't know the future. But we still want some insight into what lies ahead.

We imagine what life will be like in future. But we accept our imaginative powers are limited. What we think now will make us happy doesn't always make us happy when we get to that future.

When our imagination fails, we can either rely on the "nutty methods" or we can ask others who have been there and done it. Rather than making assumptions about will or won't make us happy we can ask those we respect and trust:

- are you happy now?
- what contributed most to your happiness?
- what major life lesson would you share?

Rather than imagine **"what will it be like"** we can ask those **"what was it like"** to draw on their real life experience and inform our choices about the future.

"Pleasure by proxy" Craig Lambert, Harvard Magazine, 2010

WHY ONE PLAN LED TO THE BAY OF PIGS AND ANOTHER TO THE SEA OF TRANQUILLITY

During his brief presidency, John F. Kennedy had the preposterous idea that the CIA could topple the government of Cuba and the equally foolish notion that the U.S. could put a man on the moon before 1970. One plan led to the Bay of Pigs, the other to the Sea of Tranquillity.

JEFFREY KLUGER

What made the difference?
Worried about Soviet plans to move into the U.S.'s "backyard", the Kennedy administration embarked on an attempt to overthrow the Castro regime. The result: a humiliating defeat at the Bay of Pigs. Stupidity? No, the operation's planners included some of the smartest people in America at the time. The administration failed because they allowed groupthink to mismanage the forces of disagreement, debate and conflict in planning the mission.

Groupthink was the dynamic behind the Bay of Pigs fiasco. Groupthink is the phenomenon which arises when teams work together but there is a need to preserve harmony. In groupthink, shared optimism about a successful outcome becomes wishful thinking.

Unlike the Bay of Pigs adventure, Kennedy's 1961 commitment to put a man on the moon by the end of the decade was realised: the eleventh Apollo space mission saw Neil Armstrong and Buzz Aldrin walk on the moon on July 20 1969.

The NASA undertaking was the coordination of a sequence of projects, with Mercury and Gemini, the precursors of Apollo, clearly defined programmes with specific goals, with opportunities to experiment, test and evaluate before progressing to the next phase. Mistakes were made, but the learning was identified to keep advancing knowledge and expertise.

Optimism about future success is important, but it's worth checking if this optimism is based on a fantasy we're sharing with others, or grounded in a practical and systematic plan of action.

WHY MESSY IMPROVEMENT MAY BE BETTER THAN MASSIVE ACTION

The path to success is to take massive, determined action.

ANTHONY ROBBINS

Anthony Robbins suggests we go beyond the limits of the possible by taking "massive action". This is self-improvement as dreaming big dreams and setting ourselves extraordinary goals. Here, presumably once we've attended one of Robbins' seminars, bought the full DVD collection and purchased the range of his nutrition products and are now wearing a Q-Link bracelet, we're good to go to begin a revolutionary transformation of our life.

An appealing prospect. Who doesn't want to be much happier, richer, popular and successful - quickly and easily?

This is the fantasy of personal change that flies in the face of psychological realities. As Oliver Burkeman notes: "we ought to consider changing our ideas about change....The reality is we change when we make small, incremental adjustments, to tolerate imperfection and bumpy progress, and not to throw in the towel in frustration the moment something starts to go wrong.... Modest action takes more guts than massive action. But it has the inestimable advantage that it really works."

Each of us in our own way wants a better life. The issue is one of tactics. The massive action of the self help gurus promises much but disappoints. Maybe the tactics that accept what is pretty much unchangeable but commits to what we can change, albeit with difficulty and the discipline of hard won habits is a smarter plan of action.

"Help!: How to Become Slightly Happier and Get a Bit More Done" Oliver Burkemann

"What You Can Change and What You Can't: Learning to Accept What You Are" Martin Seligman

"Close Your Eyes And Write A Cheque: Anthony Robbins and your inner dolphin" at NewMatilda

FUTURE

WHY WE HAVE TO WALK A FINE LINE

Reality is merely an illusion, although a very persistent one.

ALBERT EINSTEIN

Our experience of the world - how we see it, remember it and imagine it - is a mixture of stark reality and comforting illusion.

DANIEL GILBERT

If we experienced life exactly as it is, we would find it tough. We don't have to agree with Hobbes that it is "solitary, poor, nasty, brutish and short", but unless we never watch world news, we recognise there is no shortage of reasons to be miserable about the current and future lot of mankind.

But if we experienced life as we would want it to be, we would become unstuck quickly. If our progress in life is based on the assumption that all is "Mozart, sweetness and light", that we will always get what we want, and that others will fall in line with our expectations, we will be disappointed.

This is the fine line between reality and illusion. Too much reality and life is a hard place. Too much illusion and we lose contact with life "as is" and the practical problems we need to confront and tackle.

Optimists who filter out the bad news to accentuate the positives can do well in life. This is Mark Twain's law: "All you need in this life is ignorance and confidence; then success is sure." But there is good reason to believe that pessimists can also do quite well. The optimal strategy may be a combination of realistic thinking to see the issues and work out a practical plan (rather than rely on a vague concept of future success) and optimism in the implementation to persevere.

"Illusion and Well-Being", Shelley Taylor & Jonathon Brown, Psychological Bulletin 1988

"Seeing Pessimism's Place in a Smiley-Faced World" Erica Goode, New York Times, 2000

WHY DAY DREAMING IS PLEASURABLE, BUT ONLY FOR THE SHORT TERM

Thinking about the future can be so pleasurable that sometimes we'd rather think about it than get there.

DANIEL GILBERT

Daniel Gilbert recounts the study in which participants were informed they had won a free dinner at a wonderful restaurant. They were then asked when they would like to eat the meal: now, tonight, tomorrow? Most participants choose to hold fire on the restaurant trip, typically, until the following week.

"Forestalling pleasure is an inventive technique for getting double the juice from half the fruit."

We gain enjoyment from the anticipation of future pleasurable activities. Indeed, sometimes thinking about the experience turns out better than the reality of the experience.

Daydreaming can be highly enjoyable. Day dreaming takes into the world of unlimited possibilities in which our hopes and aspirations can be imagined and played out. And it is an effective tactic to "ease the boredom of routine tasks". Daydreaming has also been a powerful strategy that creative individuals from Leonardo Da Vinci to Walt Disney have deployed to create new ways of thinking about reality.

But a life pattern of daydreams may be hazardous. In another study, participants, asked to imagine themselves requesting a date with a wonderful person, were **less likely** to actually make the request, if they had enjoyed delightful fantasies about this person!

The imaginative power of daydreams can generate new and fresh insights about tomorrow's possibilities. Daydreams can also be a substitute for taking action in the face of today's realities.

"Discovering the Virtues of a Wandering Mind" John Tierney, New York Times, 2010

WHY WE SHOULD DREAM OUR OWN DREAMS AND NOT MAKE COMPARISONS WITH OTHERS

The gift of fantasy has meant more to me than my talent for absorbing positive knowledge.

ALBERT EINSTEIN

Whenever a friend succeeds a little something in me dies.

GORE VIDAL

A successful path is one that is lived through understanding and pursuing one's own path, not chasing after the dreams of others.

CHIN-LING-CHU

Are we making progress in life? What benchmarks are we using to evaluate our achievements?

It's easy to get caught up in comparisons with our peers and allow an evaluation of how well we are doing vis a vis our colleagues, friends and neighbours to shape our judgement of our personal success and happiness.

At best, peer comparisons trigger a positive competitive spirit that avoids complacency and keeps us alert to what is possible. At worst we find ourselves playing a "fool's game". Because everyone's past, current circumstances and future aspirations are different to our own we end up comparing the apples of our life with the oranges of our peers. It's a game we can't win.

Instead of setting a benchmark of our success that keeps looking at how far ahead or behind our peers we are, Scott Dinsmore suggests we become our own best competitor. Here we assess how well we're doing against our own standards of success:

- it will always **keep us motivated**. We know how well we did and why. We know the progress we've made and what helped or hindered us
- it prompts us to **be at our personal best**. As long as we commit to a life of continual improvement, our game can only get better

- **our coach will stick with us**. We take responsibility for how well we play the game. It is our life to be lived on our terms

When we take the "road less travelled", we define what success means personally for us. This is our own path in life, and it means our progress can only be measured by the standards we set for ourselves.

"The Best of Reading for Your Success" Scott Dinsmore

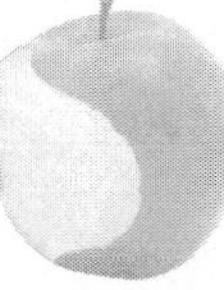

WAS THE COUNT OF MONTE CRISTO'S STRATEGY A WISE ONE

Life being what it is, one dreams of revenge.

PAUL GAUGUIN

Resentment is like taking poison and hoping the other person dies.

ST. AUGUSTINE

Edmond Dantes is in the prime of life. Good looking, a beautiful fiancé with a promising career ahead, Dantes is brought down by a conspiracy, motivated by the envy of three men. As told in Alexander Dumas' novel "The Count of Monte Cristo", loosely based on a true story, on the eve of his wedding, Dantes is arrested and sentenced to fourteen years in prison.

Treated badly by the jailors, Dantes is befriended by a fellow prisoner, the wise priest, Faria who becomes his mentor. Dantes plans their escape. Tunnelling out, Faria tells Dantes the location of buried treasure on Monte Cristo.

Free from prison with new found wealth, Dantes plots revenge on the three conspirators. One, a wealthy banker is made penniless. Another's reputation and political future is destroyed. The final rival, who through dishonesty, married Dantes' fiancé, commits suicide.

A brilliant adventure story, "The Count of Monte Cristo" resonates with any reader who has been unfairly treated and experienced wrong.

The desire for revenge is a healthy instinct for justice. We've been insulted, humiliated and wronged; we want to get even. But this natural motivation can easily become a dark fantasy that is damaging to ourselves. Think Captain Ahab whose obsession with Moby Dick cost the death and destruction of the whole boat crew.

When the "revenge fantasy" takes hold, life becomes a preoccupation with schemes we concoct and elaborate on to exact revenge. And we allow our past to dominate our thoughts in the present about a future that won't make us happy.

Realising that friends are hurt as he destroys his enemies, Dantes also recognises the impact on himself:

> *Fool that I am that I did not tear out my heart the day I resolved to revenge myself.*

"How to Get Revenge" at Mahalo.com
"The psychology of revenge" Leland Beaumont at EmotionalCompetency.com

FUTURE

WHY WE SHOULD MANAGE OUR EXPECTATIONS WISELY

The greatest hindrance to living is expectancy which depends on tomorrow and wastes today.

SENECA

It is wise to aim high so as to hit your mark, but not so high that you miss your mission at the beginning of your life.

BALTASAR GRACIAN

The creative genius Michelangelo reminds us: "The greatest danger for most of us is not that our aim is too high and we miss it, but that it is too low and we can reach it." High expectations, in igniting our purpose and fuelling our ambitions, have the potential for exceptional life success. But they also incorporate the possibility of disappointment and disillusionment if unmet.

Perhaps low expectations are preferable. Like the stoic who "expects the worst and takes what comes", we are untroubled by the striving for happiness and success. After all, even if we achieve something better, it doesn't seem to make us all that much happier. Instead, our expectations rise again to reflect our new circumstances, and we continue to feel frustrated. But low expectations also worry us. They seem to indicate a certain hopelessness to accept that "this is as good as it gets". Low expectations don't seem to represent the life force of progress.

This is the paradox of happiness. If we set our aspirations and expectations of success too high, we may live a life of unhappiness. Too low and somehow we feel we have not lived life to the full. We have that sense of having missed opportunities and possibilities and wasted our talents.

Despite the best attempts of all religious and philosophical traditions, there is no easy way to square the circle of expectations. But it may be that Baltasar Gracian's advice is the most helpful: "Keep your imagination under control. You must sometimes correct it, sometimes assist it. For it is all important for our happiness and balances reason."

"The Art of Worldly Wisdom" Baltasar Gracian
"Being a Joyful Stoic 1: How to Want What You Have" Lefty, at http://caffeine.shugendo.org

WHY GIVENS ARE BETTER THAN MUSTS

If you argue with reality, you will always lose. JOAN BORYSENKO

Albert Ellis describes the three musts - the "unholy trinity" - that often shape our expectations:

1. I must succeed
2. everyone must treat me well
3. the world must be easy

Number 1 is the flawed assumption that we should be perfect, always make progress and achieve life success. Number 2 is the mistaken belief that we are at the centre of others' thoughts and feelings and deserving of their respect, kindness and generosity. Number 3 is the view that life's events should fall into place around our desires and requirements.

There are no "musts" in life. There are however some givens. It helps if we accept:

1. we are players in a competitive game. Life isn't always win-win. Sometimes it is a zero sum game in which others' gains are our losses
2. most people aren't that much bothered about us, except when it suits them
3. the world is a complex and uncertain place that throws up difficult challenges

Musts incorporate a sense of entitlement about how life should be. Givens shift our assumptions about the dynamic of life success to create more realistic expectations.

"Overcoming Destructive Beliefs, Feelings, and Behaviors: New Directions for Rational Emotive Behavior Therapy" Albert Ellis

"Embracing life's givens" Bruce Elkin at Create What Matters Most

WHY EMPOWERED IS BETTER THAN ENTITLED

The world was here before you were.

MARK TWAIN

Entitlement is that operating mind-set that assumes:

- life should be fair
- we should succeed easily and quickly
- our plans should always come to fruition
- any setbacks are an intolerable affront

Life does not owe us a living, neither does it operate with our personal success in mind.

"Steps to Empowering Yourself" Christoph Schertler at Ezine

WHAT IS THE CHILLING REALISATION

Nothing is going to turn up.

MICHAEL FOLEY

We can go through our life with the expectation that at some point in future it will be transformed. This is the dream we have that:

- our organisation will identify our potential and accelerate our career to make us Vice President next year
- a distant relative dies, leaving us with a huge inheritance
- we win the roll over lottery next week

If we're waiting for the magical appearance of our "good fairy in life" we might have to wait.

We might get lucky but a life strategy that waits for luck might be difficult.

"The loser's guide to getting lucky" Richard Wiseman at BBC.co.uk

WHAT HARRY HOUDINI KNEW ABOUT THE ART OF THE ESCAPE

My brain is the key that sets my mind free.

HARRY HOUDINI

Is this not the true romantic feeling; not to desire to escape life, but to prevent life from escaping you.

THOMAS WOLFE

Ehrich Weisz arrived in the USA in 1876 from Hungary. As a nine year old he made his stage appearance performing the trapeze. At twelve he left his Wisconsin home for New York - "the greatest escape I ever made" - to pursue a career in magic. Joining a circus, the renamed Harry Houdini began to develop his skills in escapology. Handcuffs, straitjackets, water tanks, prison cells, coffins, there was nothing from which Houdini couldn't escape.

Houdini soon became the "king of the stage" with his theatrical displays and magical stunts on the vaudeville circuits of America and Europe; the first David Blaine or Derren Brown. There is also reason to believe that the US and British authorities recruited him as a secret agent, exploiting his access to German and Russian leaders, in the build up to World War 1.

For an individual whose career was based on escaping, it's not surprising that the psychoanalysts have asked what was it that deep down Houdini was escaping from and to where was he escaping? Was it disappointment that his father didn't fulfil the American Dream of all immigrants to make it big that motivated Houdini to achieve fame and fortune? Was it the rejection of his rabbi father's mystical tradition that led him to reinvent himself as a hard headed rationalist? After all much of Houdini's later life was devoted to exposing the fraudulent claims of the spiritualists. Aware of magical stagecraft Houdini quickly saw through the chicanery of the séances designed to contact those in the after-life.

It's easy to allow our dissatisfaction with our current life situation to become a series of escape attempts. In this we plot ways of breaking out of a reality that we are finding difficult. Before we embark on these tactics, it's worth asking:

- do we know specifically what it is we want to escape from?
- have we worked out where we want to escape to?

An escapalogist, Houdini was no fantasist. His stunts were refined over time through intense study and physical training:

> *No performer should attempt to bite off red-hot iron unless he has a good set of teeth.*

If we're planning an escape attempt we should check if we're prepared for our new freedom.

The tactics of life escapology at NewEscapologist.co.uk

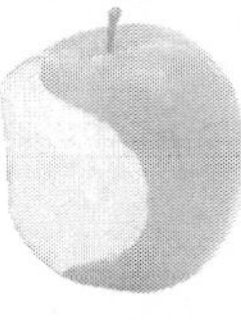

WHAT IS THE BEST WAY TO ESCAPE FROM OURSELVES?

Every person should have their escape route planned.

SIMON PEGG

I don't want realism; I want magic.

BLANCHE DUBOIS IN "A STREETCAR NAMED DESIRE

But it's a funny thing, escapism. You can go far and wide and you can keep moving on and on through places and years, but you never escape your own life.

.J. MAARTEN TROOST

Despite the human tendency to think that we are brilliant, and the life we're living is the best of all possible worlds, from time to time we want to get out of ourselves and head off somewhere else. This explains the appeal of a book that can transport us back in time to Regency England, a computer game where we are a fearless soldier behind enemy lines in World War 2, and the popularity of sites such as Second Life where we enter a new world and choose an avatar that projects our desired persona.

We can take short cuts to escape from ourselves. We can:

- simply spend a lot of time sleeping and master the art of lucid dreaming
- live the life of a couch potato and work our way through sets of DVDs
- fall hopelessly and helplessly in love and pursue an infatuation with that person who will fulfil our every fantasy
- consume huge amounts of alcohol or drugs
- lose ourselves in the music of our favourite band at Glastonbury

These experiences provide an escape route to free ourselves from the "burden of our self consciousness". Freed from the tough reality that keeps reminding us of our failings and shortcomings, our new world avoids the mundane of rubbish bins on a cold Monday morning, the tedium of a project meeting that will go round in circles, or the need to fire that objectionable member of staff who is making life a misery for the team.

But these escape routes are short cuts with side effects. As Michael Foley points out: "Being out of your head is fun but not practical - and the longer you stay out the harder it is to get back in."

We escape ourselves when we lose ourselves in something important and significant. This is the sense of transcendence that comes to:

- the artist who has mastered their craft and achieves that insight that opens up a new and fresh way of looking at the world
- the scientist who, after the toil of trial and error experimentation, generates a breakthrough innovation that will transform others' lives
- the mathematician who solves that complex problem that has defied centuries of intellectual effort
- the person of faith whose dedication, diligence and meditation brings them close to the ultimate

It seems that escape to the exaltation that genuinely takes us out of ourselves has to be earned.

"The Age of Absurdity" Michael Foley

"Tactics we use to avoid facing the truth" Brad Paul at Guru Habits

"Escape Attempts: the theory and practice of resistance to everday life" Stanley Cohen & Laurie Taylor

FUTURE

HOW SECOND LIFE REVERTED TO REAL LIFE

The saddest aspect of the fantasy world is that it is coming to resemble the real world.

MICHAEL FOLEY

Second Life is the multi-player on line world that allows users to create alter egos to pursue a life of self expression. In Second Life we can be what we want to be, and do what we want to do; it's an experiment in fantasy living.

Launched in 2003, Second Life was anticipated to be a platform to allow:

- galleries to open up to exhibit the work of new painters
- emerging talent to play at live music venues
- universities to extend their reach to make content available to new audiences
- work places to be created for employees to attend conferences and training sessions
- governments to establish a presence to encourage a wider debate about policy

At its peak major corporations, like Microsoft and IBM, were creating offices within Second Life to build their brands. Second Life even had its own currency to allow users to buy, sell, rent and trade goods and services with other users. Anshe Chung became the first Second Life millionaire through the buying and selling of virtual properties.

A few years later, and one former user returned to Second Life, and wondered where everyone had gone. It turns out that gambling and pornography and real estate became the big industries in Second Life, and the good guys had pretty much headed off.

"It might try to pretend that it's a melting pot of creativity, business and academia, but ultimately it serves no purpose." Or as another user observed "half the time you're just wandering around talking to weirdoes".

"Get a First Life" Robin Walsh at Spiked, 2007
"Whatever happened to Second Life?" Barry Collins at PC Pro, 2010

HOW THE DYNAMIC OF FANTASY IS PLAYED OUT

Every fantasy requires a constant supply of new images and sensations for the illusion of self gratification to be sustained.

CHRISTOPHER BOOKER

We have fed the heart on fantasies, the heart's made brutal by the fare.

W B YEATS

I think the more stressful our times get, the more we look for fantasy escapes.

JERI RYAN

Fantasy of course is a wonderful power within our creative imagination to transport us to new worlds. It also has the potential to detach us from reality.

Christopher Booker analyses the trajectory of fantasy in literature and society.

It begins with **anticipation**. This is the moment of hope when unhappy with our current situation we look for a better life. We don't know what or where, but we look for escape from our current predicament. The fantasy then moves into the **dream** phase. Here excitement arises as everything seems to go well and our initial expectations are met. But the fantasy meets **frustration**. In this phase cracks begin to appear in the dream; opposing forces emerge to thwart the initial fantasy. The fantasy continues into the **nightmare** stage. Here the cracks widen as things go increasingly and unaccountably wrong. The mystery becomes menace and mayhem to move to the culmination of the fantasy, the final cycle which returns us to the dark reality of **death** and the explosion of reality.

An insightful analysis of how the plots of many books, plays and films are structured, Booker suggests this pattern of fantasy is evident in biography (e.g. James Dean, Ernest Hemingway), and why societies implode (e.g. Nazi Germany).

As any project manager knows, optimism and the hope of future success are important drivers at the beginning of the exercise. They have also experienced the trajectory of a fantasy in which initial enthusiasm and the expectation of a better future moved quickly into a nightmare and project death.

When we're planning next steps, it's worth checking if we're embarking on a fantasy that can only disappoint and disillusion or a practical programme that will make a sustainable difference.

"The Seven Basic Plots: Why We Tell Stories"
Christopher Booker

WHY THE "BEST CASE SCENARIO" FAILED

I learned to embrace risk, as long as it was well thought out and, in a worst-case scenario, I'd still land on my feet.

ELI BROAD

Imagine the "best case scenario" fails when reviewing options to decide the best way forward.

Here we don't assume that our initial view is the only or optimal solution. Instead we think ahead into the future and imagine it has happened.

When we list out five reasons why our favoured option failed, we will spot more reasons when we mentally pretend it has already happened than simply thinking about what may or may not occur.

"Using Scenario Planning" at Knowledge Wharton

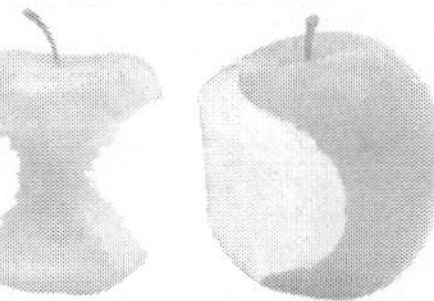

FUTURE

ARE WE SWINGING FOR THE FENCE

Do you consistently get on base or do you swing for the fences?

SCOTT ALLEN

In a baseball game, the batter is faced with a choice: play the obvious shot, the easy shot to allow the third base to run home, or go for the tougher shot, swinging as hard as possible to hit the ball over the fence and go for the home run.

The batter swings for the fence, strikes out and the team lose the game.

Success isn't a series of big shots in which we can have it all immediately.

Sometimes we need to be prepared to go for the small gains and victories.

"10 Zen Principles to Help You Live Life Better"
Wayne Allen at The PathlessPath

WHEN GOOD IS GOOD ENOUGH

We should aim for perfection but be content with continuous improvement.

Excellence is commendable but only in the things that are critical. Not everything worth doing is worth doing well. Some things can be over-done.

We can be "good enough" for the things that are important but not fundamental to our goals. The perfectionist drive, the belief that absolutely everything has to be just so (and anything else that falls short is unacceptable) is a trajectory with potential for disappointment and dissatisfaction. The signs of perfectionism:

- an exasperation with others' behaviour and a frustration with their efforts
- the feeling of being let down by others and having to "pick up the pieces"
- a heightened sensitivity to any suggestion of criticism of our work
- a fear of being made to look foolish in public
- a sense that others will find us out and expose us as a failure or fraud
- thinking more about our previous failings than past successes

Perfection is not attainable, necessary or even desirable.

It's worth asking: what would happen if we achieved perfection?

Good enough is "fit for purpose" and good enough is good enough most of the time.

"Are you a perfectionist?" at StressAbout.com
"The Rocky Road of Perfectionism" Sharon S. Esonis at SelfGrowth

WHY WE SHOULD THINK SMALL

When you set small, visible goals, and people achieve them, they start to get it into their heads that they can succeed.

NFL COACH, BILL PARCELLS

The "ultimate goal" - final victory - doesn't motivate. It might make for a good conference speech or management briefing, but it won't trigger the change that makes the improvements that progress towards success.

Instead of the quick and big change, look for the small improvements one day at a time. Karl Weick says that small wins work because:

- they reduce importance and pressure; "this is no big deal"
- they reduce demands; "that's all that needs to be done"
- they raise perceived skills; "I can at least do that"

These three factors begin to work together to make the change easier.

When you're planning your future, know what the ultimate goal is but define the small victories that will make progress towards it.

"The Nature of Small Wins" Michael McKinney, 2009
Leading Blog

IS IT BETTER TO SATISFICE OR OPTIMISE

What is an issue, indeed an important one, is 'what' should we seek to satisfice and 'what' should we seek to optimize?

MOSHE SNIEDOVICH

"At Draeger's Supermarket in Menlo Park, California, researchers set up a tasting booth. On the table were either six or twenty-four different jars of jam. When did customers stop? 60% of the customers stopped for the wider selection compared to just 40% for the smaller selection. But, for the important metric, when did customers purchase? Only 3% of all shoppers purchased when offered a wide selection while 30% of shoppers bought jam when offered a narrow selection. In other words, restricting choice from twenty-four to only six improved sell-through by a factor of 10."

Searching for the perfect decision can take considerable time and energy. And the outcomes aren't necessarily worth the effort.

Sometimes it may be better to select that option which is "good enough".

Optimisers spend life in a state of worry, concerned they haven't worked through every possible angle and analysed each option. Satisfiers get on with it, implementing solutions that are "fit for purpose".

When we're agonising about the future and its options, "Satisfice" may not be a bad strategy.

"Spoilt for Choice", Liz Hollis, The Times, 2007

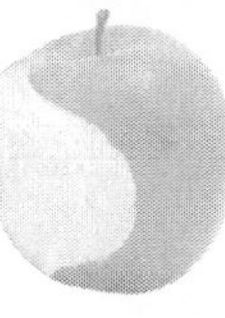

HOW WE BECOME AN OVERNIGHT SUCCESS

I did stand-up comedy for eighteen years. Ten of those years were spent learning, four years were spent refining, and four were spent in wild success.

STEVE MARTIN

It takes 20 years of hard work to become an overnight success.

DIANA RANKIN

There are very few big and quick wins. Most of the time there is a set of small gains, none of which may seem significant in themselves, but when moving in the right direction at once will make a big difference over the long run.

Sometimes we need to allow events to unfold. And at times we need to push to take advantage of the momentum of our previous efforts.

If we keep disciplined in "nudging" each of our plans forward, we might become an "overnight success".

"How To Become An Overnight Success" Conan Stevens

DO WE WANT TO BET?

Gordon Bell, IT pioneer, asks an executive team about their projections:

> *Do you want to bet? You and me, for $1000, I bet you don't make that number.*

If the individual passes on the bet, Bell knows they aren't convinced about their forecasted numbers.

Our projections shouldn't be an exercise in bravado, but realistic targets we are personally prepared to commit to for the future.

HOW TO MANAGE THE DOUBLE THINK OF OPTIMISM

Is the glass half full, or half empty? It depends on whether you're pouring, or drinking.

BILL COSBY

Are you an optimist? Some of us, by temperament, see the glass half full. Others see the glass half empty. When pessimists experience a negative event they tend to think: everything in life is going to get worse; things won't improve; and it's all their fault. Optimists, on the other hand, have a different thinking style. For them, the negative event isn't going to affect their lives, it's only temporary; and it's not their fault.

Do our levels of optimism matter? In 1946, students at Harvard were tested for their levels of pessimism. Thirty years later, the researchers tracked down the group. Those students who had been pessimistic as young adults were more likely to have experienced physical ill health as they passed into middle age.

So, is optimism the best strategy in life? Yes, but. One of the most effective ways to think successfully is a combination of optimism about achieving our goals and a realism about the problems we will have to overcome.

Optimists can be fantasists who dream of a wonderful future, but get disillusioned when things get difficult. The pessimists suck the energy out of life through a fearful caution about life's possibilities, and an acute awareness of the trials and tribulations along life's path.

Manage the art of double-think: optimism about what is possible and realism in identifying the practicalities of achieving your goals.

Are You Prone to Optimism or Pessimism? At StressAbout.Com

A review of Martin Seligman's Learned Optimism At E Consultant

"Resilience and Optimism" Harry Mills, 2005 MentalHelp.Net

HAVE WE WRITTEN THE SCRIPT

I'm waiting for that script to pop through the letterbox and completely surprise me.

BEN KINGSLEY

Have we written the script before we've experienced life?

The kind of concentrated ambition that provides clarity of purpose is important.

But not if it locks us into a path that limits our options before we've worked through what is possible.

Keep focussed but also be responsive to new opportunities that might shift your thinking to explore different career possibilities.

7 reasons to set fire to your career plan Seamus Anthony at PickTheBrain.com

FINAL THOUGHTS

Nine-tenths of wisdom consists in being wise in time.

THEODORE ROOSEVELT

The 300 or so conceptismos that make up this book do not provide a coherent theory of the psychology of time, or how our attitudes about our past, present and future shape our happiness and success in life. **Now It's About Time** is a series of questions rather than a "how to" book that provides definitive answers.

But in reviewing the mix of insights from some of the greatest thinkers of time who have applied their wisdom to the subject, the outcomes of a blossoming, if disparate, research enterprise, as well as the practical life hacks of the time and productivity experts, some recurring themes emerge:

Take time to think about time

Happiness is about three people: our past, present and future selves. When we organise our lives to anticipate future good times, enjoy the present experience, and look back with pleasure on these events, we enhance the chances of our life happiness. Easier said than done, but it's a wise strategy for sustainable happiness. We can throw ourselves into what feels fun today to "take no thought of the morrow", but a sense of regret may diminish the happiness of our future self. Alternatively, we sacrifice the enjoyments of today for a better future self, and wonder why, later in life, we feel a sense of disappointment about the way things worked out.

Boring as it may sound, it's partly about setting aside time for reflection and planning. Simply scheduling a few minutes each day, one hour a week, and a day each year to ask:

- what have I done and learnt?
- am I enjoying things right now?
- what are my plans for the future?

is an important start.

Deploying tactics to overcome the design flaws of our minds

The mental software that runs our memory, attention and imagination, are powerful programmes to manage our lives. But this software also incorporates some design flaws. Our memory can distort the past to focus on the negatives or exaggerate the positives; our attention is often divided, drawn to yesterday's regrets or tomorrow's worries rather than tackle today's challenges; and our imagination conjures up fantasies that can only disappoint, or anticipates future fears that stall us.

We're unlikely to fix these design flaws in the short-term. However we can take steps to manage around them.

To compensate for the tricks our **memory** play, it helps if we accept the inevitability of mistakes and failings, and see them as important life experiences in our learning, rather than consign them to the file of "too difficult to think about". And we can avoid the hazards of nostalgia by maintaining our sense of curiousity to keep interested and engaged in the challenges of today and tomorrow. Here we're alert to those routines and habits that are familiar and comfortable, but no longer working productively for us, and are prepared to make the life changes that ensure we keep growing and developing.

Mindfulness is an important tool to improve our powers of **attention**. It takes time and effort to quieten the "chattering monkey", but the discipline will improve our concentration and focus. A good tactic might be to start to develop the skills of "active listening", a tough challenge, but one that will improve our interpersonal impact as well as enhance our appreciation of the moment.

If our **imagination** is running ahead of reality in which pessimism creates unlikely risks that make us anxious, or optimism that assumes the best of all future worlds, **mind-management** is the best response. This isn't the outlook of the stoic: "nothing will be as bad as we fear or as good as we anticipate", but it is applying a rigour to examine the stories our minds are telling us about the future. The willingness to listen to the feedback of "wise others" and draw on their experiences also provides us with an important reality check when we are considering our plans.

Knowing our means and ends in life

How we think and feel about time is a critical dynamic of life success, but we should be clear about what success means for us personally.

Goal setting may be important to life success, but we get into trouble when we confuse the ends that matter with the means we choose to achieve these ends. As Marshall Goldsmith points out: "goal obsession is the force at play when we get so wrapped up in achieving our goal that we do it at the expense of a larger mission." Caught up in short-term goals we forget our longer-term objectives. Even worse, the pursuit of these short-term goals changes us, and in the process, we lose sight of what was once important to our life happiness and success.

Here it seems we have to shift back and forward between the past and the future to identify priorities for the present. When we view our past as a valuable source

of wisdom we begin to discover what does and doesn't matter in life and the tactics that personally work and don't work for us. When we make wise choices from the options of the future we identify a long-term purpose. And our past and future connect us to the present to feel energised to tackle today's challenges.

Walking the high wire of confidence

Fear of course makes us unsure of our capacity to cope with the pressures and demands of today. It also scans the future to translate uncertainty and change into threats and hazards. Fear then makes us retreat into the comfort of our past and what is familiar to us to avoid risk and the consequences of failure.

Confidence in our talents and skills gives us the conviction that we can overcome the challenges of today and tomorrow. This is why the gurus of the personal improvement industry like to emphasise the importance of self esteem. This is the message that "we are brilliant" and the only barriers to exceptional success in our careers and personal lives are the limiting beliefs we impose on ourselves. It is also a message that turns expectation into entitlement and ultimately disillusionment.

When we walk the high wire we balance optimism and pessimism, courage and caution, arrogance and humility. We walk the high wire when we look back on our past to remind ourselves of the times we have succeeded and remember why we failed, appraise our present to assess the difficulties but draw on smart tactics to overcome them, and make practical decisions about a future of wonderful possibilities to which we are prepared to commit, not allow our plans to remain in our dreams as fantasies.

Thomas Lombardo is right. We "are on a journey through time - the time of our life - and the light ahead of us - the light we imagine and build off of in the future will give meaning and coherence to what we are doing."

We make that journey when we recognise Aristotle's "golden mean" and combine courage and humility to walk the tight rope.

FURTHER READING

General

Stumbling on Happiness, Daniel Gilbert
The Age of Absurdity, Michael Foley
Time Lock, Ralph Keyes
Help!: How to Become Slightly Happier and Get a Bit More Done, Oliver Burkeman
The Time Paradox: The New Psychology of Time, Philip Zimbardo
Time: A User's Guide, Stefan Klein
Switch: How to change when change is hard, Chip and Dan Heath
The Dance of Life - The Other Dimension of Time, Edward Hall

Past

Memories, Dreams, Reflections, Carl Jung
If Only, Neal Roese
Hindsight: the promise and peril of looking backward, Mark Freeman
Why Life Speeds Up As You Get Older: How Memory Shapes our Past, Douwe Draaisma
Your Memory: How It Works and How to Improve It, Kenneth Higbee
A Guide to the Good Life: The Ancient Art of Stoic Joy, William Irvine
How to Write Your Own Life Story, Lois Daniel
How Proust Can Change Your Life, Alain de Botton

Present

Flow: The Psychology of Happiness, Mihaly Csikszentmihalyi
Making Time: Why Time Seems to Pass at Different Speeds and How to Control it, Steve Taylor
Getting Things Done: How to Achieve Stress-free Productivity, David Allen
Do it Tomorrow and Other Secrets of Time Management, Mark Forster
Procrastination: Why You Do It, What to Do About It Now, Jane Burka & Lenora Yuen
In Praise of Slow: How a Worldwide Movement is Challenging the Cult of Speed Carl Honoré
How to be Idle, Tom Hodgkinson
The Happiness Hypothesis, Jonathan Haidt

Future

The Art of Possibility: Transforming Professional and Personal Life, Rosamund & Benjamin Zander
The 50th Law, 50 Cent and Robert Greene
How Life Imitates Chess: Insights into life as a game of strategy, Gary Kasparov
What Got You Here Won't Get You There, Marshall Goldsmith
Goal Mapping: How to Turn Your Dreams into Realities, Brian Mayne
Future Files: A Brief History of the Next 50 Years, Richard Watson
An Optimist's Tour of the Future, Mark Stevenson
The Luxury of Time, Jane and Mike Tomlinson

INDEX

Printed in Great Britain
by Amazon.co.uk, Ltd.,
Marston Gate.